LIGHT

or

DARKNESS:

Reclaiming the Light in Sports

By
Dr. Bob Stouffer

Three Circle Press, Inc.

Urbandale, Iowa

Timberline Center

13007 Douglas Parkway, Urbandale, Iowa, 50323

Dedication

This book is dedicated to all of the parents, coaches, and administrators who are committed to providing athletes with positive, uplifting experiences in sports.

The book is also dedicated to my bride, Cheryl Stouffer, who has positively stood by me for over 28 years of our married lives.

Table of Contents

Prologue

Prologue

In this opening section of the book, Dr. Bob will describe an event at his current school. The event will exemplify the most positive model of interaction between/among coaches, student-athletes, parents, and spectators. This event will illustrate the vision for a new model of coaching in our culture.

The After Glow

The final second of 32 minutes ticked off the clock. Roars of approval emanated from the winners. Hanging heads and silence characterized everyone associated with the losing side of the scoreboard. Student-athletes and coaches formed opposing lines to shake hands. One team quickly headed to the locker room and, not long thereafter, to their school buses for the trip home. The coaches and players of the other team sauntered to the middle of the playing surface to de-brief about the game. Such is standard fare after every athletic event throughout our nation.

However, in this case, an unusual story unfolded, as it did every week at this time. A steady stream of parents, grandparents, aunts, uncles, cousins, classmates, and friends joined the assembly. No words had yet been spoken among literally hundreds of people. A reverent silence hung in the air. The coaches waited until everyone who wanted to join the gathering could do so.

The head coach began speaking. All ears awaited the words. He spoke of his pride in the effort of their team. He talked specifically about the positives of their performance on that evening. He offered constructive counsel about aspects of their play which could be improved before the next contest. He expressed unconditional regard for the team, indicating that their value did not lie in winning or losing an athletic event. He said he loved them. He was sincere. He clearly cared about everyone in this huddle. He wanted the best for his players. He wanted them to always be stretching themselves beyond their self-imposed limits, so they could increase their capacities for competition.

Then, the head coach let each assistant coach offer similar feedback to everyone in that gathering. New personalities provided a cornucopia of blessings to the players and their fans.

The head coach then facilitated the ritual of asking coaches and players to offer words of encouragement and praise to each other.

The leader of the team, for instance, had persevered in spite of numerous physical confrontations on both offense and defense. A corny ditty followed –

"Hey, Seth! Go, Seth! Attawaaaaaaaaaaaaaaaaaaay!"

Several "attaways" were offered throughout the crowd, irrespective of personality, irrespective of position, and irrespective of place on the depth chart. Starters AND third-string player who seldom saw game play, but who worked hard to prepare teammates for these contests, received adulation from their coaches and teammates.

Periodically, the seemingly hokey positive reinforcement reached different variations with a "Hip-hip-hurray!" or the exhorter calling for a single clap after "1-2-3!"

Next, the head coach asked each player to introduce friends or relatives who had made special efforts to come to the game and then to join everyone down on the playing surface for this special huddle. Young men carefully detailed the names and relations which had brought these people to the contest. Genuine thanks were offered to everyone for making this game a priority for the team which had sought to showcase their skills and abilities on that night.

The head coach made final comments about needed preparation for the next competition. The input was neither vague nor purely motivational. He was, after all, a teacher. Teachers understand that timely, concrete feedback deepens the learning. People who learn gain confidence in their abilities and are more inclined to be more successful in the future. Such was the desired outcome of this Teacher-Coach.

The head coach called all of the players into a huddle. They raised their hands together as one team. They offered prayers for injured players and any disappointments. They offered up praises for safety and excellence of performance.

And, in closing the celebration, the head coach chanted intensely, "WHAT'S OUR JOB?!" [Meaning what is the responsibility of the coaches?]

The players chanted back enthusiastically, "TO LOVE US!"

The head coach exhorted again, "WHAT'S YOUR JOB?!"

With equal enthusiasm, the players, responded, "TO LOVE EACH OTHER!"

"GO, LIONS!!!!"

Individuals and packs of people grudgingly left the celebration and drifted out into the night.

A Vision for Light in Sports

In the falls of 2009 and 2010, I have witnessed this scene played out through numerous regular season football games and play-off games. I purposefully did not reveal the actual sport, because the ritual can occur in any and all athletics.

And the picture I just painted for you occurred after a loss! To be perfectly frank, I have to admit that the scenario was almost *exactly* the same after wins *and* losses. Nary a negative word was *ever* spoken at any one of these gatherings! I heard only positive, uplifting, edifying words in victory *and* defeat. This description was the same after the team opened with three losses to ranked teams by a total of just a few points. This description was the same as after the team had won a game by a very wide margin, and after they finished their first-ever winning season, and after they qualified for their first post-season competition.

The most special gathering occurred between two Christian schools after a close, hard-fought contest. The coaches prayed for each other, and we fellowshipped together as like-minded individuals and teams. The athletic director of one team wrote, "Leadership like that can have a tremendous impact on an entire school, and I pray that the seeds these guys plant will bear incredible fruit in the immediate and distant future. Not many coaches are willing to share the stage after a game like that, but I thought it was great." It was great indeed.

During the previous season, these gatherings were so sacrosanct in my mind that I consciously chose not to join the crowd. I thought the relationships to be "too intimate" for me to "intrude." My mistake. I was missing out on a great opportunity to experience community at its best.

Yes, this is the best that sport has to offer. I am proud to say that this is my high school, and we are dedicated to making athletics positive for everyone who is directly involved; this is the ideal vision for relationships among student-athletes, coaches, parents, and spectators.

Unfortunately, my experiences as a player, coach, school administrator, and parent have not been entirely positive.

My purpose in this book is quite simple –

I seek to quickly expose the dark aspects of contemporary athletic competition and then thoroughly recommend ways to shine light on sports – through more honorable behavior of student-athletes, coaches, parents, officials, and spectators alike.

Thank you for bearing the expense and taking the time to join me on this journey.

The journey begins and concludes with my experiences, because such is what I know. During the course of this reading, I hope you will laugh with joy, cry with pain, shout with intensity, and act with enthusiasm to reclaim the light of sports in our culture.

Can an athletic team be successful by "loving each other"?

Come and see. . . .

Chapter 1

<u>*The Drover Drives the Cattle: The Author's Testimony of Athletic*</u>
<u>*Participation*</u>

*Cowboys "drive" cows on cattle drives by yelling, prodding, and
whipping from behind. "Bobby" Stouffer, the student-athlete,
enjoyed great success by the world's standards – many wins,
few losses, and even a state championship – but he had a
"hollow feeling" when all was said and done. Find out why.*

A Hollow Championship

Raucous cheering reverberated throughout the locker room at Williams
Field of Iowa State University, following Davenport West High's 4A
state football championship victory over Dowling Catholic High School
on Saturday, November 16, 1974. Trailing 10-7 at halftime, West had
overcome the deficit and a talented Dowling team in an unlikely come-
from-behind win. Players and coaches cried tears of joy after the 14-10
victory, which had included a goal line stand with first and goal at the 1-
yard-line. An 11-0 season. Seeming perfection. Jubilation reigned.
Amidst the cacophony of celebration, though, a starting linebacker sat
slumped with his back against one of the university lockers. On the
outside, he displayed happiness which comes from such a hard-fought
victory. On the inside, however, a much different set of emotions were
swirling. And that linebacker repressed the memory for decades.

That linebacker is me. All appearances would have led the observer to
conclude I was ecstatic about the state championship win on a
beautiful fall day. But ecstasy was not my predominant emotion. *Relief*
was what I most felt on that day. Certainly, I was pleased we had won
the game. I was glad I had started that season. More than being glad,
though, I was relieved that the pressure was over. My gut was twisted
in knots during the entire experience. A sixteen-year-old *boy* (with a
heavy emphasis on *boy*) often does not have the resources or
experiences to bear such pressure. As a young man in our culture, I
had been conditioned to appear tough on the outside, but I was
tenderized beef on the inside. I wasn't at a point of mental break-down,
but I was definitely fatigued enough to experience a sense of relief
more than pure joy after the championship.

Lest you believe that I am one of those former athletes who has failed to receive therapy for my insecurities or a personality disorder, and that I now want to engage in a diatribe about all which is wrong with athletics, think again. Athletics greatly impacted me in my development as a person. I learned extremely valuable lessons as a baseball and football player. With all due modesty, I was an accomplished athlete. Not everyone can claim to be a first-team all-conference student-athlete in both high school and college. Not everyone can claim to have been selected by the coaches as the most valuable player in a college conference after a 0-11 season.

However, when I should have experienced joy after that state championship game, I was simply happy that I would not have to face another practice, game, or film session. Later in this book, I will describe a very similar experience after I coached a state championship team 11 years later.

So, what's my story?

I have "seen the light." I now know a way of coaching youth athletics which would have allowed me to experience pure joy at the pinnacles of success in 1974 and 1985. Please allow me to tell more of my own story as a student-athlete and coach, and then pay special attention to my excitement about a new culture of positive participation in sports. Game on!

Husky Bob

I was the fat kid growing up. My Mom called me "husky," but we know that "husky" is simply a mother's euphemism for "fat."

From the third through the eighth grades, I lived outside the social circles of the school. I was a "have not." I was one of the "disenfranchised." Other kids made fun of me for being overweight. Compared to some schoolchildren today, I was not grossly obese, but I still did not fit the "standard mold" of the desirable body shape during any of those difficult formative years.

Because I had no friends, anger and frustration seethed in me, and my emotions would often bubble into bullying behavior. God bless my younger brother Brian for bearing with his role as a punching bag. In the only physical fight of my life, I flailed somewhat unsuccessfully at Steve Roe as we were walking home from elementary school one day, because he had made some crack about my weight. Silly him. I gave him the mumps in that tussle. God has a sense of humor.

I discovered two more appropriate channels for my aggression. First, I read incessantly. The son of a kindergarten teacher, I was an early reader, and I developed a real affinity for words. My mother read aloud constantly to me. She also modeled the habit of reading. (To this day, she reads three or four lengthy novels a week.) My earliest memories of reading included every single page of the 1963 encyclopedia, Childcraft volumes, the dictionary, biographies (especially of Adolf Hitler, interestingly enough), and cheesy sports books for young readers. Can you say *Dash to the Goalline*?!

My second outlet for my anger became athletics. My elementary physical elementary teachers marveled at my ability to climb the thick gymnasium ropes in spite of my weight. Apparently, I had some upper-body strength which allowed me to surprise Mr. Hund and Mr. Shie. Coaches can always find places for the fat kid as a flag football lineman and catcher on the baseball teams, so those were additional avenues for participation. Prior to my high school athletic experience, I showed only flashes of accomplishment, so I really didn't stand out as an athlete. In fact, I can now look back on that fact as confirmation of coaches not giving up too early on unaccomplished athletes – or me, more than the coaches, not giving up too early on myself. My best year of interscholastic athletic achievement came when I was a senior in college.

Some of my success in high school sports was a result of the unconditional love of my parents and my strong sense of perseverance. When no one else loved me, my Mom and Dad helped me navigate the turbulent white waters of peer rejection. My Dad volunteered to coach my teams. He played catch with me in the yard. Mom and Dad attended all of my games. And they were the perfect image of parents in the stands. They cheered when I succeeded, but they were never obnoxious in their support of me and my teams. They helped put athletics in perspective for me. If I failed individually, or if the team lost a game, such was not "the end of the world." The sun would come up in the morning. They instilled in me my continuing positive attitude.

A part of that positive attitude was my sense of "stick-to-it-iveness." Knocked down 6 times, I got up 6 times. Even when the whole world seemed to be against me in my mind, I never gave up. I'd have to guess that people who were watching me must have wondered whether all of my efforts were worth it. Probably, people thought I'd never amount to anything as an athlete.

A Butterfly Flutters Out of the Cocoon

Then, a funny thing happened on the way to the athletic graveyard. I took a detour. I experienced some joy and recognition from my singing in the choir. The speech teacher gave me A+'s on my oratories (even if I had written the pieces in study hall the period before). The fat kid slimmed down, and coaches started noticing my abilities. While not particularly speedy a-foot, I had an instinct, quickness, and fearlessness which allowed me to slam into bodies at the right angle on the football field. I found that I liked to hit people and that football was the perfect outlet for my pent-up anger and frustration as an outcast.

But I was no longer a social outcast! Girls started noticing me! Nancy Crow kissed me! Barb Resnick wanted to date me! And my confidence grew. I loved school, so my classes were never a great difficulty for me, and my growing competency in music, speech, and athletics all helped move my introversion into advanced extraversion. In fact, I became downright cocky!

By the grace of God, I was fortunate that coaches gave me significant playing time on teams with dozens of excellent athletes. During my varsity football competition, over 100 juniors and seniors would come streaming out of locker rooms. We were at least three deep at each position. No one played both offense and defense. I played linebacker.

Even though I had my share of injuries during my football career – multiple ankle sprains, a bruised kidney, a broken thumb, a broken nose (twice in one week), a dislocated finger, and bruises all over my body – and even though I experienced my share of adversity – I learned a great deal about myself, the game, leadership, and team play through athletics.

I definitely exhibited a linebacker's mentality. Meat-grinder drills fueled an apparent thirst for collisions, allowing me to ride an all-conference defensive career through high school. Obviously, winning a state championship while playing with the largest high school in Iowa buoyed my self-concept. Again, my parents' attitudes allowed me a perfect reference point in life. Football was no more important than baseball, nor weekend speech competitions, nor a Cappella concerts, nor English coursework, nor student council.

I wanted to play football in college, and I was willing to give the experience one year. If I didn't like it, or saw football as an impediment to my academics, I would quit. I would walk away free and clear. Seriously. Football was not the sole determiner of my identity in life. Interestingly, I did not sniff the field as a first-year player, but my love of the game was too deeply ingrained, and I decided to continue my career. As I think back on that decision, others might ask, "Why in the world did you do that?! You played on 6-34 teams in college. You were 0-11 as a senior!"*

True. True. But football continued to give me an outlet for appropriate aggression and expression of my physical talents. After all, I was selected First-Team All-Northern Intercollegiate Linebacker and the Glen Galligan Award recipient for excellence in academics, leadership, and athletic accomplishments. Through continuing participation, I refined my leadership skills and, essentially, served as a coach on the field. A Summa Cum Laude undergraduate, I could be entrusted to be prepared for and execute defensive game plans.

My coaches seemed to care about me, but they had a funny way of showing it. I enjoyed my relationships with Myron Smith, John Martin, Roger Harrington, Cy Robinson, Gary Olson, John Mullen, and, particularly Ted Minnick, since he later hired me as a coach, and we worked together as administrative colleagues. My coaches were fun people to be around – off the field, away from the film room, and after the season.

But the culture of coaching was negatively predicated during seasons. I often felt like a cow being driven to market. Coaches motivated primarily through external motivation, especially through yelling, fear, and intimidation. The "good old days" included coaches slamming football players into lockers, grabbing and yanking student-athletes by face masks, screaming epithets, blasting players with negative feedback, and running players through "killer" Burma Roads or up steep hills.

For me, the most prominent example of negativity revolved around a weekly event which I dreaded both in high school and college. I developed a psychological aversion to film sessions. Even if I had played well on the previous day, my stomach would twist in knots when I thought about the "communication" which would fly fast and furiously as the coaches and players reviewed films together. I knew that my coaches would – much to my chagrin and against the theme of the well-known song – "accentuate the negative, eliminate the positive, and not mess with Mr. In-Between." I probably over-exaggerated the length of time that the coaches would take to run the film forward-and-back-and-forward-and-back. I played in the sixteen-millimeter era. The sound of click-click-click-click-clicking of the film projector is forever etched into my grey matter. I probably don't remember this correctly, but it seems to me that my poor efforts or outcomes were played and re-played far more than my successes. My coaches did this not because they wanted to be "mean," but I'd guess because they wanted to refine my skills so I could become even better.

I have many "what if's" in my minds, though. What if those coaches had used more positive strategies to motivate me? I will never know. But such is the root of the purpose for this book.

I do not have an axe to grind with athletics. I loved sports, particularly football. Athletics contributed mightily to my development as a person. My Mom used to say that my participation in so many diverse extracurricular activities allowed "a butterfly to flutter out of the cocoon." The plan for my life was positive, one which would allow me to prosper in a more desirable future. I now know that the good works which had begun in me would be followed through to a positive outcome. But there was a definite downside at the time of my participation as an athlete. The downside was the system of coaching. Such is the topic for my next chapter.

| | | | | | | | |_____

*Funny story. A number of football players were sitting in the television lounge during a December evening after my senior season. A Wisconsin station reported that The University of Wisconsin-Eau Claire had played an ineligible back-up linebacker during the season, and Eau

Claire was forced to forfeit all of their wins. That announcement didn't set in immediately. We looked at each other. We thought some more. And we erupted in celebration for our new-found "win" over Eau Claire! Off to the bars we went! We technically finished 1-10! At least we didn't have to "cheat" to win!

Chapter 2

The Author's Perpetuation of a Negative Coaching Model

Bob Stouffer became a coach himself, coaching multiple sports and following some of the same negative practices of his mentors. Find out why.

I experienced so much about coaching during the seven years that I coached junior high and high school sports. When I was single, the athletic director saw me as an easy mark, and I coached year-round for two consecutive years – junior high football, wrestling, track, baseball, high school football again, basketball, and track (again). I married and streamlined my responsibilities to sophomore baseball and assistant varsity football, or Cheryl would have had every right to seek divorce on the grounds of my also "being adulterously wed to high school athletics."

I had followed in some rather large footsteps. I told my mother that I was choosing education as a profession, because I wanted to have the same kind of impact that my teachers and coaches had had on me. I should have been careful about what I wished for, because, as a coach myself, I basically perpetuated many if not all of the abuses I had experienced as an athlete. Allow me to come clean with some of my immature behaviors as a coach:

- I recall mocking some of my ninth grade football players for wearing earrings when such jewelry was becoming fashionable in the late-1970s and early-1980s. I questioned their manhood. (Sorry, Charlie.) Now, I hardly give earrings on men a second thought, although you won't find me sporting such bling.

- Speaking of questioning manhood, I also wondered aloud about the masculinity of my football players when they (quite naturally for their time of development) continuously touched and slapped and patted each other. One young man was aptly angry for my self-righteousness. (Sorry, Dirk.)

- I often covered up my ignorance about a teaching point in sports by shifting gears to "motivation" over teaching, yelling exhortations, rather than correctly offering counsel about a fundamental skill or responsibility in the sport. (Sorry, Herman.) More on the topic of teaching versus motivating in the book section addressed to coaches.

- We coaches once forgot about and left a special education student in a town 30 miles away after a junior high wrestling match. The student started *walking home*, and we didn't discover our error until the bus had arrived back in our city. I'm surprised I didn't face more negative consequences for that gross oversight. [Sorry, Phil (and Ron).]

- During summer football camp, I once had a senior doing a drill without pads. The drill had never been a risk before (probably because we had always done the drill *in pads*). This young man, who aspired to be our quarterback that year, separated his shoulder during the drill and missed much of his senior season. I felt terrible about that injury, but he was unusually forgiving. (Sorry, Scott.)

- I was part of the problem of applying too much pressure on players, getting overly negative when experiencing losses. (Sorry, Mike.)

- My humor tended toward the sarcastic and destructive. I would yell at kids during films. I would emphasize negatives over the positives. I often thought of winning as more important than my sophomore baseball players getting playing time. I sometimes got into unnecessary confrontations with pushy parents. I would use vulgarities and God's name in vain. (Sorry, God. Sorry, everyone else.)

I am embarrassed by the behaviors I have admitted to you. So what's my point (other than satisfying the need for a little cleansing for the soul)?

I was doing what I "knew." I was behaving as I had "seen" other coaches behave in my presence. I had experienced success as an athlete when "motivated" by an often-negative model of coaching. Such is what I knew, so such is what I repeated as a coach. We do what we know, even if we are not sure that what we know is most effective.

Many, many coaches are very positive across this great land of ours, but I would contend that the model of coaching and the model of athletics tend toward the negative, and we are not reversing this negative cycle, but, rather, perpetuating even more negativity.

If you think I was bad, turn the page.

Chapter 3

Darkness: Horrific Abuses in Sports

> *An entire book could be written on the negative behaviors of coaches, athletes, and spectators at all levels of participation, but this chapter will include only the "lowlights."*

During the very week that I began writing this book, Mike Leach was first suspended and then two days later dismissed as head coach of the Texas Tech University football program. He had ostensibly "punished" a high-profile athlete, Adam James, son of ESPN commentator Craig James, for not recovering as quickly from a concussion as the coach would have liked. Without impugning the veracity of either Texas Tech or Mike Leach, we must all agree that said incident went badly for coach, players, and university alike.

As a coach, I was a Mother Teresa compared to some of the stories you are about to read. I will offer you one encouragement at this point. With all of my power, I will attempt to leave this chapter well behind as we move through the later stages of a book dedicated to a positive vision for athletics.

Until then, though, let us become incensed about unconscionably gross improprieties committed in the name of sports. . . .

- The White Sox baseball team of 1919 became the "Black" Sox after fixing games.

- The 1972 summer Olympic games in Munich, Germany became a political bloodbath perpetrated by Arabs against Israeli athletes.

- NFL and MLB players went out on strikes in the Twentieth Century, 1982 and 1994-1995, respectively.

- Documents verified that Pete Rose bet on baseball games in 1985 and 1986, thus closing the door on his induction into the Hall of Fame.

- In 1991, Wanda Holloway, the mom of a high school cheerleader hired her brother-in-law as a hit man to kill the mother of a rival cheerleader.

- An out-of-control fan stabbed tennis player Monica Seles on April 30, 1993.

- Tonya Harding's handlers hired a thug to physically assault rival Olympic ice skater Nancy Kerrigan on January 6, 1994 (prior to the Games).

- During a game on September 27, 1996, MLB star Roberto Alomar spit in Umpire John Hirshbeck's face, resulting in three reported incidents of the same nature – in youth sports leagues. (No such incidents had ever been reported previously.)

- On June 28, 1997, Mike Tyson bit off a piece of Evander Holyfield's ear during a boxing match. (So much for Marques of Queensbury rules!)

- In 1998, both Sammy Sosa and Mark McGuire used performance-enhancing drugs to pass Roger Maris' Major League Baseball home run record for a season.

- A young woman accused Kobe Bryant of sexual assault in 2003, so he jetted back-and-forth between his Los Angeles Laker games and the trial in Colorado.

- Bobby Knight became legendary for his angry behaviors, including the tossing of a folding chair across a gym floor on February 4, 2008 in protest officiating during the Indiana-Purdue men's basketball game.

- Latrell Spewell was fired by the Golden State Warriors after choking Coach P.J. Carlesimo during a December 15, 1997 practice.

- John Daly's exploits earned him the reputation as the Professional Golf Association's "bad boy."

- Doping scandals have been discovered in various sports, including bicycling.

- In July, 2000, Thomas Junta fought his son's hockey coach, Michael Costin, at their practice. Costin died of injuries sustained in the fight.

- Drama King Terrell Owens has sought center stage on a number of occasions, including his mocking of the Dallas Cowboy star logo on the Texas Stadium field on September 24, 2000.

- In 2004, Gardener-Webb University, a Christian university in the South, was placed on three years' probation for a grade-tampering scandal that cost President Christopher White his job.

- On November 19, 2004, five players and 5 spectators were arrested for assault in a frightening brawl during the Detroit-Indianapolis NBA game.

- In 2005 alone, a California high school football coach was caught on videotape moving the sideline marker to gain a first down (and the game victory), a Connecticut man beat his daughter's high school softball coach with a bat after she had been benched for skipping practice to attend her boyfriend's prom, and a Texas parent of a high school football player actually wounded his son's coach with a .45-caliber pistol.

- 2006 Duke University lacrosse team members were accused of raping a stripper at a wild campus party.

- On July 11, 2006, famed French soccer player Zinedene Zindane viciously headbutted an Italian opponent.

- On July 18, 2007 Michael Vick was indicted and eventually went to prison for his role in a dog-fighting scandal.

- During one recent NFL season, the Cincinnati Bengals program roster often read more like a police blotter.

- On July 20, 2007, NBA referee Tim Donahy pled guilty to making calls to alter scores and shave points off the spreads of bookmakers.

- Elizabeth Lambert, a soccer player at the University of New Mexico, punched opponents and pulled at least one down to the ground by the girl's ponytail during a match on November 5, 2009.

- On February 2, 2009, epic Olympic swimmer Michael Phelps admitted to taking hits of marijuana from a bong.

- The always famous and now infamous Tiger Woods will no doubt still be navigating the murky waters of rehabilitation after his Thanksgiving, 2009 driveway "accident" and eventual sex addiction treatment.

- On New Year's Eve – December 31, 2009, NBA basketball players confronted each other in the locker room – *with guns*.

- By text message, Robin Alcaron, varsity high school girls soccer coach, 35, invited a 14-year-old player and a friend to a sex orgy with him and his girlfriend on January 8, 2010.

- On February 15, 2010 in Burnsville, Minnesota, a player's father punched the president of a basketball league, breaking his jaw, because the Dad thought the keeper of the clock had started the clock too early.

- On March 7, 2010, 19-year-old 6'8" Baylor University basketball player Brittany Griner punched Texas Tech's Jordan Barncastle in the face.

Hazing, gambling, cheating, doping, fighting, drugging.

Various sports. Various levels of competition. Various personalities. One unfortunate truth – athletics remains a venue of abusive, inappropriate behaviors. And we should not be surprised, since flawed people are involved.

These were very specific allegations and proven charges, but let's direct our attention to the more general abuses of athletes, coaches, parents, other spectators, and officials in sports.

General Abuses of Athletes, Coaches, Parents, Other Spectators, and Officials

What are the general abuses of athletes?

- Arrogance, self-absorption
- Hypocrisy
- A downright unwillingness to be a positive role model for younger athletes
- Concern more about individual statistics than team play
- Bearing grudges
- Laziness, underperformance, reliance on pure talent, not seeking to expand capacity
- Starving themselves (particularly females) in order to achieve at higher levels
- No dedication to excellence
- Sour, critical, negative complaining
- Dirty play
- Cheating
- Addiction to money, drugs, alcohol, sex or some other activity intended to numb pain
- Gossip about teammates and coaches
- Quitting
- Playing the victim and blamer when underperforming; failing to take responsibility for poor decisions and play
- Yelling at opponents, opposing and team coaches, officials, teammates
- Unrepentance when wrong
- Joy for the injuries of other athletes; happiness when others fail
- Being a sore loser and arrogant winner

What are the general abuses of coaches?

- Primary coaching emphasis on "motivating" (versus teaching)
- Providing vague, untimely feedback about the performance of athletes
- Improper conditioning of athletes

- Inadequate prevention and care of injuries
- Unclear expectations and antecedents for "playing time"
- Inconsistency in enforcing expectations and rules
- Uncaring, unloving attitudes
- Correction long on punitive measures, rather than "restorative justice"
- Addressing concerns with students, parents, and officials publicly (rather than privately)
- Speaking negatively about coaches and players
- Unforgiveness
- Demanding too much time of athletes, including the "off-season"
- Placing inappropriate amount of pressure on athletes
- Failing to balance life personally
- Assigning value to players based on their performance
- Playing favorites
- Working only with "stars," not substitutes
- Stealing signs and teaching student-athletes to "fudge" on rules
- Win-at-all-costs mentality, including the cost to integrity
- Yelling incessantly negative comments at officials, players, opponents

What are the general abuses of parents and spectators?

- Negativity
- Out-of-control behavior
- Poor sportsmanship, thus modeling poor sportsmanship for others
- Yelling – at any or all in the path of anger
- Unwillingness to lovingly confront inappropriate behaviors of fellow spectators
- Gossiping
- Unwillingness to speak directly to someone to whom in conflict
- Inappropriately pressuring children
- Taking children's lives out of balance by over-emphasizing sports
- Shielding children from pain, disappointment, heartache, and negative consequences of their own behavior.
- Physically confronting officials, parents, and/or coaches
- Providing only negative feedback about the play of athletes after practices and games
- Emphasizing the needs of their children over the team

What are the general abuses of officials?

- Incompetence or lack of discernment about the action, rules, and progression of the competition
- Out-of-control emotions during the heat of competition and/or at the point of controversial judgments
- Drawing attention to self through overly flamboyant or aggressive movement, gestures, or comments
- "Baiting" athletes, coaches, or spectators to anger through verbal or non-verbal means
- Failing to listen actively during disputes, thus escalating many arguments
- During disputes, using inflammatory words, focusing on emotion, rather than the specific rule or reason for judgment about enforcement of the rule
- Unfairness; making calls against coaches and athletes whom the do not like or respect
- Too close in relationship with coaches or participants, risking even the appearance of favoritism
- Unwillingness to seek the assistance of fellow officials, when necessary
- Arrogance – willing to stand by an incorrect or missed call even if wrong

Darkness. Very dark descriptors for a culture of sport. We do not want to "go there" anymore. We want to leave the darkness and walk into the light. Light invades the darkness, and the darkness disappears.

Thus is the purpose of this book. We can change the dark aspects of sports. We can shine light on the darkness. We can call ourselves to more honorable behavior.

Championship high school tennis coach Kirk Trow agreed with my assessment of darkness in contemporary sports: "Sports are a bigger deal than they need to be. In sports, something significant needs to happen soon. Some of the purposes of sports have become deluded. There has to be a different way. Everyone relates to sports. It's such a big deal. We need to use something that has the eye of the culture, and change the culture of sports." Perhaps we can even change the shortcomings of culture through sports.

Kirk continued, "I'm a human resources guy. If I want someone to change, I change the job description. If we want to change sports tomorrow, then the athletic directors need to get together and create a job description for which the coaches are accountable. You want a different outcome? You need to change how you do your work. Change the expectations for the student-athletes and coaches. There are too many implicit expectations."

We do need to change our current culture "job descriptions" in sports. We do need to make our positive expectations more explicit. There will always be darkness in sports, because there will always be people who cannot restrain their nature. But, I believe there are many reasons for hope, so please read on to explore the "light," a new model for athletics, one of which we can all be proud.

Chapter 4

<u>Light: A Better Way of Coaching Sports</u>

The shepherd leads the sheep. "Come and follow," the shepherd and effective teacher-coach says. In this chapter and subsequent chapters, Dr. Bob will detail the main precepts of the edifying model of athletics (with an abundance of concrete examples from his research).

A Refreshing Model of Coaching

Cowboys drive cattle from behind. Shepherds lead their sheep up ahead. I am espousing a model of athletics which places adults firmly up ahead of the athletes, teaching them about the sport, rather than driving them from behind in a primarily motivational model, leading them to a more desirable future in sports.

Allow Coach Scotty Kessler to offer a definitive description of this coaching model to which we should all ascribe. I will be paraphrasing Coach Kessler's philosophy of coaching, as detailed in his recent presentation to a Fellowship of Christian Athletes group in Indiana. I am grateful to Coach Kessler for organizing and clearly communicating these principles to me and to others.

All of us are essentially educators. And, as educators of others, we have a responsibility to learn from our mentors and to pass along the most valuable lessons of those mentors to others. As Coach Kessler says, "We all stand on the shoulders of others. No one stands alone."

These principles of coaching are true regardless of a person's spiritual orientation. All of us are spiritual. Our spirituality is a matter of our worldview and in whom or what we place our faith. I can believe in Jesus or Buddha or Mohammed, but certain truths cut across people types and cultures. The law of gravity is absolute truth. Jump off a cliff, and you will discover the truth of gravity.

Key Questions to Determine the Worldview from Which We Coach

As coaches, we must determine our worldview. A series of questions can help us determine an explicit understanding of our worldview.

- Who are we?
- Why are we here on this earth?
- Why do we have value and purpose in life?
- What ideas, values, and beliefs form the filter through which we discern, speak, and act?
- What are we attempting to accomplish by working with athletes?
- What about our own experiences flavors our coaching (both positively and negatively)?
- How will I effectively deal with unresolved issues in my own life, so I can be successful as a coach and mentor?
- To what extent are relationships more important to me than victories? How can I make relationships more important than victories?
- How able am I to coach with absolute integrity, knowing that integrity and honesty may result in defeat?
- What is our honorable vision for sports?
- What is our plan for realizing that vision?
- How willing am I to seek an honor which shines like gold (more than championship rings, trophies, plaques, and awards)?

Coach Kessler offers strong words for us, and I must quote him – "If we win championships and don't teach individuals intentionally and strategically how to prosper in marriage and family and relationships and work, I would contend that we should seriously evaluate whether we should continue in this profession." So be it!

Four Principles of Coaching with Honor

I am drawn hard to Coach Kessler's four principles of coaching in this positive model. Please explore them with me.

1. *Focus on the Long-Term Over the Short-Term.* "Do we want a great wedding or a great marriage?" Coach Kessler asks. Our answer to that question should guide all of our decisions in sports.

2. *Focus on the team over the individual.* "There is power in selflessness. Selfishness destroys, but selflessness builds," Coach Kessler points out.

3. *Focus on the inside person versus the outside person.* Win the hearts of athletes, and athletes "will follow you wherever you take them," he says.

4. *Focus on "the weak" over "the strong."* We should be caring for the athletes who are seen as cast-offs to other coaches. We should care as much about the player who will never see the field of competition as we do the athlete who plays every minute. NBA Coach Phil Jackson has always been expert at this key, finding ways to meld a team of superstars like Michael Jordan and Kobe Bryant with role players who are just as important to the success of the teams, particularly if everyone is clear about his role.

Critical Coaching Considerations

Coach Kessler also offers critical coaching considerations in this model.

- *Team-Building.* He calls coaches to "cross-pollinate" players of color, position, age, geography, socio-economics, and talent at all times. Athletes should "be together" and "doing together" constantly outside of practices and games. Non-sport activities should provide balance for athletes away from competition. Pure fun events such as movie nights, video game championship, wiffle ball competitions, bowling, skits, and retreats can build team chemistry.

- *Constant Motion.* Athletes should "learn by doing more than learn by talking." All care should be given to avoid "standing around time."

- *Coaching Enthusiasm.* Energy "begets energy."

- *The Power of Words.* Accentuate the positive. ("Catch the ball!') Eliminate the negative. ("Don't drop the ball!")

- *Feedback.* Coach Kessler calls feedback "the breakfast of champions" when offered in specific and timely ways.

- *High Expectations.* The performance of athletes during practice is as important as play in games. Coach Kessler states, "Graciously demand maximum effort and focus at all times [and] in all things" at practice. Teach athletes how to have a "want to" rather than a "have to" attitude. Great performance in practice will result in great performance in games.

Coaches should be seeking to "bless, not curse" everyone involved in athletics – opponents, fans, referees, bus drivers, equipment personnel, cafeteria workers, administrators, and parents. And we should be looking to equip leaders among all constituent groups.

Excellence in coaching brings a set of high demands. Greatness takes sacrifice. We must be willing to give the time and energy for success.

Cade Lambert, the head football coach of our school, Des Moines Christian School in Iowa, offers additional points to this mix of the ideal sports program –

- "Love is the cornerstone. To the degree players believe their coaches love them – to that degree will players respond to the coaches' authority – with immediacy, great effort, and smiles on their faces. Players must do more than simply respect each other; they must care about each other together more than they care about themselves individually; only then will a team be truly a family."

- "Power manifests itself when individuals die to themselves for the sake of the team."

- "We must watch the power of our words. Words are the simplest means by which to build-up or destroy our players. The tongue has the power of life and death. . . .Everything we say is either an investment in or a withdrawal from the bank accounts of our players' lives."

- "Humility is the mark of greatness."

- "Servant leadership is key to success."

- "Emphasize people over productivity."

- "Athletes should compete against their own best selves."

- "We promote attitudes, not rules. We are looking for changed hearts, not blind obedience. Playing is a privilege. We talk in terms of responsibilities, not rights; when we become part of a team, we give up individual rights and gain corporate responsibilities."

- "We make all that we do as fun as possible. Happy players play better – both in practice and in games."

Losing and Failure: Winning and Success

What is our perspective on "failure"? How do we define "failure"? In my mind, failure is not measured by losses. Some of our greatest learning comes through "losses." In "winning" we can even often miss the point of our participation.

"Winning" and "success" entail subordination of self to the team, obedience to authority, impeccable sportsmanship, maximum use of ability, joy in the competition, emphasis as much on the journey as the destination.

After all, Abraham Lincoln – now considered by many as THE greatest President in U.S. history – was defeated in countless local, state, and national elections before being elected President of the United States. Thomas Edison experienced over 1,000 "failures" before he made the light bulb work. His attitude made him a success: He had discovered 1,000 ways that the light bulb WOULD NOT work! Colonel Sanders of Kentucky Fried Chicken fame lost dozens of jobs before starting his famous franchise, and he created a multi-million dollar success! Michael Jordan missed more than 9,000 shots, lost almost 300 games, and missed 26 game-winning shots in his basketball career. In regard to all of this failure, Jordan remarked, "I've failed over and over and over again in my life. And that is why I succeed." (From *The Compassionate Samurai*, pp. 171-172, by Brian Klemmer)

A parent in our school showed great wisdom when writing reflections about big losses he had observed during the year –

"As I reflected on [a state tournament basketball loss] and a playoff football game, both were riddled with mistakes that were out of character for our boys. I told my son that such is the reason practice is so important. Any little weakness will be magnified and exploited in the tough games. First, you have an adversary who is working his tail off to exploit the weakness, and then we also have our own anxiety and self-created pressure. The real kicker is how similar to life this is. How easy it is to get angry and say things inappropriately when the pressure is turned on, or to not apologize when tempers are high. Well, if we are not practicing diligently in the good times, or when the pressure is not on, do we feel as though we can perform at a high level when the pressure is on? Finally, what do we cheer on? I sat among thousands of people cheering every basket made or steal taken, and I saw people rise to their feet all game long to cheer on athletic prowess. Can you imagine the reaction of the crowd if it were announced that one player witnessed effectively to a friend that day, of if another player apologized to his Dad for something said, or if yet another player forgive his brother? Shouldn't the roar be louder? It probably is – in heaven."

Well said. Well said.

A school community member commented about our 2010 state basketball tournament loss – "Maybe it's not about us. Yesterday, before the game, in our pep rally, we declared that we would play with honor. None of that has changed, after the game. Today we get to display the credibility of that testimony. We lost, and I am grieving that loss of our State Championship dream with the team. I love our students, and I am still proud of them and their commitments to discipline and teamwork. I have fond memories of watching both the girls and boys compete all season. I have equally great memories of football, marching band, show choir, jazz band, and packaging food with students for the people of Haiti [a country ravaged by an earthquake and poverty]."

I believe we can all agree that all is not doom-and-gloom about athletics. We can't throw the baby out with the bathwater. Sports offer many positives. Bernie Saggau, well-known national leader of high school athletics and former Executive Director of the Iowa High School

Athletic Association shared several plusses of activities: "The fellowship. Common goals. Teamwork. The best thing in a really good program is there are no rich kids or poor kids or white kids or black kids. They're all the same. The responsibility is for the coach to build that unity. Some coaches do better with that, and it may have to do with the sport. Right now, our coaches are the better than they've ever been – ever. They're doing a better job."

I enjoyed a recent experience with a coach who is "doing a better job."

Now, hear his story. . . .

A Very Different Kind of Coaching Clinic!

Joe Ehrmann was a free-spirited and successful player for the Baltimore Colts in the 1970s and early-80s. His young brother died, and, at that crisis point, he thought more deeply about how he could be more purposeful with his life. He went to seminary. He began preaching to congregations about truth in social justice issues. He started a foundation to help boys become men in a culture which sends messages with false criteria for manhood. He coaches high school football, and his coaching model is counter-cultural. And he now speaks to coaches all over the country about the underpinning philosophies of effectively working with athletes, their parents, and communities built around the same positive culture. How serendipitous that, during the writing of this book, he presented a full-day seminar at the University of Iowa. I attended. Coach Ehrmann's coaching clinic was like none other I had ever attended. See why. . . .

I attended a lot of clinics and seminars during my seven years of coaching. I have stood on The University of Iowa and Notre Dame football fields with coaches who manifested proven expertise. I have sat in lecture halls, listening attentively to the most successful coaches in the country draw up the X's and O's of their sports. I have watched as drills and schemes were effectively demonstrated by coaches and players.

However, in my 31 years as an educator, I have never experienced an athletic coaching clinic like the one in Iowa City, Iowa on Wednesday, June 16, 2010. Not a single X was drawn. Not a single O was discussed. The full-day seminar was entirely philosophical and relational in nature. I was refreshed by a presenter who sought to help us discuss the "why" behind the "what" of athletics. Men and women of various sports benefitted from his teaching.

Our host was The University of Iowa Football Program, and our presenter was Joe Ehrmann. Joe is the founder of a Baltimore, Maryland community center known as The Door. He is co-founder of a Ronald McDonald House for sick children in Baltimore. He launched a racial reconciliation project called Mission Baltimore. He is Pastor of the large Grace Fellowship Church. Maryland Governor Robert L. Ehrlich, Jr. once said, "He's a lot of things to a lot of people. He's really an opinion leader. And what I love about Joe – it's not just the messages. It's the messenger. He's a very unique man. Gentle. Principled. Committed. And effective." (Marx, p. 1)

Coach Ehrmann is a "coaching evangelist" who is seeking to change many negatives of athletics one-coach-at-a-time, one-program-at-a-time. As Defensive Coordinator of Gilman High School in Baltimore, he is living the model he espouses. He brought credibility, character, creativity, concern, content, and challenges to the 100-some coaches in attendance. I was touched by Joe Ehrmann's words at a deep and spiritual level. I think you will be similarly inspired by his perspective.

I was most impressed that Head University Football Coach Kirk Ferentz committed himself and his entire staff to every minute of the seminar on this day. (Coach Ferentz's wife, Mary, sat next to her husband through the entire clinic as well.) June was a busy month as Big-Ten coaches were preparing for the upcoming football season, but these coaches seemed as committed to building a positive culture in their sport in the same way that they seek excellence in their schemes for offense, defense, and special teams.

Coach Ferentz [pronounced FAIR unz] introduced Joe Ehrmann [pronounced ER muhn]. Coach Ferentz knew Joe in 1996, when Kirk was coaching with the Baltimore Ravens. Kirk and Mary's son, Brian, played two years for Joe at Gilman. Coach Ferentz and his entire family have been influenced positively by the book, *Season of Life*, by Jeffrey Marx, published in 2003; *Season of Life* was written by a former Colts ball boy turned journalist, who shadowed the Gilman football team during an entire season. Many of the following ideas are also detailed in that book.

Joe Ehrmann is on a mission to "preach" a message which changes boys into men, girls into women, coaches into mentors, and athletic programs into powerful platforms for changing more than just athletes.

Joe's materials inspire: "The mission of [his] InsideOut Coaching [approach] is to inform, inspire, and initiate individual, communal, and societal change through sports and coaching. The goal of InsideOut Coaching is to create a tipping point in the world of sports where coaches and institutions support and implement the idea that the physical, social, emotional, and moral well-being of players are no longer considered beyond the scope of what sports and coaches can or should accomplish."

Joe excelled as a high school football player in Buffalo, a college player at Syracuse University, and a professional athlete for 13 years with the Baltimore Colts; but he is not living in the past; he lives for relationships in the present, and he looks to a more positive vision for sports in the future. Joe Ehrmann works hard as a coach to help his athletes compete fiercely for wins, but the bigger "wins" for Coach Ehrmann happen in the hearts of his players, parents, teams, and community.

A product of the 1960s, he is wired to address issues of social justice, so he is attempting to "evangelize" a culture to a new way of thinking about sports, and he sees coaches as the men and women who have the most influence to impact the culture through sports.

Coach Ehrmann is a deep thinker. Just as his coaching clinic was certainly not your typical seminar, he is not your typical coach. His vocabulary is large. His experiences across venues are rich. His wife is a psychotherapist, and her influence has invaded his written and oral communication. He formed a foundation to address the issues of fatherlessness and false cultural conditioning of gender identity.

Joe and I agree that coaches need to truly understand themselves and the purpose of their coaching. I asked former IHSAA Executive Director Bernie Saggau the question, "What can we do to redeem abuses in athletics?" He told me, "One of the solutions is to hire coaches who understand why they're coaches. That's the key. The parents will object at first. But the parents will see coaches who are developing character and should ultimately support those coaches. I recently heard Paul Rhoads, the new Iowa State University Head Football Coach speak for 15 minutes. After hearing him talk, Paul Rhoads can run my butt off! Here's a guy who was a scholar. He's done marvelous things with kids. However, in four years, if he doesn't win, they'll fire him. Kirk Ferentz, The University of Iowa Head Football Coach, is that kind of guy. He's a good man. But if he won three games in a season, they'd all roll the drums on him."

Coaches need to understand their players. My Dad coached my Little League teams when I was 9 through 12 years of age. As you have already read, I was the "fat kid" during this time of my life, so I carried a lot of pain into any activity which stretched me outside my comfort zone. I did not want to call attention to myself for additional public "deficiencies." Another coach might have barked at me for my awkward abilities, but my Dad never criticized me. He gave me opportunities to play when I was not liked by my peers. He didn't judge me. He supported me. He didn't know as much about baseball as my high school coach, but he understood far more about *me*. He played catch with me when he could. Because of my Dad's relationship with me, and because of his coaching behaviors, I felt safe, loved, and valued for who I was – not what the culture would have defined me to be. I don't know what I would have done if my Mom or Dad would have "given up on me" as an athlete in such a massive system of people. My Dad loved me unconditionally. He believed in me. I understood that he valued me as his son. My Dad was the best coach I ever had, because he clearly valued me as a person (more than as a player), and he took the time to help coach my team, even though he was a very busy elementary school principal.

If I were still a full-time coach, I would understand my purpose as a coach is to help boys become men and girls become women, so they will positively impact the culture. It's Malachi 2:15 for me. We have children in order to raise the next "godly generation."

If I were still a full-time coach, I would be unconditionally committed to building a sense of positive community. In an article authored by Jeffrey Marx, essentially Joe's biographer, Marx wrote, ". . .Gilman football is about living in a community. It's about fostering relationships. It is about learning the importance of serving others. . . .accepting responsibility, leading courageously, enacting justice on behalf of others. 'I was blown away at first,' says Sean Price, who joined the varsity as a freshman and is now a junior. 'All the stuff about love and relationships – I didn't really understand why it was part of football. After a while, though, getting to know some of the older guys on the team, it was the first time I've ever been around friends who really cared about me." (Marx, p. 2)

Former Iowa High School Association Executive Director Bernie Saggau understands the need for coaches to effectively mentor their players through such life-on-life relationships: "Student-athletes need values to be strong people. The values they receive from athletics are not the running, jumping, and throwing. The values are dedication, loyalty, pride, teamwork. We need to teach disappointment in losing, or how can they handle bigger losing – like the loss of human life. There's got to be something stronger than just words. Today, we need people we can believe in. Role models are important – parents, yes, but not all parents – kids need role models. I speak to the boys at the American Legion Boys' State, and, after my talk, I could stand and listen well into the night; kids have told me about their suicide attempts. If a stranger can turn them on like that, a coach who is with them every day can turn them on. We're heading in the right direction. You don't have to beat on people mentally and physically. If you take the fun out of whatever you're doing, the kid will quit. You've got to make it fun. Athletes have got to love who they're playing for and with. Think about the number of kids whose dads don't love them, but the coaches can be their mentors. Coaches are teachers." Administrators should expect that all of the coach's words and actions be constructive. Correction should center on positive affirmation and teaching. The student-athlete must be able to improve her performance as a result of the coach's teaching.

Let's review the nuggets of Joe Ehrmann's coaching philosophy and practices.

"To Be a Better Man:

"Recognize the 'three lies of false masculinity.' Athletic ability, sexual conquest and economic success are not the best measurements of manhood.

"Allow yourself to love and be loved. Build and value relationships.

"Accept responsibility, lead courageously and enact justice on behalf of others. Practice the concepts of empathy, inclusion and integrity.

"Learn the importance of serving others. Base your thoughts and actions on 'What can I do for you?'

"Develop a cause beyond yourself. Try to leave the world a better place because you were here." (Marx, p.3)

Joe Ehrmann's coaching seminar was like none other. Parched coming in, I drank living water from a fire hose! All of America should be supporting Joe Ehrmann's efforts to change the culture of sports. As a result, we could see positive change in the cultures of our families, neighborhoods, churches, communities, states, and nation!

Now that I have hopefully established "a better way" for sports – a framework of participation which results in a more positive experience for everyone involved – let us concentrate our attention on the most important participants, the athletes themselves.

What do the participants say is important about athletics?

Read on.

Chapter 6

What Do the Kids Say?

*Recent research details the desires of student-athletes and
what they desire from participation in sports. What they desire
and what parents and coaches desire are sometimes
diametrically-opposed, and, in that regard, Dr. Bob will review
data in this chapter.*

Peter Barston, 15, is a student at Fairfield Prep School in Darien,
Connecticut. Most people in the community of scholarly research and
analysis would dismiss Peter as a researcher and his research as
perhaps invalid and unreliable. But let's not be too quick to dismiss
Peter's body of study, which is apparently growing larger by the day.

Peter had read Michigan State University's Institute for the Study of
Youth Sports study of 11 reasons children might have for playing
sports. Since August, 2009, Peter had been intrigued by the question,
"Why do kids play sports?" So, rather than allowing that question to
remain locked in his mind, he took action. He started asking kids, "Why
do you play sports?" His was a simple, but you'd have to agree, clear
question. Like the Michigan State researchers, he asked respondents
to assign points based on the importance of the reasons. He polled
255 fourth through eighth graders of the Darien Junior Football League.
He queried 470 boys and girls in the same grades of the Darien YMCA
basketball league. In 2010, he had already begun to survey players in
the local softball program, and he has similar plans for baseball and
lacrosse players.

What has Peter Barston discovered to this point? His research is
consistent with Drs. Martha Ewing and Vern Seefeldt's Michigan State
study. The most important reason young people gave for playing
sports was *to have fun*, no matter how the data was broken down.
Ninety-five percent (95%) of the boys and 98% of the girls wanted to
have fun in sports. His research had confirmed the data of the
Michigan State body of work; that 1989 study of 28,000 boys and girls
around the country determined that "fun" was the top reason for playing
sports, followed by "to do something I'm good at," and "to improve my
skills."

"Winning" did not even make the top ten motivations for playing sport in Peter's study. His data indicated that "having" fun was twice as important as "winning." Peter was enlightened by the research; he said, "It shows kids are out there to get away from their lives and have a good time with their friends. They're not there just to win." Dr. Ewing expressed a glint of pride in Peter's replication of her Michigan State research: "It's a great project. Within communities, parents and sports organizations need to do more of it – talk to the athletes." Peter has also been praised by parents and officials of the Darien youth leagues. Junior football league board member Guy Wisinski pointed out that the survey provided "a touch of reality" for the adults in their community, concluding, "It reminds us why kids play sports in the first place. It's not about winning a championship in the fourth grade and having that be a life achievement."

To be a bit more detailed in my analysis, including longitudinal study, I now turn to research conducted in my own home state of Iowa. During the 2008-2009 school year, the Iowa High School Athletic Association conducted its sixth survey of athletic participation in schools. The IHSAA is so firmly committed to listening to the state's high school athletes that the organization's Constitution and Bylaws mandate this study. In 2008-2009, the IHSAA asked schools to randomly select and anonymously survey 20-30 student-athletes in their respective high school buildings. A total of 3,306 student athletes from 130 (of 500) schools represented sports participants from around Iowa. The break-down of respondents included 53% males, 47% females, 27% ninth graders, 26% sophomores, 26% juniors, and 21% seniors. A systematic (and hopefully interesting) executive summary of that study is in order, and I hope not to bog you down in a morass of numbers.

The vast majority of students participate in athletics "because they want to" (as opposed to participating "because their friends do," "their parents want them to," or "coaches talked them into participating"). The number-one benefit the athletes believe *should result from* sports participation was "teamwork and cooperation with peers." "Fun" was their number two benefit overall, which is change from 1998-1999 and 2003-2004, when "fun" was the number one benefit, and "teamwork and cooperation with peers" was their second perceived benefit. There was no statistical difference between boys and girls with their top three reasons (#3 was "self-satisfaction in setting/accomplishing goals").

The number-one benefit they have *actually experienced* through high school athletic participation is also "teamwork and cooperation with peers." Again, they experienced "fun" as the second highest benefit, and "good sportsmanship" cracked the top-three benefits. There has been an interesting rise of experiencing good sportsmanship since the surveys were given in 1998-1999 and 2003-2004, perhaps due to the state associations' intentionality in addressing sportsmanship as an issue. A vast majority (9 in 10) believe "sportsmanship is a priority" at their schools.

The student-athletes responded that they "feel more pressure to play well than to win" at a high rate (3 to 1), and a positive trend exists in that regard since 2003-2004.

From whom do they feel that pressure to *play well* and also *to win*?

(1) Themselves, (2) their coaches, (3) their teammates, (4) their parents, and (5) their communities – in that order.

What is their attitude toward winning?

1. "Win within the rules."
2. "Nice to win, but more important that the team plays well and has fun."
3. Nice to win, but more important that I play well and have fun."
4. "Win at all costs."

I found it interesting that the boys were more willing to "win at all costs," and the girls were more interested in the team and individuals playing well than winning. They perceived their coaches prioritizing playing well over winning, winning within the rules, and winning at all costs, a sign of health from 1998-1999 to present.

The student-athletes were also asked about negative experiences resulting from their participation in high school athletics. The top three negatives were (1) "too much time away from studies," (2) "too much pressure to win (from parents/self)," and (3) "no breaks between seasons." One very interesting change from earlier surveys is the dramatic shift of one perceived negative; in 1998-1999, "Athletic participation" wasn't fun" was the #4 negative experience for student-athletes, but it dropped to #8 in 2003-2004 and 2008-2009.

What qualities *should* a coach demonstrate, in their opinion? (1) fairness, consistency, and a positive attitude, (2) a person whom players should be able to look up to as a role model, and (3) effective communication. The rest of the possible responses included good teaching, dedication/unselfishness with their time, respectfulness, trustworthiness, and caring. Role-modeling and teaching have gained traction over the years of the study.

What qualities *are* your coaches actually demonstrating? (1) fairness, consistency, and a positive attitude, (2) dedication/unselfishness with their time, and (3) effective communication. Over time, student-athletes in Iowa (although not the same athletes who took the survey on the two other most recent occasions) are noting a dramatic improvement of coaches who are unselfishly dedicating time to coaching, and they noted role modeling as markedly lower in actuality than at the athletes' desired levels.

A trend also shows that coaches, given actual observed behavior, are significantly less trustworthy in 2008-2009 than they were in 1998-1999. Females are perceiving coaches to be role models less prominently than do males.

The survey respondents were also asked about the top five concerns they had about their coaches:

1. "Coaches who have favorites"
2. "Coaches who have unreasonable expectations of my time"
3. "Coaches who expect me to practice/compete year-round"
4. "Coaches who don't substitute when appropriate"
5. "Coaches who think a loss makes them look bad"

Other possible responses were coaches who "give too few compliments," "don't' exhibit good sportsmanship," "overlook team rule violations," and "swear at players." I was personally encouraged by the low incidence of swearing, since I can vividly recall regular vulgarity during my playing career in the 1970s and my coaching career in the 1980s, and I was encouraged by the shrinking incidence of "coaches who give too few compliments." Still, coaches would be wise to pay attention to these respondents' top five concerns about coaching behaviors.

Former IHSAA Director Bernie Saggau reinforced his concern about coaches expecting players to dedicate too much of their time and energy to one sport: "One of the biggest abuses is expecting kids to spend too much time on athletics. Is our goal to develop college players or develop just good people? How many people play Division-I or Division-II schools? We burn kids out. Coaches expect kids to be in a sport year-round. Tonight, I speak at American Legion Boys' State [a simulated government and leadership program for top high school juniors in Iowa, lasting four or five days at a military training base]. I had to write a letter to the baseball coaches one year, asking those coaches to allow their players to attend Boys' State after so many players were threatened [with the loss of their position or playing time]. I guess it worked. Fifty more kids showed up for Boys State the next year."

What were the top five ways that parents supported their children's participation in athletics?

1. "They encourage me."
2. "They attend most of my games."
3. "They let me choose what sports I want to participate in."
4. "They support me when we lose."
5. "They reinforce the value of my participation in sports."

The data had not changed much since 1998-1999, although a trend exists for one of the descriptors. Students are seeing a rise in parent attendance at most of their games. In one sense, that phenomenon is good, in that parents are more involved in the athletic lives of their children; in another sense, that increased involvement could be a negative, if the parents are overly involved. I can make no conclusion in that regard, based on the survey results.

At least 9 of 10 student-athletes participate in voluntary pre-season workouts (such as open gyms and "captains' practices"). I am not surprised that the percentage has increased significantly since 1998-1999 and even 2003-2004, since there is greater pressure to spend more out-of-season time preparing for participation. The number-one reason for participating in these pre-season workouts was "to keep my position on the school team," followed by "I participate when and how much I want to" (which is a reassuring notion), and "my coaches tell me I should participate."

Large percentages of student-athletes have also "participated in non-school competition while also participating in another high school sport (61%)." Mostly, such participation is for "fun," but there is also apparently some pressure by coaches, and athletes feel compelled by parents, coaches, and themselves to participate in non-school competition "to keep or improve position on the school team." Large percentages of student-athletes have also attended summer camps hosted by their high school coaches (73%), again for the same reasons stated about non-school participation, although "fun" becomes less of factor with summer camps. The data is similar for non-school competition during the summer, although "fun" is a greater factor (their #1 reason).

Respondents were asked to indicate whether the length of high school sports seasons were "too long," "not long enough," or "just fine." High percentages of girls basketball players, wrestlers, baseball players, and softball players indicated those seasons to be too long. High percentages of football players, boys golfers, volleyball players, boys soccer players, boys tennis players believed those seasons to not be long enough. And the student-athletes who were most satisfied with the lengths of their seasons were the cross country runners, girls swimmers, girls golfers, and all track and field participants. Lengths of practice sessions are seen as reasonable, and that trend has improved since 1998-1999 and 2003-2004. Student-athletes clearly favor voluntary (rather than mandatory) practices during the winter vacation days (unique to Iowa, since the energy crisis in the late-1970s established a still-mandated no-competition rule during this time period).

Three in four schools allow participation in more than one sport during any season, but only 1 in 4 student-athletes actually participates. The students are split on specialization ("participating in only one sport year-round"): 43% believe specialization to be good, and 57% believe it not to be good for the student-athlete. Athletes of all sports offered in Iowa athletics were asked if specialization was "necessary in order to participate" in high school, and responses varied from 19-34% saying yes. Iowans would be wise to watch that data, so students' athletic or overall lives do not become imbalanced.

The athletes "have been informed of the possible risks involved with athletic participation" (8 in 10), and the sources of such information, wellness, and nutrition were their coaches, parents, physicians, school's athletic trainer, and school's athletic director (in that order). Large percentages of student-athletes had "used nutritional supplements in the past year to improve [their] performance" (67%), but that number has been on a rollercoaster ride since 1998-1999 (25%) and 2003-2004 (96%). A significantly higher percentage of boys used nutritional supplements than did girls in 2008-2009. What nutritional supplements had they used? The largest percentages were sports drinks (96%), vitamin supplements (47%), weight gain products (31%, although the larger number being boys), and meal-replacement bars (23%), so concern about illegal nutritional supplements should be at a minimum (although 14% of males admitted to using Creatine in the last year).

What can we conclude from this Iowa data?

- Students have a balanced view of their participation in athletics. Teamwork, cooperation with peers, and fun are expectations for and actual results from participation in athletics.

- They have healthy attitudes about winning and sportsmanship.

- They perceive their parents' participation in athletics in positive ways.

- Student-athletes have generally positive attitudes about their coaches, lengths of practices, durations of seasons, and expectations for out-of-season participation.

- And they understand the inherent risks of sports and the need for proper wellness practices.

Such are the views of student-athletes in one state, although I would have to believe that Iowa's data is generalizable across the nation. Every state in the union should collect such data to better understand the attitudes of student-athletes about their sports experiences, parents, teammates, and coaches.

I hope we can agree that positive experiences in athletics carry-over to most fulfilling lives when we reach greater maturity. In 2008, the Iowa Girls High School Athletic Union conducted a survey of associations between participating in high school extracurricular activities and adult life experiences. Specifically, participating in sports during high school was associated with all of the following for high school graduates:

- Engaging in vigorous physical activity during the week
- Reporting very good or excellent emotional health
- Having higher self-esteem
- Not experiencing short- or long-term depression
- Feeling satisfied with progress made toward goals in domains of family, career, and general life
- Making active use of discretionary time outside the home
- Volunteering in the community
- Voting in state and national elections
- Knowing the names of U.S. Senators from Iowa
- Accessing news outlets every day
- Completing a four-year degree
- Having an annual household income greater than $50,000
- Not having trouble paying bills

Let's shift gears now to carefully review a subject which should be a focus of athletic participation for athletes, coaches, parents, spectators, referees, and sports administrators alike – *relationships*.

Information about research by Peter Barston and the Michigan State University Institute for the Study of Youth Sports was obtained from the following source: "A Survey of Youth Sports Finds Winning Isn't the Only Thing," by Mark Hyman, New York Times, 31 January 2010, http://www.nytimes.com/2010/01/31/sports/31youth.html?pagewanted=print.

Information about research by the Iowa High School Athletic Association is found in "Athletic Participation Survey, 2008-2009: Students Give Their Views," published by the IHSAA.

Chapter 7

The Great Sports Relationship Experience

Dr. Gary and Barb Rosberg, America's Family Coaches of Des Moines, have designed a "culture" (not program) for schools teaching K-12 students how to seek and develop great relationships through the six keys to godly relationships of commitment, service, forgiveness, boundaries, perseverance, and joy. The Rosbergs call this approach to relationships by the name of "The Great Relationship Experience." Dr. Bob will make a case that athletics must also teach student-athletes how to engage in great sports relationships, the perfect venue for such authentic learning. He calls this approach to relationships in sports by the name of "The Great Sports Relationship Experience."

The Great Marriage Experience

Please allow me a brief diversion away from sports to a discussion of marriage, so I can meander through an application of relationships to sports.

My horrible marriage was, in large measure, rescued as a result of Dr. Gary and Barb Rosberg, America's Family Coaches. (Can there be any better title for an organization within the framework of this book?!) I was an awful husband from Day 1 of my married life with the lovely Cheryl Butler Stouffer. I had no clue about my responsibilities as a husband. I was selfish. I tended to focus primarily on my own schedule and ways of dealing with the natural ebb and flow of life. My Mom and Dad never argued in front of my brother and me, so I had no idea how to resolve conflict with Cheryl. Actually, since my Mom never argued with my Dad, I was dumbfounded that any wife would ever disagree with her husband!

But disagreements were regular for Cheryl and me from the beginning of our married life, starting with my holding the Columbus, Ohio newspaper as a barrier to conversation on the morning after our first night as husband and wife. Early in our marriage, red hot anger resulted in yelling matches. Once we determined that such negative emotion was not working, red hot became white, smoldering silent treatments and depression (anger turned inward). Cheryl and I could have easily been divorced in year 1, 2, 5, 10, 12, or 17 of our marriage. We were emotionally divorced during too large a share of our 28 years together as husband and wife. I am grateful that Cheryl has been as equally committed to the institution of marriage as I. Our parents had trained us well. We had made a promise to each other – a promise which must be honored, even if the relationship was loveless.

In the 12th year of our wedded life, enter America's Family Coaches, a ministry dedicated to strengthening the relationships of married couples for the sake of the next generation of children who need the security of intact marriages. Enter also CrossTrainers, a ministry dedicated to equipping men to be better husbands, fathers, members of the workforce, and leaders in their places of worship. Enter, too, Homebuilders, a division of Family Life ministries, and several Bible studies dedicated to improving family relationships. Finally, enter PromiseKeepers, a men's ministry which ignited a passion among men to honor their rightful place to be servant leaders of their families.

My life started changing. Certain behaviors took a 180-degree turn. I quit slamming doors and yelling as an immediate response to non-compliance of others, including my bride. I quit swearing; cuss words literally even left the grey-space of my brain. While I do not begrudge the choice of others to legally and responsibly use alcohol, I quit drinking as well.

The old man must die, but the new man has some difficulty overtaking years of poor habits to become the new man. Old behaviors die hard. Such was true of me. I was challenged to rid my life of dysfunctional behavior. Cheryl was justifiably guarded with the new man Bob Stouffer. I had to build up trust. That has literally taken years.

Through those years, America's Family Coaches ministered to Cheryl and especially to me. In Year 17 of our marriage, we participated in Gary and Barb's first-ever "divorce-proofing campaign" at our church. As a part of that seminar, we were asked to identify behavior indicators which placed ourselves on a "marital map," reflecting honestly about the health of our marriage. Even after all of my efforts to be a better husband, I could not honestly conclude that our marriage was a positive witness for other married couples. I describe this moment in my life as a "two-by-four upside the head." My heart sunk, but I experienced new resolve to take bolder action for the sake of my wife, our marriage, and our family, including my daughter Molly.

As they continued to receive God's vision for their ministry, the Rosbergs wisely re-named "divorce-proofing" as "discovering the love of your life all over again," with positive vision and expectations for marital relationships. Barb and Gary did exhaustive research for their books and radio programs, determining six keys to godly relationships: (1) commitment, (2) perseverance, (3) forgiveness, (4) boundaries, (5) service, and (6) joy. The six keys became "The Great Marriage Experience."

The Great Relationship Experience

As a result of my friendship with the Rosbergs – and the creativity of their Chief Operating Officer, Dr. Clint Grider – we birthed "The Great Relationship Experience" (TGRE) for America's Family Coaches at Des Moines Christian School. If Gary and Barb could help strengthen marriages – to prevent divorce and to give examples of excellent marriages for the sake of the next generation – why couldn't Christian schools throughout the world also teach children how to find, keep, and nurture godly relationships with others?! TGRE also resources the parents of schoolchildren with tools to improve their marriages as examples to their children. Parents have the ultimate responsibility of mentoring their children, so the next generation is characterized by great relationships. The vision is for children to eventually seek spouses who share their belief in relationships characterized by commitment, perseverance, forgiveness, boundaries, service, and joy.

The Great Sports Relationship Experience

So, now, in the context of this discussion about athletics, why can't we also consider these six keys as pivotal to successful relationships and performance in sports? A natural extension of TGRE in Christian schools should be "The Great Sports Relationship Experience." Truth has a way of moving us in a direction which will allow us to experience great abundance in life. Let's now consider an application of TGRE to athletics.

Commitment

We can agree that great athletic teams are characterized by commitment. The commitment is to team over individual. The unselfish player sacrifices individual statistics for the sake of the most important statistic of sports – winning the contest. The coaches are committed to the players. The players are committed to their coaches. Players are committed to each other. Parents and other spectators are committed to supporting their children and the coaches as they pursue team goals. Trust and mutual respect are at the heart of this successful community. No trust and respect? No full commitment.

As a college football player, I was committed to my sport and to winning, but I had difficulty committing to coaches and teammates who were not as dedicated as I (at least in my mind). Every player was not committed to the sport or winning. Several of the players were committed to being high on drugs as their way of juicing-up for the intensity of the gridiron, and many of them also drank themselves silly on weekends after games to numb the pain of our poor performance. We're all going to be committed to something, and the objects of our commitment must be worthy, meaningful, and noble.

As a high school football coach, I worked with coaches and players who WERE absolutely committed to excellence, and our unranked football team was able to win a state championship with a group of young men who really had no business beating four ranked opponents, including the second place school, a consistent state champion for the past 30 years. Even though championship-caliber teams have talent, commitment *to the team* and team system trumps talent every time.

Perseverance

Commitment at all levels of competition fits hand-in-glove with perseverance. Coaches, student-athletes, and parents who are committed to success will persevere through even the most challenging circumstances. In that same regard, why did my marriage survive such inauspicious beginnings? Perseverance. Cheryl and I persevered. We simply did not give up, no matter how poor our marriage. People associated with successful athletic programs will persevere. We don't give up on each other. We learn and grow from adversity. We don't whine. We don't blame others. We don't play the victim. We overcome the conflicts, problems, challenges, tragedies, heartaches, and disappointments.

Such happened with our championship football team when I was a coach. We had been used to winning at a very high percentage. One year, we started the season 1-2 against some extremely talented football teams. As is typically the case with even a short string of losses, grumbling ensued. A few parents were angry about the playing time of their sons. A father was heard loudly berating us coaches in the stands during a loss. After the second defeat, our senior quarterback, who had started every game as a junior, dropped all of his gear in the coaches' office after Saturday films, telling us he had "had enough." The coaches were discouraged. In one sense, we wanted the season to "be over" at that point. But a more noble spirit took over. We really had no other choice than to determine a way of overcoming the despair all of us were feeling. We inserted an inexperienced (but quite intelligent) sophomore quarterback, we coached our hearts out, the players played with gusto, and we ran the table of 9 consecutive games on the way to our unlikely championship. What was a key to our success? Perseverance.

Forgiveness

Forgiveness is a major part of successful relationships, and forgiveness also plays a role in athletics. Sports involve a great deal of stress. Losses exacerbate negative emotions. Playing time becomes a central issue to everyone involved. In the heat of practices and competition, all of the constituents can lash out at each other. Egos are wounded. And pride prevents us from resolving our differences. Girls and women seem to have particular difficulty resolving their emotional differences. Boys and men disagree, punch each other, pick themselves up, and become fast friends. Girls and women disagree, emotionally punch each other, over and over again, and then engage in all-out guerilla warfare on sometimes multiple-front emotional wars!

Gary and Barb Rosberg teach through their "Loop of Forgiveness" as a critical part of a relationship which thrives, rather than simply survives. When a person perceives a wrong which results in hurt, he goes to the person wronging him, calmly states the perceived offense, and seeks to resolve the matter. The relationship is always more important than the issue in a good relationship. Hopefully, the other person offers genuine apology, and the relationship can continue, perhaps even stronger from overcoming the challenge. Gary and Barb talk about this process as "closing the loop." Unclosed loops of conflict will fester, growing the offense to even greater proportions, so that the unforgiving parties are locked in their prisons of their grudges.

Athletes need to learn how to forgive each other, their coaches, and parents for the mistakes they have made. They need to learn how to close their loops of conflict. Students should be able to speak with their coaches if treatment is harsh or playing time less-than-anticipated. As I indicated earlier in the book, I once allowed a football player to do a physical pre-season drill without shoulder pads, thinking there was no threat of an injury. In the monkey drill, three players leave their feet, rolling on the ground, as they weave in place, back-and-forth. I had overseen the drill hundreds of times before, and not a single injury had occurred. However, on this one *and only* occasion, the athlete, a promising senior who was seeking to be our quarterback, rolled at a bad angle, separating his shoulder. Of course, he was crestfallen, as was I. I felt terrible during the entire length of the injury recovery, which resulted in his loss of games during the season. I empathized with him, because I had missed several games of my senior high school football game as a result of a broken thumb. I was very fortunate that this player chose to forgive me. If he had not done so, I would have probably lived with his (and my own) disappointment to this day.

Boundaries

Sexual intimacy is one of the six keys to The Great Marriage Relationship. This key to godly relationships is adapted in schools as "boundaries." Boundaries are obviously quite necessary in The Great Sports Relationship Experience. Rules establish the parameters in which coaches coach and players play, and sports officials are charged with keeping all participants within the rules; left to their own devices, coaches and players would always push their limits, so objective "outsiders" are necessary to keep everyone from falling to those temptations.

Effective coaches define their expectations for athletic participation, and they enforce those high standards, so everyone is treated fairly. Student-athletes and parents will immediately "cry foul" if a coach is not consistent with her expectations, rules, and consequences. Playing time becomes the top subject of dispute, so the coach observes the efforts of her athletes during practice in order to fairly assign minutes or participation in competition. Normally, everyone involved with athletics can see if one athlete should win a spot over another, especially if the boundaries of that participation have been clearly defined in advance of participation.

Without boundaries, sports run amok. Without boundaries, relationships in sports run amok. In the same way that mission, governing values, visioning, and goals guide the successful organization, so, too, do athletes and coaches need to understand the purpose, guiding principles, individual goals, and team goals as the boundaries for success. Coaches like Tony Dungy, John Wooden, and Pat Summit have been successful because they have created cultures with clear boundaries.

Service

Service? Serving others? The Rosbergs call this key "serving love." People in relationships attempt to "out-serve" each other. The relationship is not 50-50; the relationship is 100-0 from the server to the served, and both parties should have that attitude. How does service contribute to success in athletics? I reiterate the need for team goals to supersede individual goals. By caring more about what is best for the team, a student-athlete and parent "serves" the others on the team. Why did a football coach instruct his defenders to clear a lane on the field for a mentally-challenged running back to score his first and only touchdown at the end of his high school career? Serving love. Why did a women's college softball team pick up and carry their injured opponent all around the bases, so she could score the record homerun she had just hit? Serving love. Why did a Christian high school coach instruct his own fans to cheer for the players on the opposing prison football team, instead of his own? Serving love. Why did track officials allow a British father to help his injured world-class sprinter son to the finish line in the Olympics? Serving love.

There are no boundaries for love in sports. Members of athletic teams should care for and about each other. Competition is not simply about showing up, competing hard, and earning wins. The wins and losses will be long forgotten, but the depth of relationships and the shared experience of good times and bad times will enrich the souls of those who poured their lives into each other. The coach is responsible for nurturing this mindset. Student-athletes must "get with this program." Parents should unconditionally support a coach and team which aspires to The Great Sports Relationship Experience.

Joy

I believe the final trait of The Great Sports Relationship Experience is both a key and result of the other 5 keys. When I commit, persevere, forgive, stay within boundaries, and serve while participating in athletics, I experience true joy, including times when I experience defeat. When an athlete gives her best effort, keeps plugging away through hard times, harbors no resentment toward others or losing, honorably competes within the rules, and serves the others associated with her team, joy results. And joy is also key to the positive and successful athletic experience. The athletes, coaches, and parents must bring an attitude of joy to their roles in sports. Attitude and motivation have a great deal to do with long-lasting enjoyment of sports participation. Extremely talented athletes with "stinky" demeanors are no fun to be around, and their personalities will not meld with the team. Give me an athlete with less talent and great heart every time. Coaches have a huge influence on joy (or lack thereof). Remember my story of winning two championships but being filled with relief, rather than joy? My coaches could have helped me experience more joy by encouraging me more, pointing out my strengths and positive accomplishments on many more occasions. An attitude of joy is absolutely essential to The Great Sports Relationship Experience.

What I am writing about truly is an "experience." I am not talking about a "program." Programs are designed and executed step-by-step. The word, "program," can take on a connotation which I do not support in the athletic setting. I favor the word, "experience," because a coach cannot "program" effective relationships. We are complex people. We are fearfully and wonderfully made. Not one of us thinks, speaks, or acts in programmatic ways. But we do *respond* to each other through relationship. And those relationships are experiences which will leave lasting impressions on us. Everyone will remember a special team with special chemistry, even if that team does not win a championship. Much can be learned through a positive *culture* – not *program* – of living life to its fullest. More than *success* or our own *happiness*, we seek *abundance* of life. Such defines The Great Sports Relationship Experience. And that is why I believe extension of The Great Relationship Experience to sports is a natural fit for all schools, especially Christian schools. Public schools and sports leagues certainly can steer clear of the overt biblical references and still effectively teach about the importance of commitment, perseverance, forgiveness, boundaries, service, and joy in athletics.

Practical Applications

1. Christian schools should contact America's Family Coaches immediately to become The Great Relationship Experience Schools (www.thegreatmarriageexperience.com).

2. Athletic programs should use The Great Sports Relationship Experience as a focus for all athletes, coaches, parents, spectators, and administrators.

3. Schedule Dr. Gary and Barb Rosberg to do a conference for all of the parents of your school or league, centering on the importance of relationships in sports.

4. Hang TGRE banners in prominent locations of the school or athletic complex. Sell affordable TGRE rubber bracelets to students who enjoy collecting those bracelets. Sell affordable TGRE t-shirts to people who are interested.

5. Fund and partner with an international school or sports league as fellow The Great Sports Relationship Experience schools/leagues.

6. Consider serving as a financial sponsor of and partner with America's Family Coaches.

7. Hold regular school or league assemblies around the traits of TGRE.

I believe I have stated an airtight case for the importance of great relationships in sports. Now, we must apply those principles of relationship-building to the constituents who are most closely impacted through relationship, the first of whom is absolutely necessary for sports to exist – *the athletes.*

Chapter 8

This chapter challenges players to new heights of honor in athletic competition. Readers should also consider the written pledge for honorable behavior of student-athletes in the Appendix.

The Prototypically Honorable Athlete

I love Tim Tebow. I love Tim Tebow even though I have never met him. I love Tim Tebow in every sense of the word. I love him as a fellow Christian brother. I love him for his abilities as an athlete. I love him as a leader. I love him as a missionary. Most importantly, I love him for his character, authenticity, and humility.

I was taken aback one Sunday at my church when I declared my love for Tim Tebow and a young woman, whom I respect greatly, expressed certainty that Tim Tebow was too bold in expressing his faith and perhaps "too good to be real." She viewed him as "plastic" – anything but authentic.

I beg to differ. Tim Tebow has done nothing to dispute my positive perception of him as a person or athlete. A freshman, he started as a Bowl Championship Series quarterback for the University of Florida. He has excelled at the highest level of athletic competition, helping to lead the Gator football team to two National Championships, an extremely difficult task. He is the first-ever sophomore winner of the Heisman Trophy, an award reserved for the best player in college football. In fact, I became a Tim Tebow fan when I heard his comments prior to and after announcement of that award; he had a humble confidence about his abilities, deflecting credit away from himself and always toward his teammates, his coaches, and his God.

Tim Tebow also consistently lives out the biblical truths cited on his now-famous eyeblack "undershadow." He joyfully serves with his parents and other family members as a Christian missionary to the Phillipines. He regularly speaks and ministers to prisoners. Most of us would be scared spitless about such invitations, but Tim Tebow understands the ways that he can be used in this platform of sports. He is a witness for his faith no matter where he is and no matter his circumstances. I have never heard or read a word which is inconsistent with his faith. Tim Tebow is not perfect. I'm not putting him on a pedestal. He'd have no part of that. When he has not performed to a level anticipated by himself or football fans, he has taken full responsibility for his performance, vowing to improve in the future. He made good on his tearful "promise speech" after a 31-30 defeat to Ole Miss. In fact, one journalist, Clay Travis, wrote about that defining moment – "In responding to defeat, Tebow became more interesting than he ever was in victory." And Tim Tebow delivered on his promise; I have no doubt that he worked harder than anyone on the Florida team to improve his own play and to improve the overall play of the team.

Allow me to heavily depend upon Mr. Travis – *a Tennessee fan* – to speak of his high regard for Tim Tebow:

"Let me be clear. . . .I love Tim Tebow because he is the most authentic figure in sports today. Maybe, in all of American public society. Too often our sports heroes like Tiger Woods or Mark McGuire are steeped in artificiality. The same is true of our political figures, or religious leaders. . . .virtually everyone in the public arena today is selling us something that has nothing to do with reality. . . .I love that Tebow is refreshingly honest, direct, disarming, a man in full. . . .Tebow isn't playing a role. Because his role isn't to be cool, or to be calculated, or to do anything like that. . . .it's to be as real as real can be. . . .I asked Tebow if he was saving himself for marriage. [Tebow immediately said yes.] And all his answer did was burnish the mythological and otherworldly image of Tebow. But what it also did was provide still further evidence that Tebow was refreshingly honest, someone who is willing to live his faith and continue to propound the faith even when it might not be cool. . . .In my experience, some of the biggest hypocrites on earth are those who profess themselves religious and evangelize for their faiths. But Tebow's different. . . .Tebow cried [at the end of the Alabama game in the 2009 SEC Championship] even though Alabama fans cheered his crying. . . .he just reacted as he saw fit. . . .For four years, Tim Tebow wasn't better than us. . . .he was honest with us." ("After Memorable Sugar Bowl, Saying Goodbye to Tebow Is Sweet Sorrow," FanHouse.com, 02 January 2010)

Tim Tebow was not afraid of career or life backlash to the 2010 Super Bowl advertisement he and his mother did for Focus on the Family (even though the pre-game hype garnered more attention than the ad itself). He did what he felt was right. Why wouldn't he tell his story as a testimony of life? Doctors had told his missionary mother and father to abort her baby in the Phillipines, since a tropical disease could result in birth defects. She and her husband said no. Their faith informed them that the child was "fearfully and wonderfully made." The baby was born. The baby was Tim Tebow.

All of this talk of Tim Tebow is an introduction to a chapter which is aimed exclusively at the athletes in this reading audience – student-athletes who should be carefully considering their behavior as they represent themselves, their families, and their schools. Tim Tebow is the quintessential example of exemplary student-athlete. In my mind, he is the "vision" to which every athlete should aspire. He is a man of integrity. He is a man of an outstanding work ethic. He is a man who has a proper life-work balance.

What about you, student-athletes? Whether you are four or forty years of age, you have a responsibility to conduct yourself with honor.

Student for Life

While you are still in school, your highest priority is school. Such is why I so frequently use the term, "student-athlete," in this book. Even those who have concluded their high school and college programs are still "students" in every sense of the word, or they would not be successful in higher levels of athletics.

I learned this lesson well in my own life. The son of a kindergarten teacher and elementary school principal in the same school district has no choice but to do well in school, particularly when he is a first-born people-pleaser! I often heard about my school day missteps at the dinner table, and I never learned about the "sources" who had informed my folks about said incidents! Realizing that my mother and father were paying for my undergraduate education, I went overboard in my studies. I was all studying and football, but I made nearly no time for anything or anyone else. The drive allowed me to graduate with honors as a high school, undergraduate, and graduate student. My first point to student-athletes is that we NEVER stop learning. You are a student for life.

Code of Honor

Athletes of honor live by a code. In that regard, you've got to love the "Husker Prayer" of University of Nebraska Football –

"Dear Lord,

The battles we go through life,

We ask for a chance that's fair,

A chance to equal our stride,

A chance to do or dare.

If we should win, let it be by the code –

Faith and Honor held high.

If we should lose, we'll stand by the road

And cheer as the winners go by.

Day by day, we'll get better and better.

The team that can't be beat

Won't be beat."

Amen! Amen! And amen!!

Work Ethic

Uncommon athletes display a distinct work ethic. NFL Referee Scott Helverson pointed to Kurt Warner as a man of honor in their league. "Nothing was given to him. He worked himself up the ladder the hard way," Scott told me. Honorable players can also be creative about substituting good habits for bad habits. Ted Barrett talked to me about Mel Mussana, a journeyman catcher who won't cuss in such a culture of cussing. Ted said, "Mussana makes up words at the point of swearing. It's code-cussing!"

Team

I asked Major League Baseball Umpire Tim McClelland how the game had changed from the start of his illustrious career to today. He responded, "When I was starting, it was all 'team.' Now, it's all about

61

'what can I do for myself, and how can I get the big contract?' Players will say it's about winning the world championship, but it's not all about that world championship. It's all about the money. The purity of the game is lost. I doubt if we can get it back. It's a sign of society. It's me, me, me. It's quick-fixes. It's drive-thru." Players of honor emphasize team above individual. The only statistic which is truly important is whether the team has been successful. Players of honor are about us, us, us.

Celebrity Does Not Change Them

Athletes of honor remain humble and don't allow fame or money to change them. MLB Umpire Mike Everitt pointed to two players whom he admires – David Eckstein and Brandon Inge. These players' names are not immediately recognizable to the general public, because they do not rack up statistics, but an objective umpire sees them as the upper-echalon of character in the game of baseball. Mike said, "I remember when David Eckstein made it to the major leagues with the Anaheim Angels. He was 5'8". He didn't look like a MLB player. He didn't behave like a MLB player. He went to the library every day to use the library's computer. He drove an old car. He hasn't strayed from that very much. He kept in touch with a kid who died of cancer in my area. Brandon Inge is a talker. He likes to talk. He takes life as it comes. That's a rarity." MLB Umpire Eric Cooper also mentioned Brandon Inge in complimentary terms.

Love for the Game

Tim McClelland commented on a few Major League players who communicated a pure joy and love for the game of baseball: "Robin Yount stands out to me. He has respect for the game. He enjoyed playing the game. He never argued with or questioned an umpire. He played hard. In spite of our famous 'disagreement,' George Brett also loved to play the game and enjoyed the lifestyle. Today, Brandon Inge is like a mini-George Brett. He enjoys his association with umpires and the game. Ken Griffey, Jr. is another good guy. He loves to play the game. I've never seen him argue with an umpire. His dad helped him to be a good role model. He plays hard."

Great athletes have fun when they are playing a "game" for "work"! MLB Umpire Mike Everitt made a startling observation when speaking to me: "I spoke to the local little league team this year. You know what

I noticed? The kids didn't have a look of fun in their eyes. Now, a kid picks a sport and does it year-round. Where did we lose the fun? Of course, you want to win at the state tournament level, but the kids are afraid to lose."

Respect for the Game and History of the Game

Great players of honor respect their game and the history of their game. Tim McClelland told me, "The players [today] don't have an idea of or a respect for the history of the game. One of the Major League players asked a pitching coach who had an 8- or 10-year Major League career, 'Did you ever play in the big leagues?' When you lose the history of the game, you lose a sense of the purpose and meaning behind the game."

Accountability

Players of honor tell the truth and are accountable for their behavior. Major League Baseball Umpire Ted Barrett told me, "Matt Herges has been in the big leagues for a long time. He was exposed for using H.G.H. I love how he handled it. He admitted it. His elbow was hurt. Rehab didn't improve his health. He told the truth to his agent, the GM, the media. He owned up to it." That's refreshing honesty and character in a culture which is more often treated to examples of dishonest denials, blaming, and failure to take responsibility for mistakes.

Sportsmanship

I once received an e-mail from an opposing team's parent. She wrote, "I wanted to compliment your girls on their good sportsmanship. Unfortunately, my daughters had previously had a bad impression of Christian schools. . .their language and dirty play was worse than any public school they have played (at least in years past). . . .My impression of your school is that they are being 'raised well.' It was nice that your team lived up to my expectations – they backed me up! My girls said they played good, hard ball and just didn't turn the corner into smack talk, bad language, and dirty play. Nice to hear." Nice for the administrator of a school to hear about his school's athletes, especially from a fan of the opposing team! Music to my ears.

One of my school's grandmothers pointed to the sportsmanship of a young group of athletes. The fifth grade team, of which her grandson has been a part, finished a successful season at 22-6 overall and 10-0 in the league, with two tournament championships. She wrote, "During the season, the boys played with competitive intensity, but also with such outstanding sportsmanship that it drew comments from officials at some of their games. . . .Because of their composure, it was often hard to tell who had won or lost. They accepted victory or defeat with the same great attitude. . . .These boys and their coaches have done a great job in representing their school, their families, and their faith during the season, and you should be proud of them." I am most certainly proud of them and proud to receive such communication!

Players of honor acknowledge the talents and abilities of their opponents. One of our parents observed the behavior of our best basketball player after an outstanding opposing player had fouled out in the last game of his high school career. She wrote an e-mail to our young man's parent: "My husband and I were sitting directly across from the opponents' bench. We had the privilege of watching your son and his teammate show an amazing act of kindness toward a player who was obviously upset. . . .your son's behavior is a great example of the leadership that is shown at home. . . .We felt so proud to be 'on his team'! We hope Branden and Ryan realize the impact they both make on our children and on us, as parents."

A basketball official pointed out the following to our school after a hard-fought and tense game: "I want to commend your girls and boys, your staff, and fans. I have officiated nearly 200 games over the past two years of varsity, junior varsity, junior high, and AAU ball, and I have never seen such mature young people on the floor. The boys were in an especially hostile situation, with a hostile opposing crowd, and opposing players that were playing very rough, despite our efforts to keep the play in-check. Your players certainly had reason and opportunity to lower themselves to the level of the situation, and they did not. I give a great deal of credit to those kids, their parents, the coaching staff, and your crowd for staying above the fray and trusting the officials to keep things under control. Your kids should be proud to wear the name, Christian, on their uniforms, because they embodied that spirit last night."

Earlier in the book, I alluded to one of the most magnanimous examples of sportsmanship ever, coming from Mallory Holtman of Central Washington University:

"Western Oregon University's Sara Tucholsky had no idea that the first
– and, as it turns out – only homerun of her career would cause ripples
that would make her last swing of the bat as a college softball player a
national media sensation.

"With two runners on and her team down a run to Central Washington
University, Sara hit a homerun to centerfield. As she rounded first
base, she missed the bag. When she turned to tag the base, she
injured her knee. Able only to crawl back to the base, Sara was told
that she would be called out if her teammates came to her aid. If a
pinch runner checked into the game, her homerun would count only as
a single.

"Players and fans alike were stunned when Central Washington first
baseman Mallory Holtman, the conference's all-time homerun leader,
asked the umpire if there was any rule against opponents helping an
injured player around the bases.

"She was told there was not. Together, Holtman and shortstop Liz
Wallace picked up Tulchosky and carried her around the bases,
stopping at each bag to allow Sara to touch it with her good leg. 'It was
the right thing to do,' Holtman said in an interview on national
television, after the respectful act of sportsmanship had been
witnessed by millions on ESPN and had become a YouTube sensation.

"The three runs sent Western Oregon to a 4-2 victory, ending Central
Washington's chances of winning the conference and advancing to the
playoffs.

"'It's a great story,' Western Oregon coach Pam Knox said, "Something
I'll never forget – the game's about character and integrity and
sportsmanship, and it's not always about winning and losing.

"As it turns out, the players who helped Sara had no idea of the
circumstances surrounding the at-bat, or that the story would make
headlines around the country. 'We didn't know that she was a senior or
that this was her first homerun.' Wallace said. . . 'That makes the story
more touching than it was. We just wanted to help her.' The gesture
left Sara's Western Oregon teammates in tears. 'I hope I would do the

same for her in the same situation,' Sara said. Central Washington coach Gary Frederick called the act of sportsmanship 'unbelievable.'

"In the end, it is not about winning and losing so much,' Holtman, who initiated the act, said. 'It was about this girl. She hit it over the fence and was in pain, and she deserved a homerun.'" (Simple Truths website, www.simpletruths.com)

If your eyes haven't moistened, you don't have a pulse. Athletes are role models whether they want to be or not. How refreshing that these Central Washington athletes had the right perspective on winning, losing, and sportsmanship.

Margin

I was proud when my daughter Molly graduated from college. I was proud that she had met her very godly husband while in college. I was proud her for being spiritually mature after four years of college. I was proud that she had graduated with honors. At college graduation, I was also very proud of the number of strong friends in her life. To be frank, I had personal regrets when I watched Molly walk across the stage. I wish I had sacrificed a few As in classes and a few work-outs as an athlete to invest in friendships which would last a lifetime. Molly enjoys the dividends of her investments. I not only didn't invest; I didn't do my part to save such memories.

Kelly Smies understands the dilemma of limited margin for the student-athletes. We need margin of time and energy to live out the busy lives of the Twenty-First Century. Consider the entirety of a column she recently wrote as a reporter for her college newspaper:

"Athletics are a plague. . .contagious, quickly spreading, indiscriminate, showing no mercy.

"The plague is a silent killer. . .it shows no obvious symptoms, but eats away at families across the nation.

"This may seem ironic coming from the pen of a collegiate athlete currently writing this from the stiff seat of the coach bus traveling ten hours. . .in order to get on the field and run for 90 minutes.

"Ironic, yes, but I'll keep writing anyway.

"I live in Oostburg, Wisconsin. Oostburg eats, sleeps, and breathes basketball.

"Their dedication is displayed proudly in the case holding six golden balls representing six state championships.

"In Oostburg, basketball hoops are like mailboxes. Every house has one.

"There is no off-season. Sixth graders are placed on select teams and travel statewide to compete.

"Kids as young as 2nd grade trade in their Saturday cartoons for 6 a.m. basketball camp.

"Athletes who succeed become instant celebrities, receiving profiles in the local newspaper.

"For Oostburg the plague is basketball – but in other towns it attacks as football, volleyball, soccer, hockey, or any other organized sport.

"Society approves athletics because they build character, encourage teamwork, form friendships, and improve confidence. Boys and girls learn sportsmanship, self-discipline, and time management.

"Local newspapers create the perfect environment where the plague festers and grows.

"There are multiple pages devoted to reporting the statistics and scores of the previous night's games.

"Full color action shots plaster the front of the section, while other articles cover the favorite classes, movies, and foods of the player of the week.

"What about music or theatre? No one ever sees the tuba player's profile or the actor of the week. Rarely do we see these performances advertised or celebrated in the same way as the athletic events.

"My own family undeniably suffered from the plague.

"Once upon a time we all sat around the table, ate together, talked together, and laughed together.

"By the time I reached middle school, dinner – if homemade – was in the car while Mom drove from my basketball practice to my sister's basketball game, while Dad was watching my brother's game.

"The plague stole away our family dinners.

"It's true that athletics have their benefits. However, problems surface when our life activities scale is heavily weighted towards sports."

Special Points About Christian Athletes

Christian athletes must walk the talk. Unfortunately, their behavior is not always consistent with their stated beliefs. And people are eager to pounce on any example of hypocrisy. In this regard, Jocelyn Meinders, Varsity Coach of the Pella Christian High School Girls and Boys Cross Country teams in Iowa, understands the importance of helping Christian athletes to understand their special responsibility as witnesses for Christ: "We emphasize from day one that we are to use the talents which God has given to us. One of my runners picked up on this idea and wrote on his Facebook page when he was frustrated by people who have so much talent, and they're not using their talent." Coach Meinders was greatly encouraged by the growth of an athlete in her program: "My senior captain was phenomenal last year. He admitted to the team that he had not worked as hard as he could have. He felt bad about that. He had found a verse from the Bible indicating that God knows when you're not doing your best. He said to all of his teammates, 'He does know. That made me feel terrible. I feel badly that I haven't put my very best effort forth. Now, I am working harder. I feel better for not wasting my talent.' I respected him for admitting that to his team." Coach Meinders concluded, "The main goal of our team is to honor and glorify God." Such is authentic Christian community, trust, and mutual respect among a coach and her athletes.

MLB Umpire Ted Barrett, a committed Christian, pointed out to me, "You'd have no idea these players were Christians by their behaviors. Here's the problem with some of these guys. They think that, between the lines, when they're playing, they have a license to act differently than when they're not playing. We need to honor God during every second of our day. Some of the players don't realize that. It's a macho culture. Mike Messini found that balance, getting respect from their teammates [and still exercising his Christian faith]. So I've called some of these guys out on their behavior. When I acted poorly as a Christian, I got called on my behavior. That's why I call out the behavior which is not consistent with their profession of relationship with Christ."

Practical Applications

1. Student-athletes, carry and use a planner which prioritizes your school work over athletics. Athletics are important, but athletics are a privilege, not a right, and school must take precedence in your life

2. Act on the intention of making at least one teammate look good during a practice and game. Sacrifice individual statistics for the sake of the game.

3. Lead an effort to assemble refreshment bags for opponents to take home after contests.

4. Form a group of two or three teammates as an "accountability group." Regularly check in with these group members, asking for honest feedback about your attitude and performance in sports.

5. Send an e-mail of appreciation to your coach or teammate after you have experienced honorable behavior on their part. Such

pieces of writing should be a part of any young person's experience; My friends Jennifer and Scott Erickson have always encouraged their two daughters, Emily and Anna, to offer thanks to the coach after every game and practice; their girls also thank their orchestra conductor after each rehearsal and concert. Jennifer concluded, "What deposits of goodwill and appreciation you see from this habit; everyone is blessed as a result."

6. At the end of a season, go beyond simply chipping-in for the coaches' gifts. Carefully compose a card or letter in which you specifically express your regard for your coaches. Very few athletes do this, so you will stand out for the care and love which went into this expression of appreciation.

7. Buy and send a card to your parent, expressing your appreciation for their appropriate behavior during games.

8. Athletes, be direct with your parents when they have passed over the boundaries of propriety when they are "shouting exhortations" at you, your teammates, opponents, officials, and/or coaches. Al Lorenzen, a former Mr. Iowa Basketball Player and University of Iowa Hawkeye star, was forced to confront the pointed behavior of his father during Iowa games, which made a positive difference in later games.

    Dr. Daniel Gould, Director of Michigan State University's Institute for the Study of Youth Sports, fielded a question from Jason, who asked, "Can you help me deal with my dad's embarrassing game behavior? I play middle school basketball, and my dad has been going crazy lately. He yells at me from the stands during games and gets in arguments with opposing parents and the officials. My teammates have even started to say things about him. It's embarrassing, and I don't know what to do. Can you help?" Such is a difficult situation for a child, wanting to honor and respect his father, while still wanting to be treated with respect. The Institute offered an effective answer:

    "First, recognize that things are not all bad. Your dad cares about you and is involved in your life. A lot of kids don't have that. . . .This does not mean that your dad's approach is the right one or that it is not embarrassing to have your dad constantly yelling at you and getting into arguments with opposing parents and the officials. . . .talk directly to your dad about the situation. . . .wait until you are away from the gym and in a relaxed setting to talk to him. . . .be very respectful. . . .say something like, 'Dad, I need your help. . . .When I am playing, I am having trouble concentrating. It's hard to stay focused out there, because I am trying to listen to you and play at the same time. What makes it even worse is that I worry about letting you down, and that makes me screw up even more. What should I do? Not only am I messing up, but playing isn't much fun anymore.' . . .someday, when you are an adult and have or coach your own kids, remember how you feel right now. Be sensitive to the young athletes' feelings. Recognize that adults need to provide young athletes with honest feedback and instruction, but in a positive, nondestructive manner." (www.edu.msu.edu.ysi).

Austin Helmink understands the honor he is seeking as an athlete. In 2009, Austin was a sophomore football player from Spencer, Iowa. After reading *Season of Life* by Jeffrey Marx, a book I referenced earlier in my book, Austin entered an essay contest, and he was honored by the Poet Laureate of the state. Jeffrey Marx had been a ballboy for the Baltimore Colts. Joe Ehrmann had been a wild and untamed Colt who treated Jeffrey with kindness, but the story goes that Joe Ehrmann found Jesus, became a Pastor, started a foundation to help boys become men, and coaches exclusively with positive action.

As I have indicated, Joe Ehrmann is a wise man, but listen to the wisdom of a 15-year-old boy in a prize-winning essay about that which is really important about sports. He has written Jeffrey Marx, thanking him for writing a book which so profoundly impacted his life. I am grateful that Austin gave me permission to reprint his essay in its entirely. You will be blessed by his words.

"Dear Jeffrey Marx,

"I worry. I worry about what my obituary is going to say, what my legacy will be. Will there even be one? Will people remember my name when all that is left is a headstone? Will my life have mattered in the overall scheme of things? Will my life be just another couple of lines in the obituary column? But these are good concerns because I am not lying on my deathbed wondering them. I am doing so as a fifteen-year-old with my entire life ahead of me and a chance to shape my life any way I choose. Your book, *Season of Life*, gave me my decision. I want to be a man built for others; I want to make a difference.

"Before reading *Season of Life*, I would have thought that football, a sport I play, and love, had absolutely nothing in common. They couldn't have been more incongruous. Isn't the whole idea of football to hate your opponent and try to bury them in the ground? Your book showed me that, while football is about knocking people down, it can also be about helping them up. You have used a violent sport to show how men and boys should dare be afraid to look for love.

"Through sports and entertainment my culture teaches me that to be a 'real man' I must be strong and athletic and have the most girls and money. I didn't believe this before, but reading your book added a different insight. Coach Joe Ehrmann's message was built around striving to be men built for others, to be others-centered. He talked about speaking at funerals and having to manufacture something good to say about the person. I don't want my eulogy to be 'manufactured.' I want it to celebrate the true impact I had on people and give my family comfort in thinking about the difference I made. But this is much easier said than done.

"As I read your book, I did a lot of self-examination, searching for Joe Ehrmann's aspects of a true man in myself. According to him, being a man means emphasizing relationships, having a cause bigger than myself, accepting responsibility, and leading courageously. It means that empathy, integrity, and living a life of service to others are more important than points on a scoreboard. It means understanding the pain of others and what causes it. I agree wholeheartedly that true masculinity is all of these things. The academic and athletic awards sitting in my room, the number of admirers I have, and the amount of possessions I own are not going to be remembered nearly as long as my actions that impact others. Why is it that people are willing to spend several thousand dollars to attend the Super Bowl, or that Hollywood is dishing out tens of millions to create the next blockbuster? I now realize just how skewed my culture has become. I now understand that my trophies will end up dusty and uncared for, my admirers long gone, and my belongings dispersed, but my actions could live on in the lives of others.

"Through your description of the extraordinary football program of the Gilman Greyhounds these messages really sank in. I realized that the key to being a successful team is the same as the key to life: love.

One of the characters, Napoleon Sykes, is a perfect example of the transforming power of Coach Ehrmann's philosophies. After Napoleon broke down in the middle of the Mount St. Joseph's game, because of the death of his friend Ryan, Coach Ehrmann took him aside and prayed with him. Napoleon then proceeded to dedicate the game to Ryan and haul in a 67-yard interception. This was inspirational in itself, but, during halftime, Napoleon's teammates told him how much they loved him, and this again shocked me. This was football?

"Your book, *Season of Life*, contained messages of masculinity, love, and making a difference that will be sifting through my mind for a long time. The path of a true man is narrow, but, in the end, it will be worthwhile. Thank you for showing me the simplest answer to what it truly means to be a man: love.

Sincerely,

Austin Helmink"

I am proud to say that Austin Helmink was a student at my Christian school just a year before I came to Des Moines Christian. How maturely he has expressed himself about athletics. He understands what should be bringing him joy through sports.

Players experience more joy in athletics if they are on the same page of the playbook as their parents. I can't think of a better segue to the object of our next area of study – *parents*.

Chapter 9

To Parents, Guardians, Grandparents, and Other Spectators

This chapter challenges parents, grandparents, and other relatives to be encouragers, not needlers who endlessly hover and live out their athletic failures vicariously through the "successes" of the children. Take special note of the written pledge for honorable behavior in the Appendix of the book. .

Indulge a parent's pride. My daughter is scary fast. Hannah is lightning in a short, compact brown bottle. She knows it. Everybody knows it.

Defenders scramble and back-pedal to catch-up when she's roaring down the sideline as a forward in soccer matches. Her biggest challenge is controlling that speed, breaking down, and using foot skills to find freedom and score goals. Natural ability unfortunately sometimes causes the athlete to rely more on inherent talent and raw power than finesse. Hannah is definitely NOT a finesse athlete. She's pure, unadulterated, unleashed energy.

Sprinters see her first out of the corner of their eyes, then into the peripheral vision, and finally, most of the time, in the distance at the finish line in very short races. She has run only one 400-meter dash, as a seventh grader, and, if she wasn't so "lazy" about this "longer" race, she could really excel at the distance. (She beat her older sister's personal best in the event – seventh grader to senior! My apologies to you, Molly.) One hundred and two hundred meter dashes are Hannah's forte. She has an instinct for exploding low out of the blocks, accelerating at amazing bursts with relatively short but muscular legs, drawing momentum mid-way through any race, and then allowing her competitive juices to fuel the final breaking of the tape. In that sole 400 she ran, a girl in an outside lane was five meters ahead of her two-thirds into the race. Hannah was having no part of that; she fired her after-burners and smoked all of the competitors in the end.

Before I go overboard with arrogance about my daughter's abilities, allow me to put her talent into perspective. She's fast. She's talented. She quickly picks up any sport. (My favorite is softball, which is now in her past, but her catching, throwing, and batting styles were almost picture-perfect even without coaching.) Hannah's self-image expands when she experiences success, although, counter-intuitively, she is her most humble when she is her most successful. (Conversely, she is her most angry and arrogant when she senses herself at her least competent. Makes sense.) Athletics shapes who she is and how she perceives herself.

But sports do not define her anymore than her vocal talents as a singer define her. (That's an entirely different source of parental and Hannah pride!) What would happen if Hannah experienced a season- or career-ending injury in soccer or track? Could she take the adversity in stride? Is her self-esteem tied too much into athletic performance? Could her mother and father love her as much as if she were not so accomplished in these sports? These are convicting questions for performer and parent alike. Such is why I must address parents in very frank terms. I personally temper my pride in Hannah's athletic abilities by not placing my own identity or Hannah's identity in those abilities.

Too many parents live out their own failed athletic experiences through their children. They vicariously push their children to early entry, multiple sports camps, travel teams, hours of practice, and over-programmed competition. These are the same parents who sit at many practices, talk to the coaches before and after any session, frantically roam sidelines as the play moves up and down the field, express frustration when the competition is not going their way, and yell far too loudly for the circumstances. I have a very uneasy feeling in my stomach when I am around these parents, wanting to distance myself from hovering moms and dads who put too much pressure on their kids.

Our culture has changed so much in the last 40 years. I started playing baseball when I was 9. I first played flag football in the fourth grade and didn't start playing tackle football until I was in the eighth grade. The lengths of seasons for athletics were brief and entirely local. Moms and dads socialized on the sidelines, allowing the volunteer coaches to have free reign in their oversight of the competitors. After each contest, everybody sat down to the leisurely drinking of a soda provided by families on a rotational schedule. Summers were reserved for play which was not organized; kids had almost three months to swim at the neighborhood pool, and only one sport was scheduled per season. I used to play baseball for hours on the Peterson Park playground, armed only with a beat-up bat and balls that would long be discarded today.

Except for the "treat schedule," everything is dramatically different in contemporary youth athletics. My daughter started playing soccer when she was four, so she had been playing competitively for almost 11 years until her 15th year, when she stepped away from soccer. Kids have multiple opportunities for sports within any one "traditional" season; in other words, in the fall, a female athlete could be playing "in-season" volleyball and "out-of-season" basketball, often causing coaches from those multiple sports to be at each other throats. Schedules are no longer compacted; my daughter played soccer year-round for the last several years of her career. Summer is not a time of rest, so kids could be kids, but, rather, the off-school-months are quickly snatched up by greedy coaches (and bloodthirsty parents) who want to gain the edge of additional practices and tournaments. Parents are willing to pay thousands of dollars for fuel, hotels, and restaurants at far-away cities, giving athletes more exposure to better competition and "scouts" who might determine scholarship-worthy competitors.

Every parent believes their child is capable of earning a full-ride scholarship to the top university, yet the data is quite clear that only a small fraction of high school athletes have the abilities to compete at and earn a scholarship for colleges and universities in our country.

The lives of parents and children are so busy they have no time for fun as a family, church on Sundays, or rest to refuel the souls. Many parents, stressed-out from the over-activity, yell and scream at anyone in their sight, overwhelmed by their own competitive desires for victory and success as lived through their children. And when the wins are not coming in large enough numbers, or the playing time just doesn't seem "adequate," they pull power plays through political league leadership, and there are incessant conversations between the disappointed parents and harried, pressured coaches.

At a required meeting of parents prior to a new school year, Al Lorenzen asked several pointed questions of the parents: "How have we gotten to a place where anger is accepted and celebrated in sports? Are we modeling accountability for our children? Are we expecting accountability from our children in athletics? How do we regain our focus on core values? And will we allow athletics to help connect us with our children?" Mr. Lorenzen speaks with credibility. He was the first Iowan to be both a High School All-American basketball player and McDonald's All-American at Cedar Rapids Kennedy High School in Iowa. As a college player at The University of Iowa, he competed in four NCAA basketball tournaments, finishing in the Sweet 16 once and the Elite 8 once. During his junior year, the UI basketball team was ranked #1 for several weeks. Al worked for a recruiting service, and he saw the emotional and outrageous expectations of parents. Al also served as the commissioner of an international basketball league, which included the responsibility of resolving grievances; he received letters about officials *from both teams in the same game*! While serving as Director of External Affairs for Drake University, a booster once appeared at his front door one Sunday at 9:30 a.m., angry because he would have to walk across the street to the athletic facilities from his newly-reassigned parking space. He saw the best and worst of athletics as director of the Des Moines Area Sports Commission. Al Lorenzen wants to help parents and everyone else in sports to get their lives back in perspective. Before I share some of his answers to the questions he asked and the solutions he believe will redeem sports, may I please name other abuses among parents, guardians, grandparents, and other spectators?

- Angrily yelling negative comments at referees, their own children, other parents' kids, and parents of the opposing team

Major League Umpire Tim McClelland knows the sting of absorbing the criticism of spectators: "My younger daughter's basketball team lost a game. There was a lot of yelling at the officials. It was a close game. No one cheered for their team. Kids need encouragement. Let's redirect the energies needed to yell at the officials by cheering for our own teams. We spend so much time yelling at officials. I feel more bothered about such situations, because I know what those guys are going through. I have to sometimes walk away from yelling parents. I've made some harsh comments to them. It does bother me. When I'm at a high school game or little league game, and spectators yell at officials, I say to the yellers, 'Is your daughter playing at a WNBA level? The best officials are working in the major leagues. The next best are working at the college level. The next best are working at the high school level. The next best are working at the junior high level, and so forth.'"

Ted Barrett, MLB Umpire, piggy-backed onto Tim's observations by telling me, "I don't care if some idiot who has had 10 beers is yelling at me. A little kid yelling at me, though, is learning that from his Dad or Mom. At all levels, competition has gotten twisted. I've been involved in church athletics. I called out a pastor's behavior at his son's game! I see completely sane people behaving that way everywhere else but sporting events! It's disturbing. It's epidemic."

Tim and Ted's counterpart in the NFL, Back Judge Scott Halverson, pointed out to me, "Parents need to focus on their own children's behaviors and not other people's children. Cliques form. It's sad. Parents are trying to live their lives through their kids."

Corbin Stone, director of coaching for the Iowa Rush soccer club said, "When the parent acts out, it's not only embarrassing for the child, it also sends mixed messages. Most kids will internalize those feelings, and it will cause anxiety and indecisiveness on the field. Some will simply want to quit. There are rare cases where kids seem to excel under parental pressure. But it's not the norm." (*Blue* magazine, Welmark, Inc., Spring, 2010, p. 20)

As Iowa's director of girls sports in high schools, Mike Dick has major concerns with the sportsmanship of adults: "Our sportsmanship with coaches and athletes has never been better. Our adults or spectators have never been worse. We watch too much television, and we think we have to act that way at junior high and high school level. Coaches are sometimes guilty, too. They all lose their perspective of what they're really there for."

- Passively ignoring or not holding others accountable for outrageously inappropriate behavior

We sit in bleachers, and we stand on sidelines. We observe some of the most outrageous behaviors from people who purpose to be adults. Yet we never say anything. That which is not addressed is blessed. I am as guilty as the next person. I will often get up from my seat or walk away from my position on the sidelines when people are behaving poorly. Shouldn't I be lovingly confronting those people to possibly extinguish the behavior? Depending upon the context of play, my "confrontation" can be as simple as the following: "In my humble view, we should be using all of our energies to cheer *for* all of the kids on the floor/field and not yell at the referees. Any negative behavior on our part will not endear us to the officials."

- Gossiping about or being unreasonably hyper-critical of players, coaches, parents, officials, and administrators.

Essex High School Athletic Director Ed Hockenbury of Vermont was pointed when he observed, "The irony is that perhaps the most negative aspect of the high school sports experience on a regular basis today is the criticism directed at coaches (or more often behind their backs) by the very people who expect them to be so positive with their kids. . . .At times today, high school coaches are in a position where they coach student-athletes who go home after games and practices and are either reinforced, or even told, that their coach is bad, that their coach cost them the game, [that] their coach was not fair, etc. This is certainly not true of all kids and parents, but it seems the number is increasing, and rather than helping kids develop character and accountability, parents contribute to a culture of finger-pointing and excuses." ("Learning From the Negative: A Positive Perspective on High School Athletics," *High School Today*, February, 2010, pp. 12-13).

- Turning a community against a coach

Such gossip can results in riptide momentum, resulting in the coach's undoing. I remember once when a prominent parent said to me, the school adminisitrator, "I don't want to spit on Santa Claus, but. . . ." The big *but* came after a disingenuous commitment to dignify the departure of a coach who had been a legend in the community. Even if he was not intending to spit on Santa Claus, he was doing precisely that. Parents have a remarkable ability to engage in clandestine combat, never having to be accountable for being the rabble-rousers who ignited the firestorm. Parents form the Parking Lot Mafias and B.M.W. Club (Bitchers, Moaners, and Whiners). Pardon my French, but it's the truth.

- Unwillingness to directly resolve conflict with coaches, using gossip or e-mail instead of face-to-face conversation

With tongue not entirely "in cheek," Major League Umpire Ted Barrett told me he has the perfect sport to effectively deal with the crossfires of conflict in sports: "Cross country is the sport. The runners go out and run. No one complains about 'running time.' There are no officials. No one can yell at the official. *This* is what youth sports is all about for me!"

- Choosing to bear grudges against coaches, other parents, and administrators

Our country apparently has an aversion to conflict resolution. We would rather stay locked in our prisons of unforgiveness than to speak honestly and politely to the people who can help us resolve our conflicts. None of us likes confrontation, but we need to get more comfortable about resolving our differences. Too many grudges silently continue and grow; hence, the quality of our relationships suffers.

- Believing that confrontation of an issue will result in repercussions to the student.

If I've heard someone voice this perspective once, I've heard it a thousand times. That's hardly an exaggeration over my 30-year career in education. I don't deny that negative consequences periodically do occur to the families which confront someone over perceived or actual misbehavior, but, in the vast majority of cases, problems can be solved and conflicts resolved, when confronted. Again, I believe this is an excuse for people who do not want to confront other people. When not confronted, the problem and/or conflict continue/s.

- Physically confronting officials and coaches in the heat of the moment

We have all seen this unfortunate occurrence. You might even have a queasy feeling in your stomach over a memory of such an altercation. They're ugly. Normally, self-control is the key to a person checking emotion at the pass gate. We cannot be perfectly-behaved robots at games, never showing our emotions, but, as I stated earlier, our culture seems to be angrier and more emotional than ever before. Emotions always raise the stakes in conflicts, making solutions and resolutions more difficult to reach.

"The most important thing is to remember it's not about winning and losing," says Corbin Stone. "See the big picture. Ultimately, you're preparing your child for facing the challenges of adulthood. When you lose perspective, it teaches your child an unhealthy lesson: winning at all costs, demonizing your opponent, disrespecting authority." (*Blue* magazine, p. 20)

- Concentrating more on the individual child than the team

We naturally should love our own children. But far too many of us parents love our children at the exclusion of other people's children, the team, and community. Some fixated fathers are singularly focused on

80

only that which is best for their kids. Some mothers hold the umbilical cords to children, never wanting to let go. If we're not careful, our children can become our "idols." We need to take the wide angle shot, not the super-close-up. Where is the forest when we are so enamored by the tree?

- Riding in on a white horse to rescue students from pain, disappointment, and negative consequences.

When I was a kid – here comes a geezer story – I was twice as much trouble at home with my Dad if I were in trouble in school. Today, *the school* is in twice as much trouble than the kid. Parents are not helping their children to learn valuable life lessons by being accountable for the natural and logical consequences of their behavior. We want to protect our children. We shield them from the negative consequences and then expect everyone else only to offer positive consequences to them. Real life involves challenges. Cutting a larva out of the difficult and confined space only kills the insect. Allowing the full struggle within nature's pouch produces a glorious butterfly! To use another metaphor, the refining fires burn off the useless dross of our lives.

As I began writing this book, a controversy brewed in Central Iowa at the end of the high school basketball season. Police had detained a varsity basketball player at a party where alcohol was being consumed by under-aged drinkers. (The parent-owners of the home were out-of-town, the perfect opportunity for the ubiquitous teenage kegger.) The student-athlete in question claimed that he not only did not consume alcohol in this home but that he was unaware of alcohol even being present at the party. He said that he was fatigued enough to sleep for two or three hours in one of the bedrooms during the party. He told the police and school officials that he left the party without anyone knowing but that he willingly returned, because he "had done nothing wrong and wanted to act responsibly." (*Des Moines Register*, 06 March 2010)

The Good Conduct Policy of this high school stipulated that a student's presence at a location where alcohol is being consumed is grounds for athletic suspension. Several student witnesses told school officials it was inconceivable that this student-athlete would have failed to see all of the alcohol at the party. This athlete's parents appealed the athletic suspension to Polk County Court. The judge initially issued an injunction against the suspension but then later "dissolved" his ruling when he learned more facts from school officials. The student, parents, and attorney followed due process with school officials to ask that the suspension be rescinded, so the boy could play in the state tournament basketball game. The two-game suspension was upheld, so the athlete missed the opening round and semi-final victories of his team, but he was able to play in the state championship game.

We would be right to say that this is an unfortunate set of circumstances. I pass no judgment. None of us will ever know all of the facts of the case. But I believe we can all agree that there are some unfortunate lessons being learned in the scenario, not the least of which could be the shielding of a student from the natural and logical consequences of his choices.

- Not allowing our kids to lead balanced lives

NFL Back Judge Scott Helverson made astute points with me in this regard: "We're over-organizing and over-programming our kids. Everyone has a computer. Everyone has a TV with over 100 channels. As a parent, I should be asking, 'Am I connecting with my kids?' Balance is the correct word. Too many parents are taking kids to every event, because everyone else is doing it. I'm worried about kids not experiencing other sports. They're specializing too much and too early."

Now that I have pointed to some of the specific abuses perpetrated by parents in sports, I would like to challenge the loved ones and spectators of athletics and other activities to a higher honor.

How can Christian parents be more positive?

- Parents should get their kids involved in reputable sports leagues with the right emphasis on fun, skill development, and character-building.

For instance, "Upward Unlimited is an international nonprofit children's sports organization which has designed sports programming aimed at giving children (ages 6-12) and their family's positive sports experience. To fulfill its mission, Upward creates partnerships with evangelical churches across the country and around the world. By working with and training local churches, more than half a million children. . .participate[d] in Upward [in 2009]." (McCaslin, p. 21)   Other positive sports organizations are mentioned throughout this book.

Mike Dick, Executive Director of the Iowa Girls High School Athletic Director told me, "We regularly survey student-athletes. "Why do you play?" we ask. The kids say, "To have fun." I'm not sure that's how Mom and Dad answer the question. Parents are living out their dreams through their children's athletics. They drive their kids to the point of all-conference and scholarships. Parents assert too much pressure for the wrong reasons. Too many parents want their kids playing for the wrong reasons – scholarships, recognition. All co-curricular activities are extensions of the classroom. We need to keep that focus. Sometimes, other things get too important and tarnish the game. Parents need to be more realistic about their kids' participation in athletics – very few high school athletes get a college scholarship or become an all-stater – but they can ALL have fun and learn how to be a better person. Let's make sports fun for kids again. Let's get away from specializations. Kids are better people if they've had a more diverse, well-rounded education."

Iowa High School Athletic Association Executive Director Rick Wulkow agreed: "Many parents refuse to accept the fact that only 2% of students will receive financial assistance at colleges for athletics. The best of athletics are the role modeling, the camaraderie, and the instilling of values that athletics can provide. Those values are important immediately and for the rest of those players' lives. The coaches who role-model those values have an impact. When you get with college-age kids and people in their 20s and 30s, and you ask them to name people who have had an impact on their lives, they'll name a coach a parent or grandparent, their pastor, or an elementary teacher, but there's usually going to be a coach who is named. There are coaches who don't role model the way we want them to, but there is a much larger percentage of those who do."

- Be students of your children's personalities. Be available to your children as a source of unconditional support, expressing belief in their abilities.

The National Center for Fathering recently reported about the close bond between record-setting U.S. Olympic short track speedskater Apolo Anton Ohno and his father, Yuki Ohno, a single father who raised his son: "Though Apolo's teen years were a bit of a rollercoaster, Yuki continued to speak purpose and hope into his son's life. Apolo says, 'Above all, he told me how great my life could be. He believed it before anyone else, even before me.' Today, Apolo considers his father 'the backbone of my support group. He knows when I'm up and when I'm down.'" The National Center for Fathering wisely points out, ". . .our role [as parents] is to help our children pursue their dreams and keep giving them a positive vision for what they can be and what they can accomplish. . . .We should truly focus on what's best for them, and then give them three important things: our consistent support, win or lose; our wisdom based on experience, delivered at the right moments to help them learn from situations; and our unconditional love, no matter what." ("Coach Your Kids to Their 'Olympic' Best," The Dads @ Fathers.com, 26 February 2010).

I have been an absent Dad in the past. I passively resisted stepping into the lives of my daughters. Dr. Robert Lewis, the Pastor of a church in Little Rock, Arkansas, has produced a number of resources which allow us to better understand the negative effects of passive and over-bearing parents, and he has encouraged us to enjoy the positive results of active, reasonable, balanced parenting. Dads with sons. Moms with daughters. Moms with sons. Dads with daughters. Single parents with mentors.

- Take primary and ultimate responsibility for the character development of your children.

The sports league is not primarily responsible for your child's character development. The coaches are not primarily responsible for your child's character development. Grandparents are not primarily and ultimately responsible for your child's character development. *You* and *your child* are responsible for the child's character development. Train, train, train. Never give up. There will be highs. There will be lows. Persevere. Don't be discouraged with setbacks. Keep going. Be intentional in your teaching. Don't expect each child to get the instruction immediately. I try to regularly write letters to my daughter about any number of topics related to her maturity, including issues related to her participation in athletics. She has stored-up over two years worth of these letters in a couple binders at her bedside. I know this communication is important to her, because I will often find her sleep in the morning with one of the binders near her head, no doubt the result of her re-reading one of my letters. In the Appendix, I have included an example of my April 30, 2010 letter to her a day after a track meet.

Al Lorenzen takes primary responsibility for teaching his daughter (and eventually his infant son) about the great value of teamwork, work ethic, overcoming adversity, winning with humility, and losing with grace in sports. He believes the drive times to and from practices and games affords parents with excellent "windshield time" to talk with their kids about sports and a variety of other developmentally-appropriate subjects in their maturation. "You've got a captive audience," he said. "It's awkward at first, perhaps, but they will grow to like it. Build relationships. Teach. Athletics, when channeled in the right way, ware powerful. Leave a positive legacy through the ways that you support your kids in athletics."

- Model effective behavior for your child. Show self-control. Keep your own behavior under control. Act with no hypocrisy.

The National Center for Fathering rightly asserts, "Make sure your behavior is consistent with what you expect from your child." ("Coach Your Kids to Their 'Olympic' Best," The Dads @ Fathers.com, 26 February 2010). Children have "bologna meters." They can recognize hypocrisy a mile away. Enough said.

Parents should ask their children how they should behave at practices and games. And, then, parents need to listen, respect, and respond to their children's desires. Al Lorenzen learned this lesson the hard way. His father was a West Point graduate who earned his MBA at The University of Chicago; but he, shall we say, lacked objectivity when evaluating the performance of officials at basketball games. He was an achiever. He was intense. At first, Al could not articulate his embarrassment about his Dad's courtside behavior, but, eventually, he told his father that he could no longer act like that at games. Al has asked his own athletic daughter how she wants him to behave at her games, and he has respected her boundaries for his behavior.

- Offer only positive, constructive shouts of encouragement to your own children and teams. Stifle all yelling and negative comments directed at players, coaches, parents of opponents, and officials.

I dream of a day when I experience a little bit of heaven on earth! What if the fans on my side of the athletic competition engage in only one behavior – cheering positively for our coaches and players?! But, noooooooooo! We allow our emotions to get the better of us. We scream at the official. We mock the opposing coach when he engages in inappropriate behavior. We jeer at the opposing player who plays too hard and perhaps even cockily in our minds. And all that negative behavior does on our part is to ignite similar behaviors in our own stands and, typically, an equal and opposite force from the fans of our opponents. Major League Umpire Eric Cooper offered good counsel: "As much as I like to watch my son play baseball, we should drop our kids off at the games, and come back two hours later, so the coaches don't have to deal with critical parents. It sheds a negative light on the parents. Every parent thinks their kid is going to be a superstar. It's unneeded pressure. Part of life is learning how to lose or deal with disappointment. That builds character. Both parents and coaches should be positive with athletes. Some things are done better with sugar than with spice. Pat 'em on the back. Encourage them. Younger children get discouraged when they don't succeed. Kids change so much from when they're 7 or 8 until they're 14. It takes them awhile for them to grow into their bodies. I see parents and coaches stuck on winning, rather than teaching fundamentals, and allowing kids to have fun. It's very disappointing to me."

Bruce Brownlee, a soccer coach and referee in Atlanta, believes parents should memorize and make six statements before and after each game:

Before the game:
- ➢ "I love you."
- ➢ "Good luck."
- ➢ "Have fun."

After the game:
- ➢ "I love you."
- ➢ "It was great to see you play."
- ➢ "What would you like to eat?"
  (In *Blue* magazine, Welmark, Inc., Spring, 2010, p. 20)

- Encourage sportsmanship of others.

How often do we look for the positive? We thrive on pointing our fingers at the negative. "You, you, you, you, you, you, you!" we chant! Should we not be more interested in setting an internal level in finding positive behaviors of players, coaches, opponents, and officials?

- Hold others accountable when behavior is inappropriate.

Here is the opposite of failing to confront inappropriate behavior of others. Here is where we are willing to engage in the sloppiness of life, not automatically assuming disaster when confrontation occurs. Speaking the truth in love is sure remedy for being able to live with self and hopefully to at least plant seeds in the hearts of those who need to be positively corrected.

> ➤ Teach your children how to communicate with coaches. Help the athlete to confront a misunderstanding or gross unfairness during the season, ignoring the possibilities that confrontation will result in repercussions to the student.

According to Corbin Stone, ". . .when your child is old enough, even at 9 years old, he or she can personally talk to the coach about a problem. 'If it's difficult for you or your child, go together. You might start the conversation, but allow your child to deliver the main message. The real lesson here is to empower your child to have a relationship with their coach, their teacher or other trusted authority figure. These are simply good life skills." (*Blue* magazine, p. 20) Des Moines Sports Commission Director Al Lorenzen speaks out against "helicopter parents" who protect their children from disappointment and failure: "We need to allow our kids to fail and to be there for them," he said. That's accountability for the kids and for the parents.

Athletes are quite understandably reticent about confronting a teammate and, most certainly, a coach about issues. Again, "confronting" is preferable to "ignoring," even if resulting in some awkwardness, anxiety, or downright fear. Life is short. We should give people the benefit of the doubt. We should have a positive expectancy of confrontation. Again, speaking the truth in love allows us to do everything in our power to live at peace with everyone.

- Speak directly with others to resolve conflict.

No more rumor-mongering. No more Parking Lot Mafia. No more B.M.W. Club. I've got a beef with a coach, the athletic director, principal, or (God forbid!), the superintendent, I go right to that person. Again, in a loving manner, I express my concern, and I leave it at the doorway for that person's action. The person could slam the door in my face. I answer for my actions. He answers for his actions. Yet no resolution – no closing of the loop – can occur unless the issues and conflicts are confronted – by those who are concerned – and preferably in privacy.

- Forgive others. Bear no grudges.

Forgiveness is in short supply nowadays. The sun would shine much brighter, and the flowers would smell more fragrant, if people were more forgiving. Life is too short. The unforgiving person is not only failing to reconcile the relationship, but he is making his own individual existence less enjoyable.

- If at all possible, wait until the end of a season to resolve a personality conflict with a coach.

Too much drama is borne from mid-season confrontations between coaches and parents. Unless a matter of physical or emotional safety, let the season run its course, and then come to the table as reasonable, calm, rational people who are dedicated to the same thing – that which is best for both the student and the program (not one over the other).

- Place appropriate pressure on the child to perform at high levels.

I was watching an athletic contest once. (I will obscure the sport to protect the innocent.) A dad was yelling at his child. (I will obscure the gender to protect the guilty.) Without mercy, this dad was riding his kid. The player could do nothing right in this dad's eyes. At a very dramatic point of the game, without a stoppage of play, while athletic competition whirled around the player, that kid, tears in eyes, took one of the most courageous stands I have ever seen taken – "DAD, LEAVE ME ALONE!" Such resulted in the proverbial quiet-enough-to-hear-a-pin-drop moment. Nary a peep from Dad for the rest of the game and, as I recall, *for the rest of the season*. We need to apply appropriate – not overbrearing pressure – on our children to perform at high levels, remembering, after all, that they are, just kids.

- Remind children to keep life in balance. Activities are not the end-all, be-all. Keep life in perspective. Do not allow yourself or your child/ren to be so tunnel-visioned in the present. Take the long view.

You have seen me write so favorably of my own parents in this regard. Mom and Dad actively supported me in all of my activities, including athletics. But they effectively taught me that these were *extra-curricular* activities. Sure, I learned many valuable life lessons from speech, music, and sports, but no one of these activities was more important than the others or the greater issues of life – like my character and maturation.

"Out of the 32 million American children between the ages of 5 and 12 who play basketball, only one million will continue playing in high school. Of those high school athletes, only three percent will compete at the NCAA level. Of that group, only one percent will make it in the NBA. The point is this: the odds of any child realizing the dream of playing professional basketball is truly one in a million." (McCaslin, p. 21)

- Do not shield your child/ren from pain, disappointment, heartache, and negative consequences of their own behavior.

"Be prepared to help your child handle failures in a positive way. Those experiences are great preparation for life." ("Coach Your Kids to Their 'Olympic' Best," The Dads @ Fathers.com, 26 February 2010).

- *Never* physically confront officials, parents, or coaches *ever*, let alone in the heat of the moment. Period.

- Give specific feedback about accomplishments during practices and games.

In their heart of hearts, kids *do not* want to hear, "Good job! Great game! Nice goal! Well done! Awesome work!" They want to hear, "You hit that double-leg take-down at the ideal point of his vulnerability!' or "I was impressed by the way you saw the entire field in directing the weave offense!' or "I was so proud of you when you went over to the bench to shake the hand of that excellent player who had fouled-out!" or "You were obviously intentional about practicing a change in your batting stance by keeping that back shoulder up when moving your hands through the strike zone!'

- Emphasize team over the individual.

Of course, you should express pride in your children's individual accomplishments, but your emphasis should *always* be on team and community and unity. Each of us has talents and abilities which must be used for the greater capacity and performance of the team.

- Let kids have fun.

I have already shared qualitative and quantitative data which indicate that "kids just want to have fu-un!" Lighten up. Smile and laugh liberally around your child's athletics. Keep your sense of humor. Delight in the profound and simple.

- Check in regularly to see how things are going.

Communicate, communicate, communicate! If you are not teaching your children about character, someone else will. Do you want her teammates and peers to be her most prominent teacher? Do you want those television programs and movies to be his most prominent teacher? Do you want their coaches to assert absolute influence on your kids? No. When your kids are participating in sports, you need to step prominently into their lives. Hands-off, laissez-faire parenting is a mistake in the same way that malevolent dictatorships also do not work. The most important elements of your involvement with their athletics are fun, improvement of skills, and learning the lessons of positive participation.

Let's conclude by providing a few more practical ideas which will help you step into the quality circle of your child's life.

Practical Applications

1. Teach your children. Engage in one-on-one instruction at teachable moments. The National Center for Fathering recommends, "Point out [specific] qualities and characteristics in your child when he or she is competing, performing, or simply interacting with others." ("Coach Your Kids to Their 'Olympic' Best," The Dads @ Fathers.com, 26 February 2010).

2. Learn from your children. Yes, that's right! You can learn from your children, if you're carefully observing their behavior and play in sports. From my older daughter Molly, I learned what it

means to have a great work ethic, to use intelligence, to be coachable, to be a team player, and to be unselfish in sports. From my younger daughter Hannah, I have learned about the fruits of a highly competitive spirit, the impact of speed and quickness, the beauty of eye-hand coordination, and the inspiration of her ADHD motor always running!

3. Ask your league officials to *require* your submission of a short form at the end of every athletic contest you observe; on that card, you should list five or more specific observations about *a player other than your own child*, writing specifically about the character, integrity, honor, or sportsmanship of the player, i.e., "You showed sportsmanship during the game when, after knocking that boy down on a block, you walked over to help him up; and, then, you played just as fiercely within the parameters of the rules." I am told that a California church centers ALL church activities around a sports league, and these sports require the practice of positive feedback after all of the games; the coach collects the cards and reads them *aloud* to every player, whether a starter or a substitute, in the presence of parents, relatives, and friends. The Positive Coaching Alliance makes parent pledges and positive game charting forms available to league organizers, coaches, and parents through their website (www.positivecoach.org). Hats off to "The Church of Positive Feedback" and the Positive Coaching Alliance!

4. Ask your children to offer regular thanks and encouragement to their coaches. As I mentioned previously, Jennifer and Scott Erickson, friends of mine, are intentional about teaching their daughters Emily and Anna to offer kind words to their coaches, music instructors, and other mentors. Jennifer told me, "In general, Scott and I try to instill with Anna and Emily that they should make sure that, at the end of rehearsal or practice, thank that director or coach, and to be a blessing with those we're with. At the end of 3rd grade, Emily persevered and offered thanks to all of her coaches, and she made a darling card for the coaches. Scott and I would always offer our thanks as well. We did so after the last game. They turned the blessings back to us, raving about how incredible Emily was. It all had to do with her saying thank you at the end of each practice. Having coached recreational sports ourselves, precious few people say thank you for your time. We were more aware of the need for encouragement, and we encouraged our daughters to do so. You don't do it for the thank yous as a coach, but those thank yous make an

incredible difference. The head coach still considers Emily to be one of his favorite players of the 700 players in the league. He's not that way with every kid. It makes an impact when you say thank you with words and cards. This kindness is appropriate for all venues. At the end of every rehearsal or lesson, Anna looks her orchestra director in the eye and says, "Thank you, Mrs. Singer." Anna is now known for being very polite. How many go up to the orchestra director to say thank you? One. Your kid stands out for a very simple thing. It's powerful."

5. Encourage your own children, teammates, coaches, and administrators *in writing*. E-mail seems to be the medium of choice, but can you imagine the effect of a handwritten note when few people ever receive anything but junk distributions and bills in their mailboxes?!

Adults must behave as adults. Sometimes, adults don't behave like adults, and that often involves parents *and coaches* – the next subject of our analysis.

Chapter 10

<u>*To Coaches: We Often Do What We Know, Not What We Know to Be Right*</u>

> *This chapter challenges coaches of athletes at all abilities – recreational and select – coaches at all levels – elementary, secondary, post-secondary, and professional – and coaches of all venues – in public and non-public schools – to clean up their language and their attitudes so that they can draw even greater performances from young people who want to win, but who also desperately want to enjoy the fellowship of team, to grow in all aspects of their lives, and, quite simply, just to have fun while they compete. In the Appendix, the reader has access to a written pledge for honorable behavior among coaches.*

The Profound Lesson Not from a Fortune Cookie in a Chinese Restaurant

I was overwhelmed by a very spiritual experience in 2004. You might think that I was in church. Or perhaps you might guess this experience occurred while I was praying or while reading the Bible. No, this extremely spiritual experience occurred with three other men in a Chinese restaurant.

My school's Elementary Principal, Cade Lambert, and I had attended an Association of Christian Schools International Conference for Christian school teachers and administrators in Minneapolis, Minnesota in September of 2004. Following that first day of seminars, Cade and I ventured over to St. Paul for a football practice of Northwestern College, his former team. I caught a glimpse of what was to follow that evening when the head coach, Kirk Talley, gathered the team together after practice to discuss what had gone well and what could have gone better during the previous couple hours. There was nothing particularly unusual about the way that Coach Talley addressed his team, but, toward the end of his commentary, he did turn to Cade for words of wisdom from the graduate who was now "working in the world." I found it refreshing that a coach would focus so much of his attention on a man whom he had not even coached but who was part of the "Northwestern family."

After practice, we snagged Cade's former teammate and then graduate assistant Jason Schmidt to grab dinner with the man who had been the head coach of Northwestern when Cade and "Schmidty" had played. We made the short drive to Bethel College, where Jimmy Miller was serving as Defensive Coordinator and defensive back coach. I was told that Jimmy's love for family caused him to put aside any aspirations of greater coaching accomplishments for the sake of his relationships with his wife and children. I hadn't even met the man, and he was already a "stand-up guy" to me. But, I was not prepared for what I was about to experience.

At the risk of overstatement, I would have to say that I did next experience relationship between a coach and his players at a significantly deep and spiritual level. The three hours in this Chinese restaurant shifted my worldview about athletics and coaching. I walked away from the experience with a new commitment to a model of athletics which was different than the one I had experienced as an athlete and coach.

What was different about Coach Miller, Cade Lambert, and Jason Schmidt? First of all, there was clearly a genuine love among these men. The stories alone caused the time to pass quickly. They laughed freely, and heartily enjoyed their reminiscences. I really don't recall much talk about exciting games or fabulous football plays. Most of their running commentary centered on relationships. They asked about their families. They talked about former players. They regaled each other with tales of hilarious road trips (which even stretched the limits of survival)! They expressed appreciation for each other, always deflecting the praise with great humility. They were eager to invite me into the conversation, but I had a sense that I would be entering sacred territory, so I unnaturally bumped the verbal volleyball back to them and their shared experiences. At the end of our time together, we sauntered to our vehicles, and that's when the spirit of their camaraderie really struck me hard. Each said, "I love you" to the others, hugged, offered warm wishes, and we departed.

Transferring the Lesson of the Chinese Restaurant to the Culture of Sports

I could hardly get into our vehicle. I was overwhelmed with emotion. Tears well up in my eyes now as I recall that evening. No coach of mine had ever told me he had loved me. No coach of mine had so warmly shared his life with me. No coach of mine had reached me at such a deep emotional and spiritual level. A rush of regret washed over me. Why couldn't I have experienced this same deep love and sense of relationship with my coaches and teammates?! Why couldn't I have been united in spirit and mind with the others in my football program?! These men had experienced "losing" seasons together, but they expressed a joy about athletics that I had never known. On that day, I vowed to do everything in my power to make sure that the student-athletes, coaches, parents, and administrators of my school would know the same culture of sports.

If you are a coach reading this book, you know that you have the power to influence young men and young women more than you could ever ask or imagine. How you use that influence will, in large measure, determine your legacy. I charge you to seek the legacy of Jimmy Miller and so many other coaches who are dedicated to this honorable model of athletics.

This first tale in my odyssey toward a more honorable culture of athletics led me to like-minded individuals – some of whom I have not personally met -- people like Coach Cade Lambert of my school's football team and Coach Frosty Westering of Pacific Lutheran University in Washington and Coach Joe Ehrmann of Baltimore and former Coach Tony Dungy of the Indianapolis Colts and Coach Chris Creighton of Drake University in Des Moines and famed Coach John Wooden of UCLA and Coach Andy Lambert of Sterling College in Kansas and Coach Scotty Kessler, former football coach at Greenville College in Indiana, who, in an earlier chapter, laid out a compelling case of coaching with honor.

What are the character traits of coaches who are characterized as men and women of honor?

Character Development Over All Else

Other than John Wooden, former Northern State Men's Basketball Coach Don Meyer of Aberdeen, South Dakota illustrates this trait better than any in my knowledge or experience. Have you heard of Don Meyer? Probably not. I've never heard of him before this year. He's not a flashy guy. Nor has he coached at prominent NCAA schools. But his win-loss record puts him at the top of the profession. He recently passed Bobby Knight as the winningest basketball coach in the history of NCAA men's basketball with 922 wins! ("Meyer Retires,"

by John Papendick, *American News*, 23 February 2010, pp. 1A, 8A)
On the occasion of his recent retirement, Coach Meyer said, "It is so important to teach kids to be the right kind of person, because, really, that is all that counts in the end. If you can't win at basketball being the right kind of guy, you are not going to win when you are done playing the game." ("Meyer Retires," by John Papendick, *American News*, 23 February 2010, pp. 1A, 8A)

The Positive Coaching Alliance (www.positivecoach.org) advocates for the "Positive Coach Mental Model." Statements on the PCA website indicate, "Mental models have power. They affect how people see, think, and behave. If one were to characterize the prominent mental model for coaching, it might be called 'win-at-all-cost.' PCA believes this needs to change. As part of Positive Coaching Alliance's strategy to transform youth sports, we have developed the Positive Coach Mental Model and will promote it until it becomes the industry standard for youth sports. . . .A win-at-all-cost coach has only one goal: to win. . . .A Positive Coach is a 'Double-Goal Coach' who wants to win AND has a second goal: to help players develop positive character traits, so they can be successful in life. Winning is important, but the second goal, helping players learn 'life lessons,' is more important. . . .A Positive Coach helps players redefine what it means to be a winner through mastery, rather than [through] a scoreboard orientation. He sees victory as a by-product of the pursuit of excellence. He focuses on effort, rather than outcome and on learning, rather than making comparisons to others. He recognizes that mistakes are an important and inevitable part of learning and fosters an environment in which players don't fear making mistakes. . . .He sets standards for continuous improvement for himself and his players. He encourages his players, whatever their level of ability, to strive to become the best players, and people, they can be. He teaches players that a winner is someone who makes maximum effort, continues to learn and improve, and doesn't let mistakes (or fear of mistakes) stop them." With those descriptions in mind, I can support a movement toward the Positive Coach Mental Model being THE industry standard!

Bernie Saggau told me, "We took a stand with the Bunger v. the Board of Education case. We won the battle of holding kids accountable for being leaders as members of the community. We can't be ashamed of teaching kids to be good citizens."

Issues of citizenship, integrity, and character take many forms. For instance, private schools are often accused of "recruiting" students away from rivals. I am not disputing that such actions occur. They most certainly do, although we non-public-school types would need to be honest about that fact that we recruit *all* of our students! Coaches of honor remove themselves from situations which would have even a hint of impropriety. Great coaches rise above compromising temptations.

Our school has had the opportunity to attract talented athletes from international locations. Such occurs in a vast majority of our nation's schools. Eligibility rules are in place, of course, slowing down even the appearance of "recruiting," but the perception can remain. Coaches of honor explore all aspects of their decision-making to insure that they and their programs are above reproach. Northwestern College Athletic Director Matt Hill told me, "Coaches must model integrity, doing what is allowable *and* right. Everything is permissible, but not everything is beneficial." (emphasis in original)

JOHN WOODEN ON INTEGRITY

"Leadership from a base of hypocrisy undermines respect, and if people don't respect you, they won't willingly follow you." (p. 16)

"The five people who first come to mind that best reflect the quality of integrity are Jesus, my dad, Abraham Lincoln, Mother Teresa, and Billy Graham. The order of the last three really don't matter." (p. 29)

"Being true to ourselves doesn't make us people of integrity. Charles Manson was true to himself, and, as a result, he rightly is spending the rest of his life in prison. Ultimately, being true to our Creator gives us the purest form of integrity." (p. 33)

"I've never stopped trying to do what's right. I'm not doing it to earn favor with God. I'm doing it because it's the right thing to do." (p. 35)

"We can become great in the eyes of others, but we'll never become successful when we compromise our character and show disloyalty toward friends or teammates. The reverse is also true: No individual or team will become great without loyalty." (p. 59)

Teaching Over Motivating

Too many coaches concentrate on motivating, as opposed to teaching. Teaching for improvement is what will have the most lasting impact on a student-athlete's development. In "Communicating with Athletes," Robin S. Vealey makes a very valid point: Coaches should "avoid using high intensity, rah-rah approaches to motivating your athletes. Why? They quickly learn that this is an act, and then in situations where you attempt to communicate intensity to them, they don't buy it." (p. 3) Teaching is the predominant behavior of the honorable coach. As you have heard from my own story, I so frequently erred in motivating over teaching as my primary coaching strategy. Studies have been done of famed UCLA basketball coach John Wooden; around 90% of his behavior was teaching. Successful coaches help athletes better understand the rules, fundamentals, conditioning, systems, and strategies of the game, so athletes can increase their competency and experience more success.

A fascinating book was recently written about the factors of physiology, talent, practice, passion, persistence, and teaching. At the core of *The Talent Code*, by Daniel Coyle is the efficacy of teaching which is "master coaching." In 1970, Ron Gallimore and Roland Tharp studied the efficacy of UCLA Men's Basketball Coach John Wooden. By observing Coach Wooden, Gallimore and Tharp pointed to four virtues of master coaches:

The Four Virtues of Master Coaches

#1 The Matrix. ". . .the vast grid of task-specific knowledge. . .distinguishes the best teachers and allows them to creatively and effectively respond to a student's efforts. . . .A great teacher has the capacity to always take it deeper, to see the learning the student is capable of and to go there. It keeps going deeper and deeper because the teacher can think about the material in many different ways. . . ." (*The Talent Code*, p. 178)

#2 Perceptiveness. The master coach develops discernment about the best coaching over thousands of practices of using teaching words and phrases

#3 The GPS Reflex. ". . .master coaches [deliver] their information to their students in a series of short, vivid, high-definition bursts. . . .they [speak] in short imperatives." (Ibid., p. 186)

Ron Gallimore: "Truly great teachers connect with students because of who they are as moral standards. . . .There's an empathy, a selflessness, because you're not trying to tell the student something they know, but are finding, in their effort, a place to make a real connection." (Ibid, p. 189)

#4 Theatrical Honesty. "Theatrical honesty works best when teachers are performing their most essential myelinating role: pointing out errors." (Ibid, p. 190)

Master coaches are "performing their most essential myelinating role"? What's that all about? In the human body, "Myelin is the insulation that wraps. . .nerve fibers and increases signal strength, speed, and accuracy. . . .The more we fire a particular circuit [through deep practice], the more myelin optimizes the circuit, and the stronger, faster, and more fluent our movements and thoughts become." (Ibid., p. 32) Talented people "tap into a neurological mechanism [myelin] in which certain patterns of targeted practice build skill." (Ibid., p. 5)

Master teaching correlates positively to talent. The second correlate to talent is "deep practice." Deep practice is the key to effective skill and thought development: ". . .deep practice x 10,000 hours = world class skill." (Ibid., p. 53)

The final correlate with "talent" is "ignition." Passion and perseverance provide the spark to ignite extraordinary accomplishments: ". . .passion and persistence are key ingredients of talent. . . [b]ecause wrapping myelin around a big circuit requires immense energy and time. If you don't love [the skill you're trying to develop], you'll never work hard enough to be great." (Ibid., p. 34)

Communication with athletes is not exclusively the content, but also the method. Coaches can send the wrong message at the wrong time ("a disaster"), the wrong message at the right time ("a mistake"), the right message at the wrong time (resulting in "resistance" from the athlete), or the right message at the right time ("success"), according to Robin Vealey (p. 1)

Vealey cites an excellent example of a coach teaching and sending the right message at the right time:

"Mary Harvey, goalkeeper on the U.S. Women's Soccer Team, who won the 1991 World Cup, gave up an 'easy' goal just before halftime of the championship game, which tied up the score 1-1. Instead of berating her or questioning her about what happened on the goal, Coach Tony DiCicco simply talked to her about the upcoming second half and what she should focus on to prepare for the next half of play. A year later, Harvey told her coach: 'I never told you this, but at halftime, when you didn't mention the mistake I made and simply told me what I needed to do in the second half, well, that had an unbelievable impact on me. It gave me a lot of confidence and allowed me to focus on the second half.'" (DiCicco, Hacker, and Salzberg, 2002, cited in Vealey, p. 1)

JOHN WOODEN ON CORRECTION

"Approval is a greater motivator than disapproval, but we have to disapprove on occasion when we correct. It's necessary. I make corrections only after I have proved to the individual that I highly value him. If they know we care for them, our correction won't be seen as judgmental. I also try to never make [correction] personal." (p. 17)

Humility Over Arrogance

We know the arrogant coaches. Faces are popping into your mind right now! Humble coaches who positively impact players stand out in the profession of coaching. Again, I turn to the example of Northern State's Don Meyer. Part of the responsibilities he assumed during his first head basketball coaching position at Hamline University in St. Paul, Minnesota was to set up and break down the gym on game days. Even lower-level NCAA coaches have specialists to complete that grunt work today! But not Don Meyer. Throughout his illustrious career, he continued to be committed to doing even the lowliest work. Journalist John Papendick refers to this phenomenon as the "Meyer Basics of Sucking Scum" ("doing jobs no one else wants to do, being sacrificial, and becoming a subservient leader"). Coach Meyer said, "Everybody has got to suck scum from time to time in your whole life, no matter what job you are in or what your position is. . . .It is about teaching kids to do the right thing. Everybody picks up trash. Everybody takes notes. Everybody says, 'Yes, sir' or 'Yes, ma'am.' Everybody says, 'Thank you.' And we always want to leave the locker room cleaner than we found it. . . .No job too small, no sacrifice too big.' That is a great statement to live by. And the coach has to be the one who sets the example." John Papendick gets the final word on Coach Meyer: "So there he was on the Aberdeen basketball court that bears his name inside Wachs Arena Monday morning: Mr. 922 wins was doing the same thing he did 38 years ago in his first days as a head coach at Hamline when he had zero wins. Picking up trash, teaching basketball, and leading by example of how to become a good person." ("Meyer Retires," by John Papendick, *American News*, 23 February 2010, pp. 1A, 8A)

The humble coach also admits his mistakes when he is wrong, asks that others forgive him, and seeks reconciliation to perhaps an even stronger relationship because of his humility.

Sport Over Self

The Positive Coaching Alliance (www.positivecoach.org) encourages a coach to be a Positive Coach who "feels an obligation to his sport. He understands that Honoring the Game means getting to the R.O.O.T.S. of the matter, where R.O.O.T.S. [means] respect for Rules, Opponents, Officials, Teammates, and Self. . . .Ultimately, a Positive Coach demonstrates integrity and would rather lose than win by dishonoring the game."

High Standards Over Low Expectations

Don Meyer "is an all-in or non-in-at-all type of guy. He demands that he, his staff, and his players live by the highest standards, whether on the basketball floor or in life." Coach Meyer said, "I can't justify being in this job and not being able to give more than expected." ("Meyer Retires," by John Papendick, *American News*, 23 February 2010, pp. 1A, 8A)

Perseverance Over Concession to "Defeat"

Coach Meyer was also characterized by one of his players, Marty Gregor, as the consummate teacher of life lessons: ". . .even when life is unfair or difficult, [life] doesn't slow down. You need to learn lessons and keep moving forward," Gregor said. ("Meyer Retires," by John Papendick, *American News*, 23 February 2010, pp. 1A, 8A)

Serving Over Being Served

Pat Summit, the famed championship women's basketball coach at The University of Tennessee has a reputation for being a servant-leader. She is not above "janitorial duties." She doesn't forget where she came from or who she is.

Regarding service to the community, I was very impressed by the following communication from Rob Newton, our head varsity girls basketball coach at Christmastime in 2009: "All I can say is WOW! What a start to the season and what a way to end the first part of our season – on a 7 game winning streak. . . . The girls are doing an outstanding job on both ends of the court, but in particular on the defensive end where we are yielding an average of 30.6 points per game in conference play and just a shade over 33 points per game overall. The improvements on the court speak to the character, heart, and dedication of each player in our program. We have made a lot of improvements during the first 6 weeks of our season, and I am excited about where this team could be 6 weeks from now. I am even more proud of the girls for our Adopt-A-Family project we did yesterday. We delivered gifts and food to a family of 7 in Des Moines. A family which has been reduced to a 1-income household, who had 4 bikes stolen from their home in a 2-day period, a family which lives in a small house, a family which had no gifts for their children and the response by the girls and our families was outstanding. They brightened a family's Christmas and ensured that a family with 4 children would have gifts to unwrap on Christmas Day. The Lord calls those who have the ability to lead to do just that. He calls those with the ability to teach to do just that. He calls us all to serve and these girls hit back-to-back-to-back 3 pointers with what they did yesterday. A big thanks to Coach Greeno for setting up this project. As we head into Christmas and New Year's we are fortunate to have our families and each other, as a team, to lean on. It reminds me of John 16:33 (NCV): 'I told you these things so that you can have peace in me. In this world you will have trouble, but be brave! I have defeated the world!' Put your faith in Christ, for today's trials are temporary. We keep our eyes on the prize - eternal life with our Father. I wish you all a Merry Christmas from my family to yours and hope to see you on January 4th!"

Very unique facilities were constructed near the Iowa Cubs Triple-A baseball park to accommodate students with physical disabilities. The all-weather field is completely handicapped-accessible, and teams from all over Des Moines, Iowa come to help and serve these students. Such is a wonderful opportunity for the disabled students *and for the students who are serving them.*

Northern State Athletic Director Bob Olson said, "Coach [Don Meyer] always puts others first, whether it is his family, his team, or his school." Coach Meyer's players have also attested to that truth. Guard Brett Newton "said Meyer taught players the importance of being a servant and that you can't have a great day without helping somebody while expecting nothing in return." ("Meyer Retires," by John Papendick, *American News*, 23 February 2010, pp. 1A, 8A)

Major League Umpire Ted Barrett talked about one of the most impactful baseball managers in his long umpiring experience: "I had Chris Bando as a manager in the minor leagues. At first, he was a 'whacky Christian.' He'd argue and get ejected. He acted like an idiot. He didn't get respect from the umpires. I saw him mature. Later in his career, he was coaching third base for the Milwaukee Brewers. I was standing close by. An alarm went off on his watch. I asked him what that was all about. He told me the alarm reminded him to think about God. He asked me how I was doing. I was struggling. I wasn't getting home to my kids. I wasn't in the Word of God. I wasn't filling myself with anything but garbage. He put his arm around me and prayed for me. Right in front of the entire stadium! He prayed! I was afraid someone would take exception with a guy praying on the field. He asked God to lift me up. When I walked away from him, I thought, *That was a useless 20 seconds.* But I was energized! From that moment through the rest of the season, I felt energized and ready to go. My wife was able to come out [on the road]. My schedule worked better after that simple prayer." Ted Barrett had the right perspective: Chris Bando "served" others.

Sportsmanship and character-building should be emphasized far more than winning. Pella Christian High School Varsity Girls and Boys Cross Country Coach Jocelyn Meinders "gets this." She told me, "I'm happy when my runners are respectful, even if they don't win. High school students don't naturally build each other up. I emphasize 'no put-downs.' Be nice to each other. I say, 'You're representing yourself, Pella Christian, and God.' They need to be setting a good example for everyone who is watching them. They need to encourage each other, build each other up, be respectful, and be nice to each other. I emphasize that with the parents as well. If they are not respectful to others, I call them on it. I'll ask, 'Was that respectful to your teammate?' I'll say, 'You need to fix this.' We run against good competition. I can't emphasize winning with such competition, or they'll get discouraged. But the boys and girls teams have both qualified for the state meet. They get it. They know how to encourage each other. They know how to get results."

The i9 youth sports program makes a special point about the coach's role in nurturing sportsmanship among the athletes on her teams: "As an i9 Sports Coach, you play a critical role in reminding our youth (and their parents) of the importance of maintaining the fundamental values of good sportsmanship. These values are essential not just to sports, but to the social fabric of our entire society. Because we are living in an age in which traditional values are often forgotten, we cannot assume that all children are being taught these values at home. As you know, we believe that teaching kids how to play the game is only half of our job. . . .Helping them develop character is the other half." The i9 program prompts coaches to teach about good sportsmanship by focusing on one of the key values during each practice and game, i.e., "I know it seemed like you weren't off sides, but I was really proud of the way you didn't argue with the referee." Intentionally addressing sportsmanship is not preaching alone; i9 programs ask coaches to make discussions about sportsmanship interactive by asking questions, giving examples, and seeking player input.

The pressure to win is highest in the professional and college ranks, but that same pressure is trickling-down to lower levels. Iowa Sports Foundation Director Jim Hallihan told me, "When I was coaching in college, we weren't making that much income; you could get fired and get another job at about the same compensation. The college head coaches and the assistants today will sacrifice integrity to win and keep their jobs, money, and lifestyles. The money puts tremendous pressure on these coaches."

Iowa Girls High School Athletic Union Executive Director Mike Dick told me, "We tolerate too much in the name of winning. I'm embarrassed how I initially behaved as a coach. I inherited a 1-37 junior basketball team, and we went 10-10. I could have been elected mayor, but I'm not proud of how I did that. I berated people. The kids tolerated it. They worked hard. They believed in what we were doing. The key is learning from mistakes and not making the mistakes again. That's the essence of athletics. I out-grew that. Later, I didn't throw tantrums. I didn't mistreat or embarrass my kids. Coaches are the ones setting the example."

NFL official Scott Helverson stated to me, "NFL coaches mistreat officials, and it trickles-down to the lower levels. Those coaches of younger kids are worse, because they're trying to climb the ladder, and they often do so by living vicariously through those athletes." When asked who the honorable coaches were in his experience, Scott talked about former University of Iowa football coach Hayden Fry, for whom Scott played: "Hayden Fry was a great guy to play for. He used to tell us to control what we can. You're going to have bad calls. Referees' calls are beyond the players' and coaches' control. As a result, I never even thought about officials when I played. My nine-year-old has told me an official missed a call. How did she know that?! Why is she even paying attention to the referee? Someone is pointing her attention to the official. The media and coaches draw the players' attention to officials." Scott continued: "I was also a fan of [former NFL coach] Bill Parcells. He was great with the officials. He didn't let other coaches yell at officials. If Bill complains, it's for a short period of time, and he walks away. If he complains, you've probably got to consider whether you made the right call or not. . . .Of course, Tony Dungy was a class act."

MLB Umpire Tim McClelland indicated to me that, if baseball managers and coaches better understood their respective roles, there would be even better sportsmanship in the game: "People need to have an understanding of what my job is. I'm not the ogre who comes out of the ground to make a call against your favorite game. I'm doing the best job that I can. I'm trying to make the game fair for both teams. A coach yelling at me is not going to make me better. It's not going to give you a better call the next time around. It's not going to make me try harder. I'm already trying as hard as I can. Coaches and players should walk in the umpire's shoes. They need to have better understanding and compassion.

Former Major League manager Tom Kelly of the Minnesota Twins comes to mind for both Umpire Tim McClelland and Umpire Mike Everitt as a coach of honor. Tim told me, "Tom Kelly stands out as a man who changed the relationship between managers and umpires. His philosophy was 'I'm going to manage – I'm going to let the umpires umpire – Let the players play.' Tom Kelly was successful in doing his job and letting the umpires do their jobs. He knew he couldn't control umpires." Mike told me, "When I was in the minor leagues, I was a hot head. When you mature as a person and as an official, you learn how to incorporate your personality – what you're going to take and not going to take from managers and coaches. Early in my career, they yelled, and I yelled back. We got nose-to-nose. The manager who sticks out for me was Tom Kelly. He was very fair."

Former Iowa High School Athletic Association Executive Director Bernie Saggau told me, "I got the idea that we should help the kids to like the kids on the other teams. One coach told me that he couldn't ask players to like the other kids. The opponents are 'the enemy' to him. Coaches feed rivalries through bulletin board material." How refreshing it will be when student-athletes begin seeing the students on other teams as "worthy competitors," as opposed to "enemies." At the end of the Pella Christian-Des Moines Christian varsity football game in 2009, I was overwhelmed with emotion when the two teams and fan base came together in one large circle of the field, singing the praises of each other and praying for great witnesses of both teams in the future. That's "winning"! That's success!

Mr. Saggau also shared an interesting story about the summer of his long tenure with the IHSAA: "Doing athletics the right way can be a 'hard sell.' Coaches believe they have to be hard-nosed. During my first year I was in the office, the summer of 1964, UCLA Coach John Wooden came to Spirit Lake. It cost the coaches next-to-nothing to attend. We had a packed house – close to 300 coaches. John talked for 2 hours. He never once mentioned Xs and Os. He talked about what he expected from his players and coaches. If a player swore, he went to the locker room. The coaches loved it. They stood up and applauded him. John promised to draw a few plays in the afternoon. One of the young guys said, "I hope he shows us how to win." These coaches were good kids. That was their mentality. He had already given them the message! He had taught them how to "win" [during the two hours he had spent talking about developing the character of players]. John Wooden put his Pyramid of Success into action."

Northwestern College of St. Paul, Minnesota is raising the sportsmanship bar. Dr. Matt Hill, Vice-President, oversees the athletic department, and he is absolutely dedicated to being a leader of honor working alongside coaches of honor at Northwestern. One of the college's coaches very much "gets it." Head Volleyball Coach Beth Wilmeth suggested to her players that the team institute a new system of "honor calls." For instance, when a player blocks an opponent's shot, sending the ball out-of-bounds – and game officials don't see the touch – the Eagles now self-report, costing the team points. Senior setter Leah Kostek said, "It was a hard thing to get used to. I'm so competitive that the first few times it happened on crucial points, I had to tell myself, 'This is a good thing! This is a good thing!' I was really frustrated, but, deep down, I knew it was the right thing to do. I'm proud of my teammates, and I'm proud to be an Eagle." Coach Wilmeth challenged her players to be a "'a legacy team,' one that left a lasting impression for the athletes who would follow." What was the result? A great legacy! In August, 2010, Northwestern was awarded the 2009-2010 NCAA National Student-Athlete Sportsmanship Award for female athletes for all classes of the NCAA!

JOHN WOODEN ON WINNING

"I [always] felt that if [the players] were fully prepared, we would do just fine. If we won, great – frosting on the cake. But at no time did I consider winning to be the cake. Winning has always been the frosting that made the cake a little tastier." (p. 79)

"I never encouraged anyone to pray for a win. I don't think our prayers should be directed to the score of a game. That seems way too selfish. I wanted my boys to honor God by doing their best, controlling their emotions, and asking for protection. Those are good requests for basketball players and for our lives in general." (p. 83)

"You are the only one who knows whether you have won." (p. 129)

The name of one of the early Christian evangelists in the Bible was Barnabas. His name means "son of encouragement." That name defined the man. He was an encourager. He was positive. I, too, have been blessed with the gift of encouragement. I constantly express my appreciation for and pride in members of my own family and everyone with whom I come in contact. We live in an era of "psychological starvation," so I believe we should be thanking and praising people more for their contributions to our communities.

Certainly, any coach should offer encouragement, thanks, and praise to student-athletes. Inherently, we know that positive communication is far more motivating than negative words. Even when we deliver "bad" news, we can "speak the truth in love." I have generally been very positive my entire life, but I am embarrassed to admit that many negative, unwholesome words came out of my mouth when I was coaching.

In a recent article of the *High School Today* publication by the National Federation of High Schools, Essex High School Athletic Director Ed Hockenbury of Vermont makes several excellent points in "Learning From the Negative: A Positive Perspective on High School Athletics" (February, 2010, pp. 12-13).

Mr. Hockenbury wrote,

"'Positive.' It's a word I hear constantly in high school sports. Everyone wants student-athletes to have a positive experience. Parents expect coaches to be positive with their kids. The athletes themselves want positive feedback and, of course, positive results. . . .Positive is a fine word, and the objective of making sports a positive experience is certainly appropriate. But, I think some of the true value in sports has been lost in the unrealistic expectation that every day of every season will be positive. The fact is sports provide such a lasting learning experience in part because [sports] are not always positive. Losses hurt, bad calls are part of the game, not getting playing time is frustrating, and resolving conflict within a team or with a coach can be extremely challenging. . . . Certainly, this is not a call for negative coaching. However, everyone involved needs to accept that, while high school sports should ultimately be fun, the fact remains that on every team in every season there will be times when things do not go the way we want. It's called adversity, and it's a good thing. Dealing with [adversity] appropriately can help develop resiliency, mental toughness, and character. Learning from the negative is, in fact, positive (pp. 12-13)." Definitely. I definitely agree.

I do, however, take exception from some of the other statements in Mr. Hockenbury's article (which I do not believe he meant to come across the way they did, but did for me nevertheless): "Our best coaches are not, nor should they be expected to be, positive at all times." (p. 12) I cannot agree with that statement. I believe that, in spite of the most negative circumstances, a coach *can* be expected to be positive. We all have a choice about our responses to negatives. We can choose a negative response or a positive response. Give me the positive every time. You can carefully word your statements in positive (versus negative ways). I am not advocating for "the self-esteem movement" here. Horrible damage has been done in the name of young people never experiencing adversity or failure. I simply believe that we *can* be positive at all times.

Mr. Hockenbury also stated, ". . .good coaches also understand they can ultimately help kids by balancing praise with constructive criticism, by challenging them to be their best, by making them earn their praise, and even at times [by] chastising them." (p. 12) I was right with Mr. Hockenbury until he pointed to coaches making athletes earn their praise. I think I know what he is trying to say, but the way I received that point about earning praise was unsettling to me. I believe he is saying that we should not dole out praise when praise is not deserved. I definitely agree with such a point. But no athlete should be forced into situations in which she "earns" praise. If praise is due, the coach should be forthcoming with the praise for the athlete. Praise should not be withheld as a motivational strategy of the coach. Recall my point that athletes sometimes believe they are valued only when they are performing well. Coaches should liberally praise their team with deserved praise, no matter the "string" of the player. I was also concerned about the statement that coaches can help kids by "chastising them." In my dictionary, the term, *chastise*, means "to criticize severely." I do not believe that is what Mr. Hockenbury is advocating for in this article. I would go so far as to state that criticizing athletes severely should *never* be used as a description of the honorable coach.

Major League Baseball Umpire Ted Barrett coached his son's junior varsity football team. Ted said to me, "One mom told me, 'You're always so positive with the players. How can you be so positive?'

'What's there to be negative about?' I said. 'Kids are playing a game."
Exactly right, Ted!

The Positive Coaching Alliance (www.positivecoach.org) points to a "Positive Coach [as] a positive motivator who refuses to motivate through fear, intimidation, or shame. A Positive Coach understands that compliments, praise, and positive recognition fill Emotional Tanks. She understands the importance of giving truthful and specific feedback and resists the temptation to give praise that is not warranted. When correction is necessary, a Positive Coach communicates criticism to players in ways that don't undermine their sense of self-worth. . . .She works to remain positive even when things aren't going well. . . .Even when facing adversity, she refuses to demean herself, her players, or the environment. She always treats athletes with respect, regardless of how well they perform."

Gilman High School Varsity Defensive Coordinator Joe Ehrmann once stated, "Coaches must always teach by building up instead of tearing down. Let us be mindful never to shame a boy but to correct him in an uplifting and loving way." (Marx, p. 3)

JOHN WOODEN ON ATTITUDE / ENTHUSIASM

"I am convinced that, regardless of task, leaders must be enthusiastic and really enjoy what they're doing if they expect those under their supervision to work near their respective levels of competency. With few exceptions, an unenthusiastic leader will keep those under his or her charge from achieving their collective best." (p. 14)

"Be slow to correct and quick to commend." (p. 18)

"I never yelled at my players much. That would have been artificial stimulation, which doesn't last very long. I think it's like love and passion. Passion won't last as long as love. When you are dependent upon passion, you need more and more of it to make it work. It's the same with yelling." (p. 19)

Relationships Over Rules

Christian evangelist Josh McDowell is well known for his statement, "Rules without relationships result in rebellion." Obviously, the coach does not desire rebellion, but he should also impose rules for the benefit of order in the program. Relationships take precedence over rules. The effective coach forms relationships with each athlete in order to understand what makes him tick, what teaching works best.

Cross Country Coach Jocelyn Meiners said, "I have to get to know the kids. Everyone is different. You've got to invest time in the kids. They're runners, but they're people, too. I care about them.

I approach them differently. One, I gave a pep talk to. The other girl, I told her what to do and how high she would finish. They both responded to different methods. I need to get to know numerous cross country runners by various means. I run with the kids. I'll run with different kids on different days. I can keep up with the varsity girls. I stretch with them. I have quality conversations during warm-ups, practice, and cool-downs. I talk to them after the race. I have goals for every kid. I record those daily goals. I give them feedback. I ask them how they feel after a race."

Championship high school tennis Coach Kirk Trow told me, "If I'm strict on the rules, I can be soft in the relationships. Tennis is a gentleman's game. We don't drop racquets. We don't swear. Offenders run the "campus mile." We solve our own problems. I tell my players, 'Your job is to maintain your opponent's dignity.' Athletes need to be good role models for others. I agree with the adult Fellowship of Christian Athletes sponsor of Urbandale High School, who told the FCA kids, 'You might be the only Bible other kids at the school read.'"

A Republic Over a Democracy

Some coaches are totalitarian dictators; some, benevolent dictators. The "players' coaches" are a bit more loose with their individual and team governance, allowing for more free expression of personality among the athletes. Certainly, I understand that governance depends upon consent of the governed, but sports are all opt-in activities, and participants should understand that someone has to be "in charge," and that *someone* is not the players. Coaches can be "too tight" or "too loose" with teams. Sports should not be pure democracies. Sports should be more like republics, characterized by a clear sense of authority, checks, and balances.

"A Positive Coach [of the Positive Coaching Alliance] establishes discipline in a positive manner. She listens to players and involves them in decisions that affect the team."

Super Bowl Coach Tony Dungy has stated, "I need to treat everybody fairly, but fair doesn't always mean equal." (p. 19, *Quiet Strength*, emphasis in original) As my doctoral thesis advisor Walt Foley so eloquently pointed out, "There is nothing so unequal as the equal treatment of unequals."

JOHN WOODEN ON DISCIPLINE

"Sometimes when I overheard one of my players using profanity during practice, I would dismiss him for the day. My boys all know that practice was where they earned their playing time, so I used the sessions themselves as a disciplinary measure. If anyone cursed during a game, I would sit him on the bench for a while. It didn't take long for my players to clean up their language. There was not trash talk on my teams." (pp. 20-21)

"Once, one of my players was asked if I ever used profanity. 'Absolutely,' [I] replied. 'Goodness, gracious, sakes alive' is profanity for Coach." (p. 22)

Positive Over Negative Modeling

Coaches of honor model honorable behavior for their athletes and fans. The i9 sports program understands this truth when addressing coaches – "Don't forget that you are the kids' best role model for good sportsmanship. Be very mindful of how you respond to game officials and/or to disagreements with other coaches. Your players will take their lead from you. . . .They're always watching!"

The mental filter of the honorable coach is to seek to understand more than to be understood. She gets to know her players. He tries to understand the unique personalities of his athletes. Academy Award-winning best leading actress Sandra Bullock illustrates the maxim of a coach knowing and positively interacting with his players when, in the blockbuster *Blind Side* movie, Bullock's character says to Michael Oher's high school football coach, "Know your players. You can't yell at him. . . ." At this point, Michael's adoptive mother waltzes from the bleachers to his side to deliver the specific "coaching" he needs to be MUCH more successful in practice!

Communicating Proactively and Frequently Over Reactively and Infrequently

Rob Newton, our school's varsity girls basketball coach is the "poster boy" for effective communication. His messages come early and often. He is positive. He states a positive vision for future performance. He keeps everyone in-the-loop. Such is the communication of an effective coach.

Positive, Private, Constructive Correction Over Negative, Public, Destructive Abuse

The i9 sports program directs the coach in the following manner: "When you observe negative behavior, it is important that you address it directly with the player in a manner that will not embarrass him/her in front of others. Your goal should be to constructively correct, never to humiliate. The best way to handle a negative situation is to call the player to the sidelines and deal with the issue privately, one-to-one."

High school Coach Jocelyn Meinders said, "I'll pull kids aside to have private conversations about any negative behaviors. I ask, 'What's going on?' Kids get frustrated. Kids have personal problems. Some students will show their frustration and personal problems by acting-out."

Mike Everitt, MLB Umpire, told me, "Athletes and coaches are under a lot of pressure. Pressure fills the tank with emotion, and eventually you've got to empty it out." Coaches of honor are self-controlled. They do not allow their emotions to get the better of them or the team. A coach of honor "empties his emotion tank" through controlled intensity. These coaches are not mild milquetoasts or doormats. They compete fiercely but appropriately within boundaries.

IGHSAU Director Mike Dick wisely pointed out to me, "The coach should be the role model, setting the tone. Kids are going to behave as the coach behaves. If the coach is wild and crazy, the kids and the crowd are going to be undisciplined. Coaches set the example. How would we react to a teacher who acted that way in the classroom? They'd get fired! That same teacher-coach goes out on the court, and they abuse the officials or kids, and, when they win, they get promoted!

My friend Jennifer Erickson told me about a coach who had a 24-Hour Rule: "One coach's policy is for upset parents to sit on their complaints for 24 hours. If they still need to talk to him 24 hours after the heat of the moment, he'll talk, and cooler heads prevail. That's wise for a coach. He knows he's not perfect. He makes mistake. Parents need to think about how they are going to confront the issue. Come with grace, if you do. That's a neat way for coaches to help parents manage their expectations and take a more mature view of the issues." Robin Vealey aptly wrote, "Consider your emotional state when communicating with athletes. If anger or frustration blocks your ability to communicate productively, wait until your emotions are under control." (p. 3)

Safety and Wellness of the Athlete Over Play

Allow a friend of mind to tell her story about a dishonorable coach who cared little about the wellness of his athletes:

"Actually, my *entire junior year of high school* could be described as a nightmare. Within a few short months of that particular year, I had two grandparents die, my future competitive swimming career was shattered, and there was a murder/suicide of two of my classmates outside my classroom door. During swim practices in the fall of that year, I began to notice some sharp pains in my left shoulder. I shrugged it off, not telling anyone, and just kept on working out. Eventually, the pain became more intense, occurred more often, and lasted longer once I was done working out. The pain was accompanied by a very hot feeling in the joint. Sometimes, the pain travelled completely down my left arm, rendering it useless – or at least that's how it felt."

"During one practice, when the pain was particularly bad, I got out and went to tell my coach about it. He was focusing on something else at the moment and didn't really pay attention; he just said he was sure it would be fine. So, I got back in and continued with my workout. I got out a second time to tell him about it again with a bit more detail – to let him know that I had been experiencing the sensations for some time, but that this was the first I had told anyone. I remember we were having some pretty tough workouts, so I really believe he thought I was making excuses to get out of having to do the particular timed sprints we were doing. In other words, I don't think he believed me. He told me to 'suck it up' [I've certainly heard that phrase before in my athletic career] and finish the work out. *So I did.* He never followed up with me, and I don't remember going to him about it again. I did tell my parents what was going on, and they were concerned. By this point, I also was beginning to have pain in my right shoulder as well.

"At the swim meet that followed this discussion with my parents, as I ended my 100 yard backstroke race, the pain was excruciating, and I remember feeling like I couldn't breathe. I felt faint and I couldn't get out of the pool on my own. Some teammates helped me get out, as my mom ran over to me, and I remember lying on the pool deck in tears, my shoulders feeling as if they were on fire. I have no memories after that moment lying on the pool deck limp with pain, until arriving at the sports medicine doctor's office the next day. The staff there took x-rays and worked me over for what seemed like hours. It was awful. The pain wasn't as intense, but I was very stiff, and the feeling of heat permeated both shoulders. My skin was even red!

"The results of what the doctor found: tendonitis, bursitis, Impingement Syndrome in my left shoulder, and tendonitis and bursitis in my right shoulder. The Impingement Syndrome was from scar tissue that had been forming over time and was now affecting my nerve – thus the pain down the arm, as well as in the shoulder area. The doctor speculated that, because I had kept swimming for many weeks through the pain, my right shoulder had been overcompensating, thus causing the tendonitis and bursitis in that shoulder as well." (emphasis in original)

Why did that swimming coach not take a more active interest in the wellness of his swimmer?!

The mom of a talented hockey player told me a similar tale which could have been quite tragic –

During her son's first year in an elite hockey league, he sustained a severe concussion and eye injury. The injury occurred after he was beaten during a hockey game when the referees lost control of the game, according to his mother, and a bench brawl had ensued. Her son was the farthest away from this team's bench, so he never received any help from his teammates. The fight did not last long, but the damage was great. He lost partial vision in his left eye. He could not read, study, or concentrate. He experienced hyper-sensitivity to light, and he suffered from vertigo. He went from being a strong student to not being able to keep up with his homework, and he was failing classes. He experienced extreme personality changes and could not process simple information. He looked "normal," but he was not normal. His hockey coach pressured her to let him return to the ice, but she refused. She researched for months and finally discovered that teenagers have suffered from this condition after car accidents and sports injuries. Post-Concussion Syndrome was not initially diagnosed; his mother believes that, if he had been diagnosed earlier, her son would not have suffered so long. She discovered that some young people suffering from the syndrome could not graduate from high school, and still others have committed suicide after suffering the ravaging effects of such injuries.

Former IHSAA head Bernie Saggau said, "Right now, our coaches are better than they've ever been – ever. They're doing a better job. They're getting away from the old stuff of running kids to death without water until they die. It's traditions. [Bad traditions.] Our kids today won't take the abusive stuff. We're getting coaches to realize that they don't have to be abusive. I had a tough defensive coach at Buena Vista. He was a little guy. He ran a hamburger drill [running through a long line of players, being tackled by each one]. I flipped the ball to the coach. "I weigh 120 pounds. I won't last through the line." He called me a name. He told me to go over to a dummy. I said, 'That's a good place.'"

A coach of honor protects the health and safety of athletes as more important to winning with an injured player. He cares about the athlete physically.

No athlete should be guaranteed "playing time." In many sports, the fastest time or "challenge match" determines who plays and who does not. But when a coach has discretion to play (or not play) athletes, I am of the mind that, except for the professional or Olympic ranks, she should "play more" over "playing fewer." For Joe Ehrmann's Gilman High School varsity football team, "Every senior plays – and not only late in lopsided games." (Marx, p. 3) Jocelyn Meinders, the Varsity Boys and Girls Cross Country Coach of Pella Christian High School in Iowa, has a good perspective on this issue: "There's no bench in cross country. I say to the kids, 'There will be someone slower than you. You can achieve your individual goals *and* contribute to team goals.'" Athletes who work hard in practices should periodically be allowed to join actual game competition. Coaches should allow second- and third-string players to experience higher levels of play, or their abilities will never be stretched. (Athletes who are lazy do not "earn" playing time.)

I have a wonderful story to illustrate that point. This year, our school's ninth and tenth grade basketball coach, Jon Mumm, was coaching against a strong rival. We lost the game by 1 point. Let's pick up the story with the Bob Sheely, the father of one of the players – "Here is where the classy part comes in. While we were up by a large margin (maybe 15 points at one time), our coach allowed the kids that had not seen much playing time to get their minutes. Then [our rival] started to close the gap, actually getting to about 4 down with a couple minutes left. Coach Mumm then put in one starter (my son) but continued to play with the 2nd or 3rd string. He put faith in those kids and let them finish the game. While winning is certainly important, I thought this loss was as important as winning. I felt that our team had a real Christ-like reflection, and I was very proud to be a part of [our school's] athletics. I am unsure of [our opponent's] record (I don't know if they have won many games – maybe they have), but I was very happy for their team as I listened to their cheering. While I hope the loss was not too disappointing for our team, I hope the life lesson that comes out of this will be remembered for a long time. I know the future will give us many wins, but I think a game I probably will remember more will be the game last night." Mr. Sheely hit the bulls-eye with his comments.

Chick Moorman tells a story in his book, *Stories for Dad's Heart*. When Chick was 11 years old, a boy named Gordon was being cast from one Little League baseball team to the next. Chick wrote, "The kindest way of describing Gordon's skills is to say that he didn't have any. . . .After two weeks of practice [with his assigned team] two of Gordon's team members – directed by their coach --- delivered Gordon this message: 'Get lost." Gordon got lost. My coach decided Gordon needed to be on a team that treated him with respect and [which] gave everyone a fair chance to contribute. Gordon became my team member. I don't think Gordon even hit a foul ball that season. It wasn't that he didn't he didn't get help. The coach worked with him a lot. I'm not sure Gordon learned anything from my coach. I know I did. But the most important lessons weren't about baseball. I learned everyone has worth and that doing what's right is more important than winning. I'm grateful that man was my coach that year. I was proud to be his shortstop and his son." What a poignant contrast between a coach who would cast off a player and a coach who would welcome the "have-not" as one who had value in his eyes!

Playing Hard Over Pulling Up

All coaches are confronted with the dilemma of avoiding the big loss or big win in games. What's a coach to do? Should starters sit early or late? Should he rotate substitutes in early or late? Should he do everything in his power to keep the score down – in order not to humiliate or to be humiliated? Of course, players should learn to win with grace and lose with dignity. But coaches should not be put in moral dilemmas because of the lopsidedness of a score. Coaches must encourage all players to continuously play hard, no matter the score. Some strategies can be undertaken which still allow for hard play, while not embarrassing opponents. Spectators and players on teams which swamp an opponent should not engage in any verbal or non-verbal tactics to humiliate the overwhelmed team; for instance, players should not engage in chest-thumping, and spectators should not cheer for 100 points, even if such scoring is a rarity. These words are spoken gingerly by the administrator of a school who saw his boys basketball team win big by scoring 100 points in a high school game in the same week that the girls team won 77-7! I can look you straight in the face and state that both coaches managed their respective games as well as can be expected.

Why take teaching from me on this subject when you can hear from a coach himself. Cade Lambert, our school's Elementary Principal, is also our head varsity football coach. He recently published an Internet piece, "A Coach's Perspective on Winning Big" (February 12, 2010).

"I can't think of any game task that is more difficult to manage than when you are winning big. When you are behind or the game is close, the job is very focused and pretty simple: use your coaching skill and instincts to get over the top. When you are up big, it's much harder than it might seem. Instead of coaching one team, you coach two. You find yourself trying to manage the feelings, emotions, and perceptions of everyone.

"I grew up in a program that now shares the 3rd longest winning streak in 11-man football history. Needless to say, we thumped a lot of people back then, and, during 'the streak,' there were several major blow-outs. One included a national record for most points scored in a quarter (72). That was just the first quarter, and the score ended up 81-0. The starters played for just one quarter, the JV scored once, and the sophomores and freshman fell down and kicked field goals the rest of the game. Despite support from the opposing coach on how the game was managed, the media and message boards lit up with outrage.

"When I first started coaching back in 2001, I was on the other end of the spectrum. It was the first time I'd ever experienced not being competitive and *getting* thumped. I remember those experiences well, and still remember vividly the one time here at [our school] we were subjected to the 35-point rule in football. Not a pleasant experience. However I looked at it as my job to get competitive. I wanted to coach varsity athletics and learned quickly what comes with it, good and bad. In other words, our players knew that, if we didn't like it, there were two choices: (1) Stop caring and giving effort, or (2) Get after it!

"It's no secret that we've got a couple of great basketball teams this year. It's also no secret we play some teams that are not so great. When those two scenarios collide, the disparity on the scoreboard becomes a matter of great scrutiny, and, in my experience, that scrutiny is often more intense than losing. The goals of the kids are sometimes hijacked by outside opinions and the tyranny of the urgent – replaced with a sentiment of anger and resentment.

"Everyone has an idea of when 'enough is enough' or 'it's time to call off the dogs.' I would encourage everyone to consider how difficult it is not only to coach one team, but two, and to remember that the goals of teams are measured in seasons and not games.

"We are bound to disagree, and that's OK. As a coach, I know I've made my fair share of mistakes. I just always hope fans understand that managing perceptions is much more difficult than managing kids. And how much I appreciate it when folks approach disagreements in a caring and godly manner. Without that spirit, winning can be miserable, and kids become the casualties.

"Let's continue to encourage each other in the process of becoming more Christ-like in our playing, coaching, and cheering!"

Absorbing Criticism of Others Over Allowing Players to Take Criticism

A coach of honor protects her athletes from undue criticism of other coaches, parents, spectators, and the media. I was recently in a situation when a group of educators were engaged in discussion which at least indirectly could have been deemed as criticism of players. All of these ideas were voiced in the presence of one of these players' coaches. The coach rightly pointed out to me, "Criticize me, but not our players."

The Journey Over the Destination

Tony Dungy wrote, "It's the journey that matters. Learning is more important than the test." (p. xiv, *Quiet Strength*, 2007) The coach of honor who adheres to this aphorism – "the journey over the destination" – will not get fixated on losses in contests and will be more concerned about preparing his athletes for competition. Also, a "journey" mentality helps the coach to avoid an "end-justifies-the-means" perspective.

Life Balance Over Life Imbalance

Our lives are busier than they have ever been. Some of this busy-ness is "done to us." We're being expected to "do more with less." Some of this busy-ness we do to ourselves. We over-schedule our time, and, as a result, our personal lives and/our our professional lives can be out-of-balance. The coach of honor leads a balanced life himself, and he encourages his student-athletes to lead balanced lives as well. Cross

Country Coach Jocelyn Meinders understands this truth: "Cross country is important, but it's not the most important thing in their lives. Academics, for instance, come first. A girl missed the first half of a meet because she hadn't finished an assignment; I supported the parents and teacher 100%. I will be flexible to a point, so they can be in the school play or other activities. 'If you miss a couple practices, I'm not going to kill you,' I tell them."

The busy coach must also determine ways of finding life balance for herself: making mental drive-time transitions from coaching to family life, venting emotion, avoiding use of electronic devices at home, asking about others, and not taking work home, if at all possible. Tony Dungy asked a convicting question in his first book, *Quiet Strength* – "How would your business do if you spent the amount of time on it that you spend with your wife and family?" (p. 143)

JOHN WOODEN ON PRIORITIES

"People don't spend enough time with their families. They get caught up in material things, thinking that those make up life. The pursuit of material possessions often takes precedence over the things that are more lasting, such as faith, family, and friends. Don't allow the lesser values to wreak havoc on your family." (p. 75)

Team Over Individual

Just as the team must be the focus of the athletes, so, too, must coaches emphasis a culture of teamwork over individual accomplishments.

JOHN WOODEN ON TEAMWORK

"I believe we are most likely to succeed when ambition is focused on noble and worthy purposes and outcomes, rather than on goals set out of selfishness." (p. 37)

> "Kindness makes for much better teamwork." (p. 54)
>
> "God created us to be interdependent. We were not designed to go through life alone. We become so much more when we come alongside others – and we make them better, too." (p. 55)
>
> "Those who primarily work alone will never become all they could become if they were working with others. Working with others makes us much more that we could ever become alone." (p. 126)

Fun Over Seriousness

"Remember that 'Having Fun is #1' in the i9 sports program!" Kids want to have fun even moreso than winning. Overly serious, hyper-focused practices and games are wearing. NFL Official Bill Spyksma stated this truth to me in another way: "A kid doesn't have to be a great athlete to have fun." Current University of New Mexico Men's Basketball Coach and former University of Iowa Coach Steve Alford used to call off practice every-so-often to play wiffle ball in Carver-Hawkeye Arena. We don't normally think of Division I program coaches even thinking about such a possibility, let alone actually taking valuable practice time to have fun.

Cross Country Coach Jocelyn Meinders knows how to bring variety and fun into the lives of her runners – "I try to make it interesting. The first Friday of practice, we go to the lake house of a runner. We run. They swim. We grill. We have a potluck. They hang out. They goof off. They play. It's huge for team bonding. It's little stuff. The beginning of the season is intense, with several meets in one week; after that tough stretch, we'll play capture the flag and I'll bring ice cream. I can tell when they're burning out, so we'll have fun games in which they're sprinting. On hot days, I'll map out a route, and we'll end up at Dairy Queen. We don't just do mileage work-outs. We also do interval work. I try to provide variety. During the first week of school, I schedule 'a picnic practice' – they all run to different stores for different items, and conclude with a team picnic. On the night before Districts, we have a pasta supper at someone's home. The JV runners help us cook. They do devotions together. They hang out together. They enjoy spending time together." *There* is a coach who knows how to make athletics fun!

Coach Jocelyn Meinders also understands that the sport may fill the need for some coaches to realize glory like a flash-in-the-pan, but she is more concerned about the life lessons of her student-athletes – "I tell them, 'You're not in cross country. You're learning *life stuff.*' This is a picture of what God wants you to be doing.' My team is very, very close – boys and girls both. This is one of most satisfying things of coaching. They will remember this closeness and community." That is positive legacy!

Tennis Coach Kirk Trow reflected upon the moments which mean much more to him than all of the championships he has won: "There are so many moments in coaching that trump a win. It's a privilege to watch kids compete and do things which are seemingly beyond them. I had a doubles pair who constantly bicker back-and-forth. Joe was getting on Mason something fierce. I said, "Joe, I think Mason needs a hug." I'm not a big hugger, but Joe walked over and gave Mason a hug. At the end of the day, that's the stuff you remember."

Coaches of youth sports should be working constantly to help student-athletes mature intellectually, physically, emotionally, and spiritually through sports. In particular, junior high, high school, and college coaches must be preparing boys and girls to enter adulthood as men and women.

Honorable coaches have the ability to touch the lives of their athletes for eternity. A recent "Wisdom for the Busy Coach" blog entry stated, "The domino effect of one solitary life touching another, then another then another. That's the whole point, isn't it? You [coaches] have been entrusted with such influence – the opportunity to profoundly touch the lives of athletes, fans, students, media, colleagues, parents, donors, and so many others. The question is not *whether* your life will touch them, but *how* it will touch them. . . for good or ill"? (emphasis added) Noted theologian Frederick Buechner understood this truth: "The life I touch for good or ill will touch another life, and that in turn another, until who knows where the trembling stops and in what place my touch will be felt."

Tony Dungy wrote, ". . .winning the Super Bowl is not the ultimate victory. . . .It's about the journey – mine and yours – and the lives we can touch, the legacy we can leave, and the world we can change for the better." (p. xv, *Quiet Strength*, 2007)

John Wooden is one of the greatest coaches of honor who has ever lived. He died just short of his 100th birthday, and, right up to his death, he spoke through his books, his excellence, and, most importantly, his character. He truly "finished life strong." His formulation of the "Pyramid of Success" is one of the most skilled assemblages of coaching points. If you have never considered the content of this pyramid, I enthusiastically encourage you to do so.

Thirty-three-year-old Brad Stevens is apparently setting the bar high for the "new school" coaches who want to make a positive difference on everyone around them. That name will sound familiar to NCAA men's basketball fans who were shocked by Butler University advancing to the 2010 National Championship basketball game against Duke University. His players feed off of Coach Stevens. Guard Ronald Nored said, "I think [his calm demeanor] affects us directly. We see him like that, and he's our leader, he's our example. So I think under any circumstance, any situation, we're the same way because he trusts in us, believes in us. There's no need to get rattled in certain situations. I think that translates directly to us." Butler forward Willie Veasley said, "He leads, we follow. When those big runs come, Coach calls a timeout and says a few calm words. Then he says he believes in us, loves us, and that we're going to win the game."

Sports journalist Jay Mariotti followed Brad Stevens through the 2010 tournament, and he found Coach Stevens' style to be counter-cultural: "How utterly refreshing to be assigned a courtside seat behind the Butler bench. . . where I could view Stevens and hear his soothing words and start to grasp why Butler is overachieving when so many coach-scalded teams underachieve. . . .Why, in the 21st century, do coaches feel the need to scream and yell at their players? . . .Nothing rattles him. . . .How is it possible to have such apolomb at such a tender age?"

Coach Mike Krzyzewski, his renowned opponent for the 2010 championship game, had high praise for Coach Stevens: "He's very smart. He's composed. . . .He has shown amazing humility, and I hope he takes all of those attributes as he attains the success he's going to attain and keeps them and [is] an example for other coaches. He'll be somebody that a lot of people will try to emulate."

I'll give Indiana Governor Mitch Daniels, the chief executive officer of the state in which Coach Brad Stevens coaches, the final word on this new model of a coach: Butler has "a lot of Hoosier kids, and they play like a team. No one hot-dogs it, and there's no real ego that you can find. And they're good students. You've got math majors and finance majors on that team, and to seem them doing what they're doing – I just think it's a message to every sports man in America." (Jay Mariotti, p. 4)

Head Drake University Football Coach Chris Creighton takes his players through a four-year "curriculum" of leadership development, culminating, typically, in a team-building trip up Pike's Peak in Colorado for the incoming seniors. Coach Creighton also works with graduating Drake players to teach them how to be good husbands and fathers in preparation for their lives away from the football field. Coach Creighton is dreaming even bigger for 2011. The football team will travel to Tanzania to play the first-ever American football game on the continent of Africa! On May 21, 2011, Drake will compete against an all-star team from Mexico under the shadows of Mount Kilimanjaro. The trip will also include community service projects for children in a nearby orphanage. The final phase of the trip will feature a climb of players and coaches up the imposing 19,350-foot Kilimanjaro, the tallest mountain in Africa! The two football teams will ascend the mountain by different routes, meeting at the summit to hoist their national flags. What a memorable experience this will be for players, coaches, and fans alike. Coach Creighton understands the value of life-impacting moments in the lives of student-athletes who will greatly benefit from such a dramatic set of experiences. At the time of the announcement of this historic journey, Coach Creighton said, "I am overwhelmed with excitement as this long-time vision is now becoming a reality. This trip allows for us to bring the game we love to a place and to a people who have never experienced it. This trip also provides a unique opportunity to serve those who are far less fortunate that we are and to hopefully make a positive difference. Finally, climbing Mount Kilimanjaro as a team will be one of the greatest challenges we will ever face. The Drake football program is about more than winning games in the fall each year. Our program's vision is to make playing football at Drake one of the most incredible experiences of our lives. This trip exemplifies who we are and what we are about. We want to do something special with our lives."

The famous football coach Amos Alonzo Stagg was once asked if his most recent season was his most successful. He responded, "I don't know. Ask me in another 20 or 30 years." Stagg's implication was that the character of his players decades after this football campaign would determine the "success" of that season and his success as a coach. Coaches of integrity concentrate less on individual seasons and more on the legacy they are leaving through the young men and young women who positively impact the culture.

Coaches of honor focus on. . .

Character Development Over All Else

Integrity Over Even the Hint of Impropriety

Teaching Over Motivating

Humility Over Arrogance

Sport Over Self

High Standards Over Low Expectations

Perseverance Over Concession to "Defeat"

Serving Over Being Served

Sportsmanship Over Winning

Positive Over Negative

Relationships Over Rules

A Republic Over a Democracy

Positive Over Negative Modeling

Listening Over Talking

Communicating Proactively and Frequently Over Reactively and Infrequently

Positive, Private, Constructive Correction Over Negative, Public, Destructive Abuse

Self-Control Over Explosion

Safety and Wellness of the Athlete Over Play

Playing More Over Playing Less

Playing Hard Over Pulling Up

Absorbing Criticism of Others Over Allowing Players to Take Criticism

The Journey Over the Destination

Life Balance Over Life Imbalance
Team Over Individual
Fun Over Seriousness
Long-Term Legacy Over Short-Term Expediency

Practical Applications

1. Intentionally concentrate on teaching as your primary coaching behavior. Develop "lesson plans" which include an "anticipatory set," desired objectives, instruction, guided practice, independent practice, and closure.

2. Equip your leaders. Drake University Football Coach Chris Creighton of Des Moines, Iowa has developed a multi-year curriculum for leadership development from the first to final year in his program. The curriculum is capped by an "Outward Bound" adventure for seniors and post-career training for young men to learn how to be effective husbands, fathers, and employees. Limited space prevents a fuller explanation of Coach Creighton's training ideas, but I heartily recommend that you contact him if you are interested in equipping the next generation of men, women, and leaders.

3. Coaches, without playing favorites, tell your athletes when your relationships with them have positively impacted you. If you're comfortable doing so, say, "I love you." (Of course, this is a platonic love which is borne of the shared athletic experience.)

4. Talk regularly about character development in practices and during games. The Josephson Institute has a number of excellent materials available online, including a priceless 10 minute, 42 second conversation between Michael Josephson and Coach John Wooden about the consummate teacher-coach (http://josephsoninstitute.org/sports). Coach Wooden is the legendary coach of the men's UCLA basketball program, and Dr. Josephson is the founder of the Institute for Character Development, Character Counts, and Pursuing Victory with Honor.

5. Schedule service projects which unite he hearts of your athletes around a common noble cause. For instance, our school raised enough money and then students, including

athletes, packaged meals together for transport to Haiti after the country's devastating earthquake in 2010.

6. Teach and expect athletes to engage in good stewardship practices in sports. They should pick up after themselves in the locker room, discarding trash in barrels and laundry in appropriate receptacles. They should not unnecessarily drain the utilities (water and electricity) of their own schools or opponents' schools.

7. Give lessons on the history of your sport, the history of your sport at that school, and the tradition of sports in your community. Tell the stories which will etch great memories in your athletes' minds. Help athletes to have a healthy appreciation and respect for their sport.

8. Work *with* your team to establish very few rules. Ask for their input. Ask for their buy-in. Have each athlete (and parents) sign a covenant of commitment to expectations. Be crystal-clear in your expectations about the behavior of your athletes.

9. Schedule a pre-season and post-season meeting with the parents, who should have absolute clarity about all aspects of your sports program. Leave nothing to chance. Positively speak to even the most sensitive of topics, including and especially playing time.

10. Consistently enforce your rules, maintaining at least some creativity in that enforcement. Don't "use a cookie cutter" approach to situations which call for disciplinary consequences. Err on the side of restorative, rather then punitive, if possible.

11. Periodically substitute a player who is not typically substituted in that situation or that time, as a way of demonstrating your pride in their practice effort and value to the team, no matter their position on the depth chart. (In 2010, Dave Stubbs, our varsity boys' basketball coach started three senior players on senior night, which is not unusual for most schools, but these boys were more football than basketball players, and our coach started them even before his own senior son, Branden, who was concluding a brilliant career. Both coach and player-son seemed pleased that the football players were experiencing their fifteen minutes of fame!)

12. Randomly contact parents, officials, and school administrators (of both your own and your opponents) to check on how you're doing during the season. Better yet, establish a "personal board of directors," people you respect and from whom you know you will get honest feedback, and meet regularly with them for the sake of accountability.

13. Encourage good officials, particularly when they are discouraged. Make a phone call. Write a note.

14. Make it clear to your players that their job is to "play." Your job is to coach and to address any concerns with officials. Athletes are NOT to give even a hint of disagreement or disrespect to officials.

15. If you are married, schedule a regular weekly or monthly date night with your spouse, including time during the season, so your spouse does not feel as though s/he is receiving "left-over" time.

16. If you have children, schedule a regular weekly or monthly date night with each child in this same way and for the same reason.

17. You cannot exclusively claim the efficiency of speaking to your entire team at all times. Schedule brief one-on-one pre-season, in-season, and post-season conversations with your athletes. Work hard to listen at least 60% of the time and speak 40% of the time. Call on your athletes to reflect outloud (or perhaps even in writing) about their practice and game performances.

18. At some point in the year, read a book, decide which of your athletes would appreciate the contents of that book, ask the athlete to read the book, and then schedule a coffee date to discuss your mutual experience. I have read that Phil Jackson often followed this practice when he coached for the Chicago Bulls during their championship era.

19. Work with your athletic trainer to establish clear protocols about prevention and care of injuries, length of rehabilitation, and when athletes will/will not play with injuries. Make sure the parents understand your protocols.

20. Stop practice for no apparent reason to hand out and enjoy popsicles or ice cream bars. Frosty Westering did this with his football players at Pacific Lutheran University in Washington.

21. Make your year-end sportsmanship and work ethic awards at least as important as the most valuable player award.

22. Write down goals which will take a long-term perspective of your legacy in a sports program. Even with baby steps, a marathon can be run and finished well. Finish well.

Coaches have had their time for reflection. Now, I must focus on people with whom coaches experience the most "interesting" of relationships – *referees, umpires, and other officials.*

Chapter 11

To Officials: How Officials, Coaches, Student-Athletes, Parents, and Spectators Should Interact

Sports officials should be called to a high standard of encouragement and accountability. Research will also include the input of Major League Baseball Umpires Tim McClelland, Ted Barrett, Mike Everitt, and Eric Cooper – also NFL officials Scott Helverson and Bill Spyksma.

The Problem Is Not with the Officials

At all levels of competition, out-of-control baseball managers aggressively charge umpires. Football coaches gyrate on sidelines, screaming for several minutes in the ears of referees who, amazingly, take the abuse without any penalization whatsoever. Basketball coaches whine and "work" officials in attempts to influence future calls. Temperamental tennis players argue line calls they could not possibly have seen from their angles. Soccer Dads and Moms spout disrespect to line judges and field judges with each questionable call (in their minds). I ought to know. I have personally witnessed all of these acts, AND I have been guilty of the same inappropriate behaviors as an athlete, coach, and spectator.

In fact, imagine the ultimate irony of the Christian school superintendent, standing courtside in his supervisory role, intense during a close competition, and angrily questioning a referee's judgment. Fortunately, I am quickly convicted about my ungodly behavior, and I "turn from my wicked ways"!

What makes players and coaches believe officials will have any sympathy whatsoever for them when "wronged parties" spew venom at them?! I am beside myself with frustration about the current level of criticism allowed against game officials. Umpires and referees do not intentionally make mistakes to provoke teams. Truth be told, officials are, on the whole, very accurate about their calls and interpretations of rules.

And I boldly state that no official ever cost a team a game. Along the way of any competition, a play could have been made by a player, a better decision made by a coach, or a mistake averted, which would have overridden any missed call by an official.

Major League Baseball Umpire Tim McClelland made a good point when I talked to him: "Some of the officiating in high schools is not really very good right now. The reason is that no one wants to be an official, because the fans and coaches are so hard on officials. Such is also the case with the behavior of people toward umpires in youth baseball. These are often volunteers! They're doing it out of the kindness of their hearts!" Tim has developed the remarkable ability to shut out the heckling of fans at the highest level of baseball competition: "At A, AA, and AAA ball, you could always hear that leatherneck yelling at you. The din of the major leagues tunes those leathernecks out. I don't even hear crowd noise. Even in a World Series game, I can't remember crowd noise. Maybe that's my concentration level. Players can concentrate and block out that noise, too. Attention is 100% focused." His colleague, Eric Cooper agreed when he talked to me: "A youth league official earns 40 dollars for 2 games, and an angry parents follows an official to his car in the parking lot?! Who wants to put up with that? Kids will think that's okay to act like that with anyone in authority."

I believe the time has come for referees and umpires to stand up and loudly proclaim, "ENOUGH!" The first hint of uncontrolled anger and unreasonable arguments from players, coaches, or spectators should result in a penalty for unsportsmanlike behavior. A second similar infraction should be met with a more harsh penalty and immediate ejection of the perpetrator.

Of course, coaches should be allowed opportunities to dispute incorrectly interpreted rules or obvious misjudgments, but the disagreement must be civil. And I believe athletes should not ever be allowed to argue calls. In any athletic competition, the players play, the spectators cheer, the coaches coach, and the officials officiate. Any dispute about a call should be handled *only* by the coaches, preferably the head coach, not players.

To a person, the sports officials I interviewed speak positively about the opportunity to be involved with sports at the highest level. They pinch themselves that they are able to stay actively involved in sports, and with reasonable compensation. Major League Umpire Eric Cooper told me, "I'm fortunate to do something which a lot of people don't get to do. There are only 68 MLB Umpires. It's a way of living which would allow my family to do things and see things we never would have been able to do or see. My office is a major league baseball game – Fenway Park, Wrigley Field, or the new Yankee Stadium, to name a few. I'm at the highest level. I am extremely fortunate to have that opportunity. God willing, I'll be able to do that for the better part of 20 more years. You can see a lot of neat things. I've met Presidents. I've worked the play-offs. I've worked an all-star game."

Officials, particularly at the highest levels of competition, are intelligent, well-trained people who do not wish to be the focus of the contest and want only to act professionally. Granted, there are some referees and umpires who love "center stage," but such is the exception, not the rule. I well believe that officials would rather not be noticed at all. The highest compliment paid to any sports arbiter is for anonymity in any given game. But officials are also realists. Major League Baseball Umpire Mike Everitt knows he will be at the center of controversial calls. Still, these officials do not seek a presence in controversy. They want to do a good job, so athletes are free to do their best without outside impediments. Mike told me, "There are games when you have to handle situations, so it's not necessarily that people won't notice the umpires. The players and fans are going to notice the umpire. The desired outcome is to 'be noticed' while making the *right* call in the pressure situation."

Professional umpires and referees have a great deal of empathy for their counterparts in all levels of sports. Major League Baseball Umpire Ted Barrett told me, "When I was coaching a junior varsity football team, the principal was a former coach, and his boy was playing on the varsity. After this principal watched me coach, he said I got the short-end of the stick on referees' calls because I didn't complain. I'm not going to ride a guy to get a call. It's not my personality or nature. You'll have a certain number of calls go against you, and you should be able to overcome that. I know what that official is going through."

Ted's professional colleague, Tim McClelland told me, "I was defending an official once, and a friend of mine, who is not an official, said, 'You've got that F.O.O. going. The Fraternal Order of Officials!' We know what the officials in the NBA and NHL are going through. It's amazing our friendships with officials in other sports. We're brothers. I know that these guys are going through." Fellow MLB Umpire Eric Cooper reinforced that idea: "I can relate to officials at the major league level in every sport. I love to hear about [NFL official] Scott

Helversen's experiences. He's interested in my job. We compare. I watch him when he works. I know what he's feeling when he has to make a tough call. Those nasty situations are filled with pressure. I have empathy for my fellow sports officials. I've had close plays. Parents and coaches come up to me at games and ask if the official missed the call. I'm extremely supportive of the officials in youth sport leagues. I know what it takes, even if it's at a different level. I know what it's like when all of the eyes turn to me in controversial situations. It's a different feeling. It's the same feeling at every level. These people are donating their time. I'm not going to criticize their work. They're doing the best they can. Our goal is to be perfect every single day and every single pitch. We don't want to miss a call. We don't want to be embarrassed. I'm paid to make right calls. I have a lot of pride in what I do. A missed call doesn't bother anybody more than it bothers me. I'm disappointed in myself. I look at the tape to see why I missed the call. It's timing, positioning, or bad luck. We're an easy punching bag. I've got to remember that sometimes coaches, players, and spectators are not yelling at Eric Cooper; they're yelling at the man in black or blue."

As with anyone in my era of athletic competition, I observed my coaches "fill the ears" of officials. Monkey see, monkey do. I did similarly as a coach. I can vividly recall the head coach of our high school football team restraining me, as his assistant, on the sideline after calls which had gone against us. Was the call wrong? Most of the time, the call was right. I was just angry that events had not been fortuitous for our team. Someone – the referee – or his call – was "standing in the way of our success."

Such is life. Not every call goes our way. Right calls should not be argued. Wrong calls should be reasonably addressed, and then the game should go on. Far too much abuse is taken by officials – from athletes, from coaches, from spectators. Now is the time for a more honorable code in athletics. Now is a time for people to show more respect for the officials in our sports leagues. I propose covenants in regard to our treatment of sports officials and officials' behavior during athletic competition.

The Ideal Behavior of Athletes, Coaches, and Spectators

As an athlete, coach, or spectator, I should agree to. . .

- Hold my tongue when I perceive a missed call to be made by an official. I will not scream epithets at referees, officials, or umpires.

Our Athletic Director, John Jones, has a healthy attitude about this issue: "I have seen coaches yell more at referees during a game, rather than coaching their team. Had the coaches spent more time during the game thinking of how to correct what their team was doing, then maybe they would not have needed to worry about the refs. Remember, we need the officials if we are going to play."

MLB Umpire Ted Barrett understands the life of the maligned official: "I stood away from everyone at my kids' games. I stayed away from my own Dad! People thought I was anti-social. People were complaining about umpires and playing time. I wanted no part of that negativity."

MLB Umpire Eric Cooper told me, "Attack me, but leave my family out of it. We're just playing a game. It's not life-or-death. After the call which cost Detroit Tigers pitcher Armando Galarraga a perfect game [on June 2, 2010], Jim Joyce's family got death threats!"

National Football League Official Bill Spyksma believes NFL players and coaches generally control their behavior: "Ninety-five percent of the coaches are professional. Officials are sent to training camps. We work their scrimmages. They film everything. We watch film. The officials are teaching rules and philosophies behind the rules. Players and coaches need to understand how officials are going to "call" games. Officials get to know the coaches better. We have sessions with the media on new rules and points of emphasis. It's more relaxed. Not pressured. We are not graded by the coaches. We are graded by administration in New York. They grade every play. You don't have to please the coaches; you need to make the right calls. NFL officials are more passive than Major League Baseball umpires. We don't want to have a visible confrontation. I take only so much, though. I'll walk back to the water cooler and say, 'Hey, this is enough. Get over it. Put this behind you.' It's a part of the culture of the NFL. Players are also really pretty good. We have some good rules to keep bad behavior from happening. You don't see much fighting. A few years ago, I was working the first Monday night game in Atlanta. We were policing the warm-ups. There was a lot of hype for this game. I could see a couple players jawing at each other. There was some hot-dogging. One lost his cool. Suddenly, I was in the middle of three guys flailing. I threw three guys out of the game before the game even started! Fans can be another story. I was working a game once, and a lady old enough to be my grandmother was really giving it to me. I said, 'Does your mother know you're talking like that?!'"

- Call to account fellow spectators who launch uncontrolled tirades against officials. No out-of-control fan should be given a "free ride" with unsubstantiated or unreasonable yelling at officials.

Dave Bosman, a parent at my school, did an excellent job of addressing the inappropriate behavior of opposing fans, stating his convictions and actually signing his name in a letter to the editor of our state-wide newspaper:

"This letter is to high school basketball fans who berate officials. Please stop. You are embarrassing yourselves, kids, school and team. I recently attended an away game, and was shocked by the hometown crowd. Many screamed verbal abuse at the referees all night long. A good referee is one who is consistent, and most are. This means the calls even out over the course of the game. But even if they didn't, isn't it good for the kids to learn that life isn't always fair? Do we scream at our boss at work or teachers at school when things don't seem fair? At most games I've seen, the sportsmanship shown by the players has been excellent. So a good start would be for fans to model the sportsmanship of the players they came to watch. This will keep you from embarrassing yourself, but it's only the beginning. The real-life lessons you teach your kids occur during the car ride home, while you rehash the game. They study you as you discuss the referees, coaches and other players. How much respect are you showing then? Be the type of person you want them to become." ("Set Example for Kids by Laying Off the Refs," *Des Moines Register*, 28 January 2010)

Again, monkey see, monkey do. The old aphorism is true. Umpire Eric Cooper told me, "You see arguments with officials, and that affects young people as well. The fans enjoy seeing an argument in a baseball game in the same way that they like to see fights in hockey and crashes in NASCAR. Fans like 'commotion.'" We need to be good role models for young people.

- Put a missed call (or made call that went against my team) behind me, living in the present, not the past.

Do you still have an ax to grind for that call some official made when you were at the very apex of your career as an 8th grade C-team star? Get over it. Move on. Eric Cooper said, "Whether I get along with a manager depends upon personality, history, and mindset; some guys can shake off a couple bad calls. Some guys generalize my abilities on the basis of a couple questionable calls."

- Reasonably address any legitimate dispute I have with officials. I understand that the coaches – not I – have primary responsibility for problem-solving and conflict resolution in such cases.

Only the coach or captain should have interaction with an official, and that point of contact should be firmly established in advance of each contest.

- Concentrate all of my energies on positively encouraging everyone involved in sports competition, including officials, rather than negatively tearing-down the participants.

Again, people other than officials should be solely concerned about *cheering for* their team, not *booing against* anyone, including the official.

(See my Appendix for the covenants made by a Christian athletes, parents and spectators.)

The Ideal Behavior of Officials

Officials should agree to all of the following:

- I will attempt to maintain sharp discernment about the action, rules, and progression of the competition.

An official's mind must be clear of distraction. An official's heart must be clear of excess emotion or residue of negative interactions in the past. Every day is full of new mercies and grace. Major League Baseball Umpire Eric Cooper told me, "Different managers and players handle adversity in different ways. Some will always lash out. They attribute that to 'I'm intense' or 'I'm frustrated' or 'It's the heat of the battle.' I'm all of those things, because there is heat-of-the-battle for us, too. You need to be right as an official. There are periods of the game when we face more pressure, and we're expected to hold our emotions in-check at all times, but that's sometimes tough to do." But keep those emotions in-check they must!

- I will keep my emotions in-check during the heat of competition and at the point of controversial judgments.

One basketball official actually sent an apology e-mail to our school after an unfortunate post-game incident. After a tightly-called game, the players were shaking hands, and one of the players from the opposing team accused this official of pushing him and then challenged the referee to a fight! Fortunately, the official kept his cool during this regrettable situation.

NFL Official Bill Spyksma told me, "Initially, take a non-confrontational approach. If you don't know the answer, don't say you do know the answer. Don't lie. Treat them with respect. Know the rules and quote them right. Don't interpret what one of the other officials did, especially if interpreting the calls incorrectly. Every single NFL official is college educated. We're educated people. We have experienced success in other professions. We are professional to start with. Roger Goodall has done a good job as NFL Commissioner. He is concerned about the integrity of the game. Our system is working hard to evaluate officials positively. The results are always so much better if positive."

- I will seek to listen actively during disputes, deescalating any argument when possible. At least so far as it depends on me, I will live at peace with everyone.

Unfortunately, emotion gets the better of us, and active listening becomes the least of our concerns in such situations. Positive expectancy about "living at peace" with everyone will better allow the official to stay in-control. To the extent that "relationships" are possible, good officials know they need to be on good terms with players, coaches, and spectators, and they appreciate the opportunities to see great athletic performance, working with any number of fine people. Iowa Girls High School Athletic Union Executive Director Mike Dick officiated state tournament games in four sports and was inducted in the Iowa Officials Hall of Fame. He told me, "In all of those experiences as an official, I developed great relationships throughout the State of Iowa. I can't go somewhere without knowing something from all of those years of officiating and coaching, and that's very satisfying."

- If I have made a correct judgment or interpretation of a rule, and a coach or player begins to unreasonably spew emotional arguments at me, I will not simply stand and take the abuse of this person. I will focus on the reasons and rules of my call, not the emotion of the moment.

MLB Umpire Tim McClelland believes that some basketball and football referees take extraordinary abuse from coaches, in particular, because any technical fouls called against those coaches could result in "marks" against the official, thus essentially "blackballing" a referee from consideration for post-season refereeing. It may also very well be that coaches talk to each other, accumulating black marks against refs. So, too often, officials stand and take the abuse, rather than being allowed to reasonably interact with coaches without reprisal. I believe referees should be able to state their cases and make unsportsmanlike or technical calls without any negative consequence from coaches or the league.

- I will not draw attention to myself through overly flamboyant or aggressive movement, gestures, or comments.

Please, no robots. And, please, no thespians in melodramas, either!

- I will not "bait" participants, coaches, or spectators to anger by verbal or non-verbal means.

Grudges are the seeds planted in the fertile ground of baiting. With each new contest, the official must give a clean slate to all participants, with positive presumptions of good behavior, unless proven otherwise.

- During disputes, I will not use inflammatory words, and I will focus on the specific rule or reason for my judgment about enforcement of the rule.

After once calling a Hall of Fame Major League Baseball player out on a called third strike, home plate umpire Tim McClelland interacted with him.

The player said, "The pitch was outside."

Tim said, "I didn't see it that way."

The player responded, "The pitch WAS OUTSIDE."

Tim said, "No it wasn't, or I wouldn't have called it a strike. Are you only looking for an argument?"

The player *was* simply looking for an argument over a judgment with which he did not agree. Tim avoided escalating the argument by getting to the heart of the player's argument, a disagreement which was not going to be resolved in either the player's or the official's mind.

- I will strive for absolute fairness of judgment, no matter my negative or positive biases for coaches, participants, or teams.

Again, negative and positive biases can develop, if the official is not careful. The goal of every official should be to get each call right, no matter who is involved. And this expectation cuts both ways. Coaches and players should not hold grudges against particular sports officials.

- I will not attempt to form too close a relationship with any one coach or participant – in order to remove even the hint of favoritism.

MLB Umpire Mike Everitt made this point with me: "We don't have a lot of interaction with players and coaches. I firmly believe that I'm there to uphold the integrity of the game. You can't pass the line of getting too close to players and managers."

- I will seek the assistance of fellow officials or technology, when necessary.

Some officials are lone rangers. Or they are too proud to ask for help. Independence and pride should not get in the way of correct officiating. Major League Umpire Eric Cooper studies tape to improve his abilities as an official: "Watching film allows me to see why I might have missed a call. It's almost unfair to watch high-definition television frozen frame-by-frame. The players are bigger, stronger, faster. The plays happen faster than you can imagine. Even with all of the pressure and fast calls, sports officiating is extremely good."

- I will not be so proud or arrogant as to stand by an incorrect or missed call. My objective will always be to make the correct judgment, even after-the-fact, if such is permissible under the rules.

Athletes, coaches, and spectators have much more respect for officials who admit when they make a mistake, or when they need help on a call. All anyone cares about is the correct call. Regarding the controversy of the missed call and missed perfect game on June 2, 2010, MLB Umpire Eric Cooper said to me, "I applaud Jim Joyce and Armando Galarraga. That player had the right mentality. The umpire apologized, but the player could have said different things to the media. That's good sportsmanship with both parties. Those are positives which came out of a horrible situation. Interestingly, that same night, a play in another game cost one team their game, but that call was overshadowed by the lost perfect game."

Perfect games are rare – only 20 in the last 130 years. In his June 10, 2010 column, "A Perfect Reaction to an Imperfect Call," syndicated columnist Leonard Pitts expressed himself well: "Joyce was reported to be disconsolate after he saw the replay. 'I just cost that kid a perfect game,' he said. What's remarkable, though, is what happened afterward. The umpire sought out the player and apologized, weeping. And Galarraga promptly accepted. 'Nobody's perfect,' he said. . . .both put it behind them and went back to work. The game might not have been perfect, but the response surely was. You will seldom see better definitions of integrity, civility, sportsmanship."

I contend that an umpire sincerely apologizing and a player magnanimously accepting that apology is far more memorable than a perfect game. I will remember the names of that umpire and player far longer for that reason than for a perfect game, because such sportsmanship is so rare in sports – rarer than a perfect game!

Jim Joyce's fellow umpire, Eric Cooper said to me, "I hope that, after this situation involving Jim Joyce, fans don't think that umpires should apologize for every one of our missed calls. I can't apologize for every play or pitch I might miss. That's part of the game." Indeed.

- At the end of a competition – whether I made correct judgments or missed calls – I will walk away knowing that I did my best, and I will not second-guess myself in future competitions.

Mike Everitt said, "Umpires have to get past the notion that people are going to say good things about them. We need to be confident about who we are." Mike's colleague, Eric Cooper told me, "This is my 12th year in the game. The names don't change. The uniforms change. I seem to get the benefit of the doubt, based on my work ethic. . . .heart and hustle can make the difference. Everyone on our staff upholds the integrity of the game. I give a total effort. You can't be afraid to interact with players, coaches, and managers, so they understand you and your personality. In my heart of hearts, I don't believe I make 'bad' calls. I might 'miss' calls, but I'm doing my best to make the right call in all situations."

(See my Appendix for the covenant made by a Christian official.)

What can officials do to contribute to a game of greater honor? MLB Umpire Tim McClelland said, "It all goes back to what you're supposed to do. What's your job? I want to do the job. I try to enjoy what I do. I do my best. Body language is huge, projecting your enjoyment and interest in the game. Tom Treblehorn commented that I had once made a call with a smile on my face. He commented it was nice that such was the case. I keep my emotions in-check, but I'm also not a robot. We are the third team on that field; media is bringing more attention to officials, especially with missed calls. We don't want the notoriety. Big-time situations will bring attention to you and your profession. It comes back to personality. People need to realize umpires and officials are human beings who are trying to do their best. I'm a really laid-back guy. People know that on the field. I don't want to lose my emotions. I want to hear what they have to say, if I have to write in a report or react to it. I will raise my voice to give direction, but not to get into an argument. If Tim McClelland yells, my partners know I am upset."

Practical Applications

For Officials

1. Don't get too close to any one player, coach, or administrator, but don't be stand-offish, either. Warmly greet sports participants at contests. Show your personality. Allow people to know you as an individual.

2. In pre-game conversations with coaches and/or captains, be very clear in your expectations, so there will be no surprises when you enforce a rule or address an inappropriate behavior of players, coaches, and spectators.

3. Ignore 95% of the commentary from spectators; only address an individual in a crowd when behavior has become inappropriate, and ask the sports administrator to address that behavior in a way which does not call attention to you, the perpetrator, or situation (if possible). Continuing inappropriate behavior is grounds for ejection from the contest.

4. Concentrate on the specifics of rules and reason for your enforcement of the rules when interacting with a coach who has a dispute with you. Resist the urge to get caught up in the emotion, which almost always clouds good reason.

5. It's fine for you to have a "style" and "personality" as an official, but do not allow either style or personality to make you a central part of the athletic contest. You are not an "extra," but neither are you to be the "protagonist" of the play.

6. Smile during contests. Laugh when appropriate. Allow people to see that you enjoy yourself.

7. "Teach" as you are officiating. Skilled NFL Back Judge Scott Helverson told me that he often teaches as he is officiating – often preventing future rules infractions.

8. Keep learning. Keep building your competency by attending clinics and reading books. As your competency grows, people will have even more respect for your abilities and performances as an official.

For Spectators

1. If you have responsibility for greeting officials at contests, extend a warm hand of hospitality to them. In a timely manner, get them situated in a comfortable locker room. Provide refreshments before, during, and after the contests.

2. Bite your tongue, if an official missed a call or made a bad call (at least in your mind). Literally, bite your tongue, and avoid the temptation of lashing-out at an official.

3. When natural opportunities present themselves, walk up to officials after contests to offer specific compliments on their officiating.

4. Once the emotion of a contest has subsided, an athletic director should call and give specific feedback to officials about effective and ineffective behaviors.

5. If an official has done a particularly exemplary job in a game or season, find the e-mail or home address of that official, and send a message of thanks with concrete reasons.

6. School and sports league administrators should emphasize the need for sportsmanship and appropriate behavior with officials during athletic competition *prior to* that competition, and, then, school and sports league administrators should be consistent about enforcing those expectations, including ejections of individuals when behavior is inappropriate.

7. Top NFL Back Judge Scott Helverson liked the idea of parents, coaches, and players signing pledges to engage in more honorable behavior during sporting events when I posed that

possibility to him. He went so far as to say that, when coaches, players, and fans gather together after a game (as is the case at our school) everyone should ask each other, "Did you abide by your pledge today." Scott said, "Hold yourself accountable." Indeed. Again, check out the various covenants in the Appendix of this book, including those which could be signed by officials.

Who schedules the officials? *School and league administrators*, of course. On to the next course of counsel for a group of leaders who are pivotal to success of a positive sports paradigm.

Chapter 12

To School and League Administrators: Organizational Impact on the Culture of Sports

Administrators of schools and organizers of sports leagues must model a culture of integrity and set clear expectations for the behavior of everyone involved in athletic programs. America's Family Coaches, Character Counts, Positive Coaching Alliance, and Institute for the Study of Youth Sports programs will also highlighted in this chapter.

As a college student, I ran a spring baseball league. I have coached sports in multiple schools and at the elementary, junior high, and high school levels. I have coached girls and boys. I have watched my own daughters play in recreational and select sports leagues. I have served as a school administrator for over 20 years, so I have watched interscholastic sports of every ilk (except for curling, downhill skiing, and rodeo, but that's a different story). One day, I hope to have grandchildren whom I can pamper when they participate in sports.

One thing I know for sure: Not one of us can escape the politics of school or league sports administration! Everyone seems to want to assert pressure in any number of ways. Like-minded parents band together and form a special interest group in the pavilion. People get elected to Boards to gain "power." Booster clubs take on lives of their own if left unabated. Folks with money or sob stories tell the administrators that "rules are great for everybody else's kid, but couldn't we, just this once, make an exception?!"

This chapter is written as an encouragement to all of the volunteers and professional administrators who are trying to run sports programs. My first exhortation to you is to rise above these politics. As you can see, I know about politics. But I am proud to say that, in all of my experience in leadership, whether "in power" or seemingly "powerless," I have never actually engaged in any political behaviors. In fact, to this point, I have resisted *any* and *all* temptation to be political.

I'm not sure why I have been able to resist the natural pull of politics in one of the most political environments ever – the American school. With a straight face, I can say that I have never attempted to use my influence or "power" to play political games, and neither should you. There have been thousands of times when I could have done so, but I have simply chosen not to travel those routes.

Unfortunately, I see politics rear their ugly heads time and time again. But I call you to seek a more noble form of leadership which is directly related to integrity and boundaries and clear communication and well-known expectations and consistency of policy enforcement. You must EARN the moral authority to lead.

Right now, our country has never experienced so much governmental upheaval. The two main political parties seem capable of cutthroat politics in pulling out all of the stops of smear campaigns. People who are supposed to be representing me and my interests are arrogantly closing their ears and minds to me and to large percentages of constituents. Promises of bipartisanship have gone by the wayside. The country is characterized by division, rancor, and chaos, in my humble opinion. And those who are "governing" don't even "get it." Even moral, upstanding people have been at least intellectually-corrupted by a system. I say, "Throw all the bums out, and let's start out with term limits for all!" Enough of the career politicians!!!

Thanks for indulging that rant, because it really does pertain to what I am addressing in the administration of sports. These negative political behaviors are leaving state and national congresses and drifting into sports leagues as well. We must resist that drift at all costs.

What's the sports administrator to do?

I'll tell you what she's supposed to do.

- Start with the right mission, premise, purpose, or objective – helping young people to develop character and integrity.

Iowa Sports Foundation Director Jim Hallihan stated this well to me, "Players, coaches, and parents are not on the same page, so things blow up. They need to work toward the same goals. The most important thing about sports is to build better citizens. Start with that premise, and you'll have an honorable culture of sports. If you start with winning as the purpose, then you will see greed and other negatives. Just playing is fun. That's what we remember as kids.

Adults now think that winning is the reason for sports. You play for the fun. If we remove the fun from sports, kids will quit sports, or they will perpetuate the negative model. We have instituted the Pursuing Victory with Honor program in the Iowa Games. We focus on awarding athletes for sportsmanship. In the team sports, officials rate the players, fans, and coaches; if everyone gets a 1, everyone earns gold medals. Everything we do in the Iowa Games is about fun and good sportsmanship. The Brian Pierson Award is given for character. We have a Character Counts coach of the year every year for both the Iowa High School Athletic Association and Iowa Girls High School Athletic Union." Should we pursue winning at the cost of character "losing of the soul," or should we pursue victory with honor? The choice seems very clear to me.

School athletic directors and directors of sports leagues should be promoting sports themselves and the participation of athletes in those sports far more than any other purpose. Mike Dick oversees the Iowa Girls High School Athletic Union as the organization's executive director; from his perspective, the best of athletics is "the Iowa Girl" – giving female athletes opportunities to perform and excel in a competitive environment. I am so proud that our state basketball tournament brings in athletes, drill teams, singers, and cheerleaders. Thousands of kids are involved besides the basketball players. We're trying to maintain that idea. It's a total school involvement." Rick Wulkow oversees the Iowa High School Athletic Association as his organization's executive director; Rick also sees the importance of student participation in junior high and high school athletics: "There is value in participation. It's not about scholarships to college. It's not about pro contracts. It's not about state championships. Our mission is to get kids involved in athletics."

- Don't allow the league or conference to become more important than each individual player. In my opinion, the school or sports league is still expected to play too central a role in a child's development. The parent must still maintain large control over the development of the child. Emphasize character development through sports; *however*, as I stated in an earlier chapter – a point which bears repeating at this point – emphasize that parents are primarily and ultimately responsible for their child/ren's character development.

- Make complainers follow the chain-of-command. Any time you, as a school or league sports administrator, receive a complaint from someone, the first question to that person *must be*, "Have you spoken directly with the person with whom you have the complaint?" If the answer is no, you must direct the complainer to that person. I do not like it when someone goes "over my head" with a complaint to my boss before I have had an opportunity to make the situation right; in the same manner, coaches deserve the opportunity to resolve disputes closest to the dispute, because, the higher the complaint moves up the chain-of-command, the less control the original disputants have, and they will generally not ultimately be pleased with solutions of the "higher-ups."

- Of course, this does not mean that an administrator chooses to cut the complainer off, refusing to listen to a single detail of the complaint. The process simply involves the administrator making no commitment and deflecting the conflict resolution and problem-solving to the people who can most directly effect a satisfactory outcome.

- Shield coaches from all unwarranted criticism. They don't have to know that you took a bullet for them. They also don't need to hear about every nit-picky complaint, many or most of which may have no merit whatsoever. I have gotten an ear-ful from parents and spectators about coaches after athletic contests. I have listened, empathized, asked a lot of clarifying questions, and requested that these people deal directly with the those they perceive to have "wronged" them in some way.

- Don't immediately address concern from a donor, spectator, or parent unless (1) the concern is a safety concern or (2) the concern is part of a pattern. We too frequently jump on the first "incident," when the coach may not have even contributed to the situation, and the perceived problem is the sole responsibility of the complainer.

- Bring down the level of organization already! Major League Baseball Umpire Ted Barrett told me, "I'm turned off on organized sports. There are just no 'disorganized' sports. I'm in my 40s. All we did when I was a kid was to play football and wiffle ball. We played hockey at a make-shift rink in the winter. All without refs. We divided up teams. That's completely gone. I never see kids even throwing the ball around outside anymore." Why? Because they're playing year-round on travel teams, and they don't have a spare moment, given their homework, school activities, church programs, work, and sleep.

(That's right! They need to be getting 8 or 9 hours of sleep each night, but they're not getting that, either, because they are over-organized and over-programmed!)

- Slow down (if not eliminate) this spiraling trend of specialization and "competition" between school sports and club sports. Mike Dick believes that girls in Iowa's high schools are being expected to spend too much in-season time with off-season sports activities: "The involvement of club non-school sports is a concern of mine. Year-round, every spare moment is consumed by sports. In my time, every sport had its distinct season, and there were no interloping coaches. Coaches are pressuring kids to do one sport year-round. I talked to a young lady who – on any given day in the summer – is lifting weights and doing separate practices in volleyball, basketball, *and* softball. The pressure is phenomenal. Student-athletes ought to be playing 3 or 4 sports. Kids ought to be able to go swimming and fishing. They ought to be able to hold down a part-time job. I'd like to see kids in sports, FFA, speech, drama – and still have conversation time at the dinner table and to go to church on Sunday." Rick Wulkow oversees boys sports in Iowa's high school supports. He agrees with Mike: "There are abuses of demands of time on kids that I don't like. We're hearing more and more people asking us to put limitations on the practice time that coaches demand on kids. We used to have good summer rules, but public sentiment forced a relaxing of those limits. We're a rural state. Small schools depend upon multiple-sport athletes. I would like to reinstitute stiffer summer contact rules which limit the amount of time which coaches can work with kids in the off-season. We can control things during the school year, but there are so many demands on kids in the summer. We have the power to control what our coaches are doing. We don't have control over the coaches of club sports and AAU leagues. This year, I'm going to challenge my staff to find a way of bringing the leaders of non-school sports together to talk about these abuses and the values we're attempting to instill. Education is the farthest things from some of these people's minds. A majority are trying to find the elite athletes and achieve the recognition of the best teams. Some are exploiting our kids for their own benefits."

- Communicate, communicate, communicate! Communication and education from league officials are extremely important to success in athletics. For instance, Rick Wulkow, IHSAA's chief executive, told me, "Our wellness department does a great job of sending educational information about nutrition supplements to our athletic directors and coaches. Coaches have to be educated about abuses. We need to keep that information on the front-burner. We can't just do it annually. We've got to keep reinforcing the message. With sportsmanship and citizenship, we've got to preach it day-after-day-after-day. We've got to get coaches to talk about these topics during practices and games. Athletic directors can address these issues in meetings and evaluations of coaches."

My school's Principal, John Steddom, and Athletic Director, John Jones, do an excellent job of intentionally putting the topics of integrity, character, honor, and sportsmanship in front of the school community. They are absolutely committed to integrating the attributes of a positive sports program into place. I couldn't be more proud of them or the coaches who are attempting to make athletics a positive memory for our athletes. Development of an honorable sports program does not occur without the support of senior level leadership and Boards of Directors.

Matt Hill, Athletic Director of Northwestern College in St. Paul, Minnesota, has a very healthy perspective on athletic competition. Take in, chew upon, digest, and be nourished by his ideas:

Sports league administrators should. . .

- Develop a brochure which explains the expectations for each sports season, addressing typical parental concerns, game behavior, consequences for inappropriate behavior, etc. "This communication sets the tone for your athletic program," Matt said.

- Establish a system of "honor points" to be honest with officials about calls they missed but about which players can honest, even if "costly" to the game's outcome.

- Train coaches in expectations for performance.

- Regulate club sports and AAU sports. Failure to evaluate those programs can result in poor coaching and officiating.

Matt said, "Coaches are out-of-control, because they have no training."

- Form a committee of coaches and student-athletes to develop a Code of Conduct.

- Direct a student-athlete to read a Code of Conduct when it's "dead-quiet." Those students should come from the Advisory Committee which developed the Code. Hence, the expectations for sportsmanship are coming from the student-athletes to everyone in attendance at the contest. "The NCAA does not require us to read such a Code of Conduct at Northwestern, but we believe we've got to live it and enforce it," Matt said.

- Insure that game management staff members are trained well in all rules and procedures. "If they don't know the rules," Matt said, "They could actually create problems for the game."

- Carefully supervise crowds at contests. They should not be afraid to confront inappropriate behavior. Game managers should be visible and active, thwarting unsportsmanlike behavior. Matt told me The University of Minnesota recently opened a new football stadium and expected season ticketholders to follow their Code of Conduct. Athletic administrators "do police the Code and do boot people," Matt said. "The U is leading the way."

- When defeated in a contest, the coaches and players should learn, and acknowledge their responsibilities for being defeated.

- Expect coaches to ask three questions: (1) Was God honored by our play? (2) Did we respect our opponents? (3) Did we win the game?" Matt commented, "If we say yes to #3 but not to #1 or #2, we have 'lost.' If we can say yes to #1 and #2, even if we say no to #3, we have 'won.'"

- Evaluate coaches on a regular basis. Monitor coaches for teaching about character, honesty, and integrity. Matt said, "Athletes should know what's right and wrong about athletics. I have a problem with coaches who don't teach about the integrity of the game."

- Regularly self-assess the athletic program to gauge the ethical approach in sports. Even in a Christian school, people might believe they are coaching with integrity, but they are not doing so. Matt said, "I see some of the worst behavior at Bible colleges and Christian schools."

How about some more practical ideas for the school and sports league administrators?

Practical Applications

1. Shape a positive culture in your sports program. For instance, the Positive Coaching Alliance writes on their website (www.positivecoach.org), "Youth sports leaders take on a major responsibility when they join a board. How many of these leaders realize that culture shaping is a major part of their job? Positive Coaching Alliance offers an interactive leadership workshop that introduces youth sports organizers and school leaders to the Roadmap to Excellence, the best way to bring an Honoring the Game culture to your organization. This road map is intended to help [leaders] to make the organization one that promotes and reinforces positive coaching rather than the win-at-all-cost model of coaching that is polluting youth sports."

2. Take advantage of resources available to you. I have obviously already pointed your attention to a wealth of information in the Positive Coaching Alliance. The Institute for Character Development, Institute for the Study of Youth Sports, and America's Family Coaches are three additional organizations which could be of assistance to you. "The mission of the Institute for the Study of Youth Sports is to provide leadership, conduct scientific research, and engage in service or outreach that transforms the face of youth sports in ways that maximize the beneficial physical, psychological, and social effects of participation for children and youth while minimizing detrimental affects." (www.edu.msu.edu/ysi). ISYS provides resources for coaches, leaders, parents, researchers, and kids alike. The Institute for Character Development is responsible for oversight of the famed "Character Counts" program in the United States. Not only schools, but also sports leagues, political systems, and entire

communities have embraced the Character Counts program. Dr. Gary and Barb Rosberg, America's Family Coaches, have numerous resources available to Christian families and Christian schools, including The Great Relationship Experience, which I have even adapted as "The Great Sports Relationship Experience."

3. Support your athletic directors and coaches when they deserve your support, even and especially when pressure seems unbearable. Make the "hard right" decision, rather than the "easy wrong" call. We should all "have each others' backs," not in a circle-the-wagon mentality, but to stand steadfast when good decisions have been made, no matter how difficult. Offer words of encouragement to coaches when they are discouraged.

4. Don't just "support" your athletic directors and coaches. Praise them publicly and privately, when possible. Send e-mails, letters, handwritten notes, e-cards – whatever will be best received by your colleagues.

5. Keep the lines of communication open. Be open to praise *and criticism*. There is usually at least a kernel of truth in any criticism. Don't be closed to negative feedback, because that negativity will always bubble-up at some other location of the organization. I always say that the health of an organization is directly proportional to the speed by which bad news travels to the top of the hierarchy. Whenever I encounter a negative piece of *signed* communication, I always express appreciation that the person was confident enough to share the criticism with me, knowing I would take her seriously, listen actively, and respond appropriately. In a recent e-mail criticizing my school (unfairly, in my opinion), I wrote back to the person, "I realize we are not a perfect school. We make mistakes. We will do wrong from time-to-time, as any school does. But I want you to know that we are committed to addressing those mistakes, owning up to them, and then correcting the problems, so they do not happen again in the future."

6. Dismiss anonymous "petitions" and communication outright. If someone does not have the guts to stand by a message – by name – you have no obligation to respond in any way. Now, you should obviously be sensitive to the content of the communication, because this might be a symptom of a larger problem. But every individual who comes out of right field to

address an issue in an unreasonable way does not necessitate a response from you.

7. If the coach has made a mistake, or could have handled a situation differently, offer counsel, particularly if you have had a similar experience. Be transparent with the coaches; allow them to learn from your past mistakes and successes.

Administrators play a vital role in leadership. They also have greater opportunities to interact with the next stakeholder in positive culture of athletics – *the media*.

Chapter 13

To the Media: Please, How About More Close-Ups of Correct Calls and Character?!

In particular, television coverage has become so sophisticated that we can watch athletic plays and calls of officials in super-slow motion, frame-by-frame. The media love to stir controversy, so we can watch missed or close calls over-and-over-and-over again. In the media moguls' minds, incompetence, controversy, and behavior of "bad boys and girls" sell. Wouldn't we find it refreshing to read, see, and hear about the positive character of the "good guys" and the correct calls of officials (which is a vast majority of time)?

Consider the media, which has the power to effect negative or positive reactions to sports.

One online blogger wrote,

"San Francisco Giants catcher Bengie Molina is not fast. In fact, he's very slow. Very very slow. You see that picture to the right? Well, that's not even a picture. That's a video of Molina running full speed.

"He's that slow.

"Okay, so it's a picture, but that's beside the point. On ESPN over the weekend they showed a highlight from the Giants game against the Marlins. From Molina's point of view it wasn't a highlight as much as a lowlight, and the way it was presented was a further insult. He even took to his blog to write about it. . . .

"'ESPN's sarcastic depiction of me running in slow motion down third base and getting thrown out at home in the Marlins' game was hard to take. . . .'

"'Until recently, I had thought of ESPN as a network run by professionals who know sports. I thought the people at ESPN, because they focus only on sports, actually understood the game and what pro athletes do to reach the highest level of their sport.'

"'In that Marlins game, which we won, Nate Schierholtz went three-for-three with his first home run of the season. Matt Cain pitched six innings of no-hit ball. And the one highlight ESPN shows of that game is me getting thrown out at home? And they're doing it just for laughs?'

"'Look, you can say I'm the slowest guy in baseball or in all of sports or in the entire world. I don't take issue with that because I AM the slowest guy. I have always been the slowest guy. I can't challenge that criticism. But ESPN's intention was not to criticize but to humiliate.'

"Now had the clip that was shown been in full-speed, Molina likely would have been upset, but I doubt he'd have written a blog entry about it. It wasn't in full-speed, though. ESPN ran it in slow motion to mock Molina's speed. With the anchors having a good time at his expense.

"So I get why Molina is upset, but at the same time, it's not really a big deal. Molina knows he's slow, he admitted it in the blog entry, so why not just laugh it off? It's not like they said he was a horrible baseball player.

He should probably just be happy that ESPN even showed a Giants clip. Sometimes I can't even tell if they're aware that there's a whole other coast in this country and that they play baseball games out there too." (Fornelli, p. 1)

This writer couldn't help but get his own dig into a baseball team which was struggling at the time of publication.

Bobby Knight is alleged to have once said, "Absolute silence – That's the one thing a sportswriter can quote accurately." (*What They Don't Tell You about School Administration in Schools of Education*, by Fenwick and English, p. 93)

In their classic book on school administration, Fenwick and English themselves point out, "Any school administrator who believes the media people sell the 'truth' or are even remotely interested in the

157

truth has a lot to learn. Reporters from papers are proctologists of print." (p. 85)

While unfair to characterize all of the members of the media in these ways, I must admit that I have far too much experience interacting with the media, and, usually, in some of the most negative of circumstances. You name the medium, and I have been thrust into the limelight. In my thirty years of leadership in schools and churches, I have been an interview subject for newspapers, magazines, the Internet, radio, and television.

I have been pressed into media service to handle any number of challenges:

- More than one student being murdered
- Accidental deaths of students
- Deaths of students, staff members, parents due to disease
- A gun being brought to school by a student
- Multiple bomb threats
- A D.A.R.E. (Drug Abuse Resistance Education) officer being arrested for possession of display drugs when soliciting a prostitute with those drugs
- Confirmed allegations of sexual abuse perpetrated by more than one "trusted" adult
- Students building home-made bombs at a homecoming football game
- Numerous outbreaks of school vandalism at both public and Christian schools
- An H1N1 flu outbreak
- Personnel decisions needing to remain legally confidential in nature
- Issues involving the hot-button topics of homosexuality, racism, and abortion
- Requested reconsideration of literature perceived to be vulgar by certain parents
- A student assault of a teacher (and subsequent expulsion of the student)
- A student "escaping" Good Conduct Policy consequences by transferring to my school to be immediately eligible in his sport

I am not surprised that professional officials in sports reserved their most pointed opinions for the media during my interviews. Consider MLB Umpire Ted Barrett's view: "The media has taken such a negative turn. And whenever guys profess their faith, the media turns away from the coverage." NFL Referee Scott Helverson adds, "The media? Miss a call, and the media is all over the call. Make a good call, and the media doesn't mention that. I don't mind our replay system. I want it to be right. One year, I missed a toe-tap in the back of the end zone. I'm all for getting it right. The college football system is horrible. Let's get it down to 3 or 4 challenges a game in college ball. The media stresses so much of the negative that it trickles-down to all of the parents, kids, and coaches. The media blames. Kids pick up on this. They criticize their teammates, rather than taking responsibility for their own mistakes."

What's the perspective of MLB Umpire Tim McClelland? He told me, "The media are becoming a huge part of sports. Now there is so much scrutiny with everyone connected to the game. There were two weeks of 24/7 coverage of the Super Bowl players and coaches. We are so scrutinized by the media. Is that good for the game? The media is generally a negative. They're looking for controversy. They're trying to knock some of these guys off the pedestal. Derek Jeter going 0 for 4 is the news, instead of the good things he does. The media comes at this from a negative perspective. Media exposure is the reason for sports sometimes being out-of-control. Everybody sees this bad behavior on TV. We didn't have technology like this years ago. That's what has branched-out this poor behavior. This is why it's permeating down into the leagues with young kids. . . .The media come to ask us about missed calls. What is the purpose of being confronted about making a missed call? I stand up and admit the mistake, and I move on. . . . The media say, 'Tim McClelland missed that call,' but they also do not say, 'The official made a good call' when I make a good call. . . . Players make mistakes. Umpires make mistakes. Referees' decisions do not affect the outcome of the game. Players need to shoot or hit better or make better throws. The media is looking for perfection."

Major League Baseball Umpire Eric Cooper agreed: "Controversy sells tickets and ads. That's the media's spin on things. From the time I've been in the game and now (15 years), I've seen a huge change in the way that MLB Umpires are seen. If you make a mistake and miss a play, you miss a play for a month. The call is re-run on ESPN, CNN, the local news. Sports officials are seen as 'not good at our jobs.' In the minds of reporters, we 'need extra media to do well.' Our sport was so pure and traditional. Human error was part of the game. The media reflects good and bad on our youth. The kids who see this stuff on Sports Center want to emulate the behavior of superstars. They flip their bats. They sag their pants. The run with one hand down. From my point of view, I can't do a lot to stop that."

Major League Baseball Umpire Tim Everitt gets the final word from the official's perspective: "Television coverage and the technology have made officiating extremely difficult. It's a no-win situation. You're not going to be right 100% of the time. It's a double-edged sword. You don't want a pivotal call to decide a game, not being able to correct it, but you also want the call to stand as called. Before television, baseball was a more pure sport. TV loves controversy. People in the media love to see arguments. At the annual meeting of all 68 umpires in January, we prepare ourselves for the upcoming season. We go over rules. This year, meeting organizers started something new. They trained us in how to handle the press. They're trying to help us to diffuse arguments. We can become better at answering questions. Most of us have a bitter taste in our mouths about the press; the media has completely mis-paraphrased interviews, and the information is wrong."

Hmm. I detect some common themes, and I'm reasonably sure that athletes, coaches, parents, and spectators would share their opinions.

- Negative news sells.
- Controversy is an attention-getter.
- We live in an age of hyper-accountability, and the media relish opportunities to focus on perpetrators. (See the Tiger Woods controversy of Thanksgiving, 2009 and following!)
- "Wars" are often ignited through the choice of poor or inaccurate words.
- The ways that we communicate can be equally as damaging as the words which are used. Body language, tone, and volume often reveal the heart of our statements.

So, what can all of us do to eliminate the negative and accentuate the positive when interacting with the media? Let's close with some practical applications for members of the media and for representatives of teams and leagues.

To the Media

- Get to know the athletes, coaches, and schools well within your area of coverage. Nurture relationships without compromising your objectivity. How? Set regular appointments to cover "human interest stories." Take time to try to understand each interview subject by listening actively and showing interest in them as people (even moreso than your interest in the stories).

- Force your predominant mental filter to be positive more than negative. Look for the positive before looking for the negative. Report on the positive in addition to the negative. Seek positive news at least as often as negative news.

- Cover "bad" or negative news – such is your responsibility – but remove as much of the opinion, editorializing, and cynicism which drips through contemporary journalistic language.

- Choose your words carefully. Avoid inflammatory language which could only be intended to enrage a portion of your audience.

- Fairly cover *all* sides of stories. Books have been written about liberal mainstream media coverage. No media outlet – whether "conservative" or "liberal" – could today be accurately described as "fair and balanced." When a liberal must be accountable for her actions, don't avoid the coverage. When a conservative must be accountable for his actions, don't avoid the coverage. Be truly fair and objective. Too much journalism today would have been found exclusively on the "opinion" pages of early-Twentieth Century newspapers.

- Be fair to athletes, coaches, and officials by covering the "right" and "good" things they do at least as equally as the behaviors and calls which "missed" the mark. You could even choose to ignore a behavior from time-to-time. While athletes, coaches, and officials have no real choice in being role models and ambassadors for their sports, they are, also, after all, human beings deserving of some privacy and consideration during the difficult times of their lives.

To Representatives of Teams and Leagues

I am indebted to my former employer, the Urbandale Community School District of Iowa for providing me and my administrative colleagues with valuable training by the famed Arch Lustberg – who used to prepare interview subjects for grillings by Dan Rather and Morley Safer on the "60 Minutes" television program – and I would like to share Arch's wisdom with you (including my own learning experiences sprinkled-in):

- Seek to nurture positive relationships with all members of the media. Proactively call, schedule appointments, and send press releases with interesting and meaningful story ideas. NFL Replay Official Bill Spyksma works hard to develop positive relationships with television producers: "Replay officiating is much different. I have to know the rules inside-and-out. Camera angles can be deceiving. I meet with the TV producers prior to every game. I know every angle. When we have a tough call, I asked the producer to give me every angle they have. Regional games don't provide me with as many angles. I can get 8 cameras regionally, 26 games on Monday Night Football. It's got to be pretty quick. I've got about 60 seconds to make a decision."

- When the opportunity for an interview presents itself, choose *one* person to serve as the central spokesperson for the school or league, so multiple perspectives are not confounding the situation. The media spokesperson should keep people within the organization informed about the latest developments, not allowing "insiders" to learn information from the media, rather than from you.

- If the media seeks to interview minors, follow policies, and seek parental permission. Know and follow all of your policies to the letter when interacting with the media.

- Before you return that phone call or speak directly with the media, construct your message. Be prepared. Type out words and phrases which will help you guide your interaction with the media.

- If confronted by a member of the media, be calm, not defensive. Don't blame others. Don't play the role of "victim."

- Smile (appropriately). Do not use humor in a serious situation, or you will be perceived as not taking the serious situation seriously.

- Provide accurate information. Inaccurate information can seriously damage your reputation and the credibility of your leadership and communication.

- If you do not know the answer to a question, say so, find out, and report back to the media when you have determined answers to their questions.

- If necessary, use your own recording devices, with the full knowledge of the media, so you can be assured that you can verify your comments, particularly in a "he said / she said" dispute. Don't pull the "hidden recorder trick," even if the media does so with you.

- A good formula for responses to the media: Simple + Brief + Clear + Concise = Easy to Understand. Avoid jargon or technical language.

- Use my 5 C's of Effective Communication as your filter – Clear, Concise, Concrete, Clean, and Compelling. Choose words, stories, illustrations, illustrations, and sound bytes which will send positive messages.

- Don't use high-powered vocabulary to prove your competence. Such typically backfires on a person, resulting in the audience perceiving the interview subject to be arrogant.

- Be positive. With positive phrasing, honestly acknowledge any problems or conflicts which should be acknowledged.

- Pause. Stop and think before you speak. TV and radio people will edit the "dead air time."

- Don't volunteer any additional information beyond that which the question asks for, and feel free to answer questions which are not asked – as a means of getting positive information before audiences. Don't provide information which might extend the life of a negative story.

- Don't speculate. Say, "I cannot or should not speculate."

- Be honest about mistakes which have been made. Communicate a sincere desire to overcome and not repeat those mistakes in the future.

- Don't repeat the interviewer's negative-connoted words, thus reinforcing the negativity. For instance, an interviewer could ask, "What are you trying to hide?" The poor response is "I'm not trying to hide anything!" Using that sound byte on the 5:00 news will not present you in a favorable light. A better response is "I want to be completely forthright about all aspects of this matter, and I will be fully cooperative during the investigation."

- If the person asks a convoluted, multi-part question ask for rephrasing or a breaking-down of the questions within the question. Blathering-on in comments posed as questions seems to be a Twenty-First Century phenomenon, so you should be prepared to concentrate well and ask that all of the questions or points be broken down into more digestible bites.

- Tell what you are doing, not what you are not doing. Stating actions in the positive come across as much more positive than what you are not doing in the situation.

- Repeat positive phrases to etch your words in to the public's mind – words which will hopefully overshadow any negative perspectives of the press or your confronter/s.

- Do not overuse any one communication strategy, or you will sound programmed in your responses.

- Be yourself. Be authentic. Be real. Don't put on an act.

- Be likeable. People who are reading or hearing your words will respond more positively to you if you are likeable. Style is often more important than substance.

- But it's not enough to be likeable. You must also be perceived as competent. Most of the people will give you the benefit of the doubt. They want to like you. But the audience will not believe you if you demonstrate incompetence during forays with the media. You must be both likeable and competent.

- Give your audience credit for being able to draw their own conclusions in judging a member of the media as an unreasonable attacker. You don't need to judge that person through your words in the interview.

- Give as much information as legally possible. If you cannot share certain information, do not say, "No comment." Say something like, "Confidentiality laws prevent me from sharing that information. I want to protect everyone's legal rights in not going beyond what is legally permissible to share. If I were able to provide you with all of the details of this case, I hope you would agree that we have taken the prudent course of action."

- There are three constituencies in your audience: (1) those who are *for* you, (2) those who are *against* you, and (3) those *who haven't made up their minds* about you. Forget the people who are for you; they will probably always be for you. Forget the people who are against you, because they will probably always be against you. Concentrate your attention on the people who are undecided. Try to help them make up their minds in your favor.

- Following your interaction with the media, reflect mentally and in writing about what went well and what could have gone more effectively to deal with the situation. Learn from your mistakes. Replicate your successes.

- Thank members of the media when they fairly and accurately cover stories.

Arch Lustberg's training occurred on the heels of an incident in which Iowa State University students dropped large quantities of anti-Jewish and anti-Black literature in my high school's restrooms, an attempt to spread the perception that our school was a "racist" high school.

The training helped me develop positive statements which resulted in much more positive perceptions of the school --

- "As has been the case in the past, we are going to do everything possible to nurture a safe, caring environment for everyone in our school and for everyone in our community."

- "A few noisy people who hate have attracted media attention and are creating a perception about this community and school which is simply not true. Ours is a safe, caring community on the whole."

- "I'm proud that so many of our students have come to me to say that they were disgusted by the drop of this literature at our school."

- "Freedom in our country means that we must allow people to express their hate. But our student body and staff have the right to see that such hate is expressed off school grounds."

The media are certainly not going away. Technology is going to get more and more sophisticated. All of us in sports should work collaboratively, rather than combatively, to enjoy the very best which sports have to offer to all participants, including the media, nearly all of whom love the sports they are covering.

Now, let's shift gears, so I can share my experience with finally coaching under the model I am advocating in this book. Read about "Dr. Bob: A New Coach."

Chapter 14

Dr. Bob: A New Coach

Dr. Bob had never himself coached under this desired model of positive coaching, so he sought an opportunity to do just that, volunteering to coach the Grasshoppers, a team of beginning softball players in the spring and early-summer of 2010. This chapter will detail the hilarity, poignancy, and lessons of that experience.

Who is right for youth sports?

Coach Lou! That's who!

In the park, and in the dark, he is no shark!

He's Coach Lou!

Who is Coach Lou, and why is this now sounding like a Dr. Seuss book?!

Apart from my pride in the coaches who are using a positive model of coaching at my school, Lou Chapko is my most consistent long-term example of exemplary performance in this positive model of athletics, while Lou was coaching my daughter Hannah in recreational soccer for several years. In this chapter, allow me to introduce you to Lou Chapko, THE poster boy for positive coaching!

Why was Lou so effective?

Lou is a very laid-back, positive, upbeat, pleasant guy. He smiles a lot. His toothy grins exude sincere warmth. He earns a person's trust right away. He obviously loves his wife, his own kids, and other people's children. I instinctively understood that almost immediately.

Lou is also a very moral guy. He cares deeply about his faith, and I could tell that he was operating from a sound moral compass when interacting with Hannah and her teammates. He has a crisp understanding of his values and makes all decisions from that core of his being.

Lou is very organized. We parents received treat, practice, and game schedules well in advance of each season. There was never any lack of clarity about proper uniforms, which can often be a source of concern for everyone involved. Even though he could have "flown by the seat of his pants" for practices – after all, he is a busy executive with Pioneer Hi-Bred International – he always had a practice plan for drills and a game plan for substitutions and strategy.

In addition, Lou is an excellent communicator. Two points here. #1 – He was *always* positive; I have never once heard an unkind comment come out of his mouth, even when he could have been tempted by irritable girls, parents, coaches, and referees. And #2 – He is the consummate *teacher*-coach. He always gives very specific feedback about fundamental skills, rules interpretations, field positioning, offensive strategies, and defense methodologies. I think I finally understood "offsides" for the first time of my life, after watching both of my daughters play soccer for years, only because Lou was such an effective teacher of athletes *and* their parents.

Lou understood that the foundation of a great feeder system is effectively conditioning the athletes and teaching them how to practice sound fundamental skills. Because of Coach Lou's commitment in that regard, his girls played better individually AND as a team.

And it was always all about team. Lou played no favorites. His daughter was clearly *the* most talented soccer player, but she received no preferential treatment. *Everyone*, no matter her ability, received playing time in accordance with the plan he set out in advance of the game. Only injuries would cause Coach Lou to deviate from his plan. Otherwise, he stuck to his plan, because he knew that these beginning soccer players needed a lot of practice in game situations.

Lou's legacy as a coach is obviously intact for me, or he would not be the featured subject of this chapter of the book! You remember people like Lou, because they are kind, loving, focused, organized teachers who greatly impact your kids *and you*.

Why so much focus on Lou? Because I want to coach young players just like Lou Chapko coached my daughter and her teammates! And I found that opportunity during the writing of this book. Yes, that's right, after a LONG hiatus from coaching – 1987 until 2010 – and no opportunities to engage this noble model of coaching – I decided that I needed to apply my own learning to an actual situation. The practical application of this chapter involved me signing up to coach in the beginner's league of a local girls' softball program!

I called the league organizer and swore him to secrecy. He loved the idea. He even recommended that I read a related book, *The Talent Code*. That book only reinforced my understanding of the importance of practice, passion, and teaching to the successful athlete.

I want to make my motivations abundantly clear at the front-end of this chapter. I did not take on this responsibility to coach as "experimentation" or a way of "testing" the model. Such would have been irresponsible on my part. Children are not "guinea pigs" in "lab experiments." I was genuinely excited to apply what I have learned about this coaching model.

And I did not want anyone to know what I was doing. I would engage my learning and the model, and, following the season, I would record my impressions of our success – based on the experiences of the girls, their parents, and other spectators. Only after I had "collected all of this data" would I reveal my intentions, because I did, ultimately, want the girls and their fans to be excited about being subjects in a book!

Here is our story. . .

The athletes of the Urbandale Girls Recreation Association (UGRA) enjoy access to high-quality facilities, coaching, and programming. The UGRA has long advocated for girls sports, offering opportunities in volleyball, basketball, and softball. My daughter Molly went through the system as a volleyball and softball player. (She tried basketball one year, but she fell off a bar stool in her friend's home, breaking her arm and ending her basketball career for good!) My daughter Hannah also went through part of the system as a volleyball and softball player.

So this commitment to UGRA was a "third generation" experience for me. The parents were old enough to be my children – the players, at 4 and 5 years of age, old enough to be my grandchildren! Needless to say, I was excited about the opportunity – not only to engage this positive coaching model with the girls, but also to enjoy these girls' first softball experiences! I had attempted to coach Molly's UGRA team when she was in fourth grade, but I am chagrined to recall that I had very little patience for the whining of the girls and the unique personalities of the team, even though I should have been thrilled to be spending time with my own daughter.

My commitment to this 2010 team was not at all onerous. Six games were scheduled. Practices were essentially on the nights of the games. We had obligation to an extra night for team photographs and an extra night for year-end awards. Rain necessitated only two re-schedulings, and no deeper than late-June. Very do-able. I consciously made the decision not to arrange more than one extra practice, since these kids needed to have their own time in the late-spring and early-summer to simply play at home and not be at practices all of the time. Such also would have run their parents ragged, too.

The most important elements of the softball game *for the girls* were (1) the name of the team, the Grasshoppers; (2) "splashes" of color (a lime green t-shirt; shiny blue shorts; and pink, black, and brown bats, spikes, and gloves); (3) the temperature of each game, 70 degrees being most optimal; (4) the chance to bat repeatedly in practices and games; (5) as many opportunities to multi-task with softball and playing in the infield dirt during the games; (6) being able to bat first in an inning, which I accomplished by rotating through the line-up from one inning to the next; (7) running the bases, *usually* in the correct order; and (7) the treat schedule and tickets for the concession stand visits after the games!!

Of course, our attitudes as coaches and parents were important to the girls, too. My daughter Molly, who had morphed from her only earlier UGRA experience as a child to this UGRA coaching experience as a 23-year-old, was the perfect co-coach for this team. She is a delightful young woman. Married. Mature. Positive. Loving. Encouraging. And she was an all-conference high school softball player who understood the game. All that could have made the coaching staff any better is if her husband Jacob and my other daughter Hannah had joined us, but we made due with the coaches who were available. And Wendy the Team Mom was a dream, orchestrating development of a treat schedule with the wonderful graphic of a very large cartoon grasshopper and periodically bringing along her own mother, a woman with an incredible work ethic who was able to serve as Team Grandmom in the dugout from time-to-time. Not every team has a Team Grandmom!

I was at a distinct advantage as a coach, since I had access to my school's facilities and equipment. And I took full advantage of those perks. Prior to our first game, we were able to use multiple batting tees and an ingenious rope apparatus with hanging wiffle balls for numerous repetitions of hitting. The girls were well prepared for their first game and every game, and it showed; all of them hit well off the batting tee. We also practiced fundamentals of fielding and throwing (with a bit less success).

What made this a worthwhile experience for everyone involved?

- I told the girls the only rule was for them to have fun and to enjoy the games. I think we accomplished that mission.

- I told them that I would be concentrating on being positive and helping them to improve their skills. I remember I only got a little testy once, when the girls seemed to be more interested in playing with the infield dirt than learning how to field and throw to first base. Molly and I tried and were largely successful in being positive on all occasions.

- I stayed in close communication with the parents prior to each game. E-mail generally worked really well. Good communication usually begets good communication; the parents were really good about keeping us well informed about their daughters' anticipated absences.

- We very much welcomed the parents' involvement on the practice field; the parents listened well to our coaching talk, repeating the same expectations at practices and at home. I could tell that some of the parents spent more time with the girls away from practices, because the Grasshoppers came back the next week with markedly improved skills. The parents were wonderful throughout this entire experience.

- I stole a page from one California sports league's playbook, in which parents are asked to write positive comments about the other players on the team; such was well-received, I believe, contributing to the girls trying even harder to do their best. Read on, since their comments were one of the highlights of my experience, personally.

- Molly and I modeled fundamental skills, and we gave one-on-one attention to the girls during practice. I can't think of a more important outcome of the first experience than building a foundation of excellent fundamentals.

- We hustled the girls on and off the field, so they nearly always got to bat first in at least one inning each night. Organization is crucial. Making sure that the girls didn't stand around for very long was important. I may incorrectly recall my own daughters' beginning experiences being much slower-paced. Girls want to be able to bat, and coaches need to push a brisk pace without rushing them fundamentally.

- The "little things" count for a lot. On one particularly hot and humid Iowa evening, I prepared an icy water cooler for use with washrags to keep on the girls' necks as a means of making the girls more comfortable in the heat. (My wife Cheryl was brilliant with that idea!) The girls thought it was fun, and the cold compresses did the trick!

What did I learn from this coaching experience?

- Pre-schoolers and kindergarteners have short attention spans! Enough said (especially of those of you with short attention spans)!

- We learned to ignore some of the consequences of their short attention spans – i.e., playing in the dirt when they were in the field – after all, that's where some of the best memories are made. I remember Molly at about the same age practicing her ballet positions in the field. As much as we would have liked to have redirected their attention and focus exclusively to every single play of the game, it was simply unrealistic, because they really were clueless at that age about the dynamics of the entire game.

- I know quite a bit about the mechanics of hitting, and I laid it on pretty thick from the beginning. I learned that you can only put 1 or 2 things in a kindergartener's head at a time. Could YOU remember all of the following at the same time?! Feet shoulders' width apart, knees slightly bent, fisted hands together on the handle, back shoulder up, hands back, eye on the ball, positioning the barrel of the bat on the ball, hitting the middle of the ball, level bat, pivoting and driving off the back foot, and following through by rolling the top hand over?!!

- In spite of my over-stimulating instruction, the girls really "got it"! They listened! They learned! They nearly always made solid contact between bat and ball. That's important, because, if a young player is discouraged by her batting experiences, she might very well quit before realizing a satisfying softball career, which can be life-long in recreation leagues.

- I wish I had taken more time to build community among the players, parents, and grandparents so they were more connected to the entire experience, and I wish I had explained more about what I was attempting to do philosophically. Basically a grand total of 10-12 hours over the course of 7 weeks doesn't allow the amount of time or activity to develop relationships or teaching to a great extent.

- I learned to be less of a control-freak. I have some definite tendencies to be Obsessive-Compulsive. I am a Type-A over-achiever. I have difficulty understanding why people are not as driven as I. But, during this experience, I gave myself permission to relax, spend time with Molly, have fun, release some of my hang-ups, and enjoy the girls.

The highlights of the season?

- CUTENESS! Have you ever been around a gaggle of darling 4- and 5-year-olds just learning to play a game?! It's a blast!

- The names of the teams! Grasshoppers. Butterflies. Lady Bugs. Fireflies. Mosquitoes. Lightning Bugs. Dragon flies. Wasps. Next year, they may be kittens or puppies, but this year, they represented insect-dom well!

- The coaches of the other teams were delightful. I didn't see a single screamer. There was nary a negative comment. Everyone was quite encouraging! Makes sense. How could you get negative with these delightful young ladies?!

- It was a hoot trying to explain simple terms that experienced players take for granted, i.e., back shoulder up, hands back, choking up, dugout, visiting team, home team, on-deck circle, batting order, force out, etc.!

- The first time one of our girls hit the ball and ran to third base, instead of first base, nearly undid me. I loved it!

- The written comments of the parents (and at least one sister) were precious, hitting the mark for specificity and positivity – "Great hustle to first base," "I like how you keep your eye on the ball," "You did a good job of keeping your glove down to field the ball, " "Love your smile," "Good teamwork," "You listened well to Coach Bob as he helped you at bat," and "Good catch on first base."

- Reading these comments to the girls after each game always brought broad smiles to each of the girls' faces, and the ritual warmed my soul as well.

- The smiles of the girls! The unbridled enthusiasm of each player. I think everyone had enough fun that they will come back for another season in 2011! Can I think of a better outcome?!

- One of the girls made a card for me, writing, "Dr. Bob, thank you for being my coach and showing me how to play softball! I like how you are nice to me." Can I ask for a better comment?!

Grasshoppers, you made my summer for 2010!!

Thanks for sticking with me so well thus far. I want to tell you, though, that you are about to read *the* most important chapter of the book, so take time to consider every word.

Chapter 15

To All – The Most Important Question of the Book

What is at the heart of this system of athletics? This may be the most important chapter in the book, either affirming your beliefs or drawing you inextricably to a new belief which has life-and-death implications.

I purposefully held back a more overt expression of my faith, because I believe some or many of you will more willingly receive my testimony of faith now, and I did not want you to close such a valuable assemblage of ideas too quickly. Now, I must be overt about my faith; to do otherwise would dishonor God, and I would be soft-pedaling or denying the very foundation of this athletic philosophy. *Please* read on to absorb *the* most important information in this book. Even if you do not agree with me, these life-or-death ideas demand your attention. I pray that I am planting the first seed, watering the plant, applying fertilizer to grow fruit, or finally harvesting this truth in your heart and mind.

I attended church every Sunday when I was a child. But I did not have a personal relationship with Jesus Christ as Lord and Savior of my life. I heard about God in the most generic and "safe" sense. But no one emphasized that my Christianity was, first and foremost, about relationship with Jesus. I experienced "churchianity" as a child and young adult. In my 20s, I was even selected to be an elder in a mainline denomination church. But as the saying goes, being in church doesn't any more make me a "Christian" than my being in a garage makes me a car.

I stumbled through life without any True North. I was, after all, a good guy, a dedicated teacher, coach, assistant principal, and principal. I seemed to have the tiger by the tail. Actually, I had the Lion of Judah by the tail, and he eventually got the better of me! As you have read, I had not been a good husband to Cheryl from the start. I was an absent Dad with my first daughter, Molly. I wanted to be a better leader of my family and a better Dad to my second daughter, Hannah. God got ahold of me through people who made the story of Jesus Christ clear to me, and I finally received the "meat" of truth through my study of the Bible. My love for words brought me to my knees when I read the Scriptures with the scales coming off my eyes, overwhelming me, and a love for Christ invaded every aspect of my life.

Did my new-found faith in Jesus change me overnight? In some ways, yes, but I had a lot of bad habits to overcome. I was (and continue to be) self-absorbed. To serve others can be quite difficult for me. But I now understood, and I was convicted by the truth of, my need for a Savior. I was like the infamous Doubting Thomas. At the point of my greatest need, I essentially cried out to Jesus, "*My Lord and my God*!" And I have been on a most interesting journey ever since that time of my 36th birthday. I now understand that my faith is not about "religion," but, rather, about relationships. I must fully love God (vertically) to find joy in my love for others (horizontally).

The true story of Christ is not complicated. God created a perfect world. He established boundaries for Adam and Eve, who were real people, not "characters" in a "myth." They disobeyed God, declaring independence from Him. Every generation thereafter has suffered as a result of their original sin. We ALL sin and fall short of the glory of God. Such is an unpopular contemporary notion, but a true proposition nevertheless. We people are not "good and perfectable" as others in this world would have us believe. We are literally the "filthy rags" Paul writes about in the Book of Romans.

Father God could not bear this break in relationship. He does not suffer sin. After all, He is perfect, righteous, and holy. *However*, He loves us so much that he wanted to reconcile human beings back to Himself. So, amazingly, He sent God the Son, Jesus Christ, from heaven to earth, and Jesus lived a fully human life as a way of experiencing our joys and heartaches. He was fully God *and* fully human, *and he did not sin*. Only a human being who never sinned could have done what He did at the end of His earthly life. He willingly allowed Himself to be crucified on a Roman cross. He bore my sin. He bore your sin. He bore the sin of all eternity. Only He could have done that for us! He died. His was a substitutionary death. You and I deserve that death! Even the thought of His brief separation from God the Father must have been excruciating. But He willingly paid the cost, because a great joy lay ahead of Him! He was put in the grave on Friday, but He conquered death and rose to life on Sunday! No other god of any other religion can make that claim, and there are hundreds of eyewitnesses to His resurrection. After forty additional days of life on earth, Jesus ascended to heaven, and he now sits at the right hand of God the Father. One day, He WILL come again, and every knee will bow, and every tongue will confess, He is Lord – to the glory of God the Father!

So you cannot escape the truth which lies before you at this very moment in your reading.

You may fully understand what I just explained, and your heart is soaring, because my words are confirmation of the faith which we share.

Or you do not believe in, and you have not submitted to Jesus as Savior and Lord of your life.

God loves us enough to allow us to make the choice of submitting your will to His will.

Through his body of writing and speaking, contemporary author-philosopher-business guru-evangelist Brian Klemmer has convinced me that our life is made up of any series of intentions. Intentions start as thoughts in our minds. Thus, the Scriptures propose that we are to be transformed first through the renewing of our minds. Those thoughts drift to our "hearts." Here is the seat of being. Here is where intentions collide. Here is where we "decide in our souls" which intentions will become most strong. We are often intent on life transformation, but another intention wins the day. And we do not change. So this choice about Jesus is really a matter of the will. At this point in your life, do you have the will to declare Jesus as Lord and Savior, then submitting to him for life transformation?

This choice is a life-or-death proposition. And it's an eternal proposition. None of us is simply "food for worms." At death, I do not simply cease to exist entirely. The shell of my body will go the way of "ashes to ashes." But my soul is an everlasting soul.

Believe, and you will enjoy everlasting life in heaven! No one can pluck you out of Christ's hand! Your eternal existence is secure!

If you choose not to believe in Jesus as Savior of your life, you are choosing everlasting separation from God!

My worldview, faith, and belief tell me that heaven is a real place. Hell is also a real place. Prior to my 36th birthday, I certainly did not personally want to go to hell, but I also had not yet declared my submission to Christ. I embraced Jesus as Lord, not as "fire insurance," but in appreciation for what He had rescued me from.

If you now believe in Christ and want to be submitted to him every moment of every day, you must find a Bible-believing church and a small group of Christians who will love you enough to lift up your arms when you're weary, pray for you when you are experiencing trials, encourage you when you need hope, love you when others will not do so, and speak the truth in love to you when you need to be directed back to the narrow way.

We live in a fallen world with so many worldviews based not on truth. These worldviews are competing for our attention. We must remain steadfast to the One who saved us and to the Truth which He and His Word in the Bible embody.

Jesus Christ is the cornerstone of my life, and I plumb my life to Jesus as I live out the roles of believer in Christ, husband, father, father-in-law, son, brother, neighbor, and Superintendent of a school. Jesus is the cornerstone and capstone of my life. Jesus is the cornerstone and capstone of my Christian school; and, as such, I must be open to His Holy Spirit guiding every decision for the school.

One of the most important sets of decisions at my Christian school involves all extracurricular activities, including athletics. Jesus Christ is central to the athletic experience – for student-athletes, coaches, parents, spectators, and officials alike. You have stayed on this road with me for quite some time. Please take another step in the journey of discovering honor in sports by considering *the greatest coach ever.*

Chapter 16

The Greatest Coach of History

Jesus Christ was certainly not an athletic coach, but he was a "coach" in every other sense of the word. In this chapter, Dr. Bob makes applications of Jesus' ministry to the coaching which should be going on in today's athletics. Readers will also have the opportunity to understand and perhaps commit to a worldview and lifestyle which will allow this positive sports participation model to be even more possible.

A legend died on June 4, 2010.

Just weeks short of his 100th birthday, the great coach and man, John Wooden, passed into his eternal existence. Anyone who has ever experienced March Madness must admire Coach Wooden's success in so many NCAA tournaments. Coaches and leaders from many other venues point to the practical application of his immaculately-crafted "Pyramid of Success." With his death, he leaves an incredible legacy of character and accomplishment.

I would not have so liberally sprinkled this book with the words of Coach Wooden if I did not think so highly of him. Without putting him on too high a pedestal, I would still have to say that he was much more than a basketball coach. Of course, he was an accomplished coach, but he was also a whole-hearted follower of Jesus Christ, a devoted husband to his wife, a loving father, a man who equipped basketball players for the "game of life," and a person who stood for honor beyond the game of basketball.

Iowa Sports Foundation Director (and former Division I men's basketball coach) Jim Hallihan had a chance to spend three days with long-time *Los Angeles Times* Sports Editor Bill Dwyer, NBC announcer Bob Costas, other members of the media, and athletic directors from major universities to discuss how to build character into the culture of athletics. They listened to John Wooden being interviewed on the subject for 2 hours, and Mr. Hallihan said he could have "sat there listening for 8 hours. His mind stayed so sharp to the very end of his life. That conversation led to the 'Pursuing Victory with Honor' program of Character Counts."

John Wooden was a great coach. Former NFL coach Vince Lombardi of the Green Bay Packers is often touted as one of the greatest coaches ever. Phil Jackson has molded numerous NBA champion teams in the Midwest (the Chicago Bulls) and on the West Coast (the Los Angeles Lakers). Walton Alston set a high standard for consistent performance as a Major League Baseball Manager with the L.A. Dodgers. But Wooden, Lombardi, Jackson, and Alston don't hold a candle to the greatest coach in history. Not only was he the greatest coach, but he was also the greatest teacher, friend, man, leader, priest, prophet, and king ever.

Of course, now, you should know that I am writing about Jesus Christ, the son of God who lived on this earth in the First Century. All time is now measured by the short time span of his short 33 years on earth. As I write this sentence, it is the year 2010 A.D. (Anno Domini, "The Year of Our Lord"). My faith compels me to think of Jesus as the ideal role model for any coach, athlete, parent, official, and sports league administrator. Why do I consider Jesus to be "The Greatest Coach of History"?

My reasons follow.

- First and foremost, He sought a vibrant, intimate, abiding relationship with Father God.

Jesus did not do anything in his life except when directed by His Father. He understood authority. He knew from whence His marching orders came. Administrators oversee athletic programs, but positive working relationships with all constituents must be the goal of every superintendent, athletic director, principal, coaches, players, parents, and community members.

- Jesus was absolutely obedient to God the Father.

Jesus understood and submitted to authority. He knew He would be blessed by God for His obedience.

Obedience and submission too often take on negative connotations in our culture, but we must all have a healthy respect for authority, because we know that all of us will be held accountable for our submission (and lack thereof). A coach is not a dictator. A coach does not "lord it over" players and parents. A coach is humble. S/he exhibits integrity, earning the moral authority to lead. Parents must not shove athletics down the throats of their children; student-athletes deserve some say in the programs which showcase them literally as the key players. Who of us would not want to follow coaches and parents who has our best interests in mind? Too many of us choose NOT to follow such people, and such disobedience results in chaos.

- He prayed for opportunities to make a difference in the lives of others.

Jesus knew that prayer was his pipeline to God the Father. He had a direct path of communication with THE power source. Prayer is also our vehicle to doing the will of the Father. To the degree that prayer is legally permissible in your school or league, prayer should be the kingpin of the Christian's life. Private or corporate prayer prior to and after contests allows participants to offer up praises and prayer to God for life and the abilities to compete for His glory. At points of injury, no person should be above offering up prayers of God's intervention, including and especially for opponents.

- He, the Father, and the Holy Spirit were one, so He was led by the Holy Spirit.

I should state the obvious: You have an advantage in life when you are God! No question about that! But Jesus still modeled the perfect human lifestyle for all of us. We must be of one mind, heart, vision, and planning when involved in athletics. Some Christians in our culture ask, "What would Jesus do?" The real question is "What DID Jesus do?" That which Jesus thought, said, and did we should think, say, and do ourselves.

- Because of his relationship with God the Father, Jesus had absolute integrity. He integrated truth and character throughout all of his thought life, words, and behaviors.

Northwestern College Athletic Director Matt Hill wisely pointed out to me, "Jesus had integrity. He was powerful, but He neither sought nor demanded power. He served others. At our school, senior athletes serve the freshmen; the freshmen do not serve the seniors. That's an example of Jesus washing the feet of the disciples. The leaders must model servanthood."

- He served others. He came not to be served, but to serve – to give His life as a ransom for many.

The Jewish people awaited a conquering king to liberate them from the yoke of Roman rule. Instead, a baby was born. He was meek, but He was a warrior. He served others, washing the feet of the disciples, as Matt Hill pointed out. He healed. He taught. He performed the tasks of a lowly servant, once even washing the feet of his disciples. He poured His life into the lives of others. He was the ultimate servant-leader. Considering equality with God not something to which He aspired, he humbled Himself and became obedient to death – death on a cross. In athletics, all of us should "die to self." We should want what is in the best interests of the team, not ourselves. We should strive to consider others better than ourselves. We should out-serve all others others. We should make sacrifices for our coaches and teammates.

- He poured His life positively into others.

Jesus invested His mind, heart, soul, and strength into his 12 disciples, even the one who betrayed Him. His circle of influence was certainly wider than that, as the Scriptures record dozens of testimonies of people's faith in Him. Jesus turned His world upside-down, reaching out to the disenfranchised "sinners" of the culture – fishermen, tax collectors, the disabled, adulterers, and those not selected by other rabbis. Contemporary relationships are too often characterized by superficiality. We call people our "friends," but we really don't know that much about them. In athletics, teammates should be "bands of brothers," willing to serve even the players who are difficult to serve. Parents should not be stand-offish, but seek to help create a community of players, coaches, and extended family members. We should be willing to bear the messiness, inconvenience, and hardness of life for the sake of others.

- He lived the sold-out, God-centered life 24/7/365!

Jesus said, "The Father and I are one." He said, "I do not do anything unless directed by the Father." He rested when the Father told Him to rest. He performed miracles when the Father told him to do so. He taught and discipled when the Father asked Him to teach and disciple others. He is the only example of a human being absolutely committed to God. Shouldn't student-athletes, coaches, parents, officials, and spectators do similarly when they are engaged in their respective roles of athletic competition? I vow that I will NOT be a Sunday-morning-only Christian! I must live for Jesus Christ in every thought, word, and deed – including when I am operating within the venue of athletics.

- He asked great questions.

When people tried to confront or corner Jesus, they often asked Him questions. The Pharisees, scribes, and teachers of the law smugly thought they could "put Him on the spot." Au contrere. Remarkably, Jesus would often answer their questions with questions of his own. He always had the perfect response or question for the situation. He taught through a Socratic method which prompted people to think at deeper levels of meaning than they would otherwise. Coaches should ask great questions to stimulate athletes' deeper knowledge of the game and appreciation for contest strategies. Parents should use non-judgmental, non-autobiographical questions to help their sons and daughters to put these "games" in perspective. While athletic participation is an important part of some people's lives, sports must be kept in balance with the rest of life.

- He told wonderful stories (parables), which illustrated Kingdom principles.

Christ is *the greatest teacher ever* in history, and one reason is that He understood the power of characters, plots, rising action, crisis points, and resolution as a memorable way for people to learn. Without a single exception, all of His parables pointed the hearers to God. Student-athletes will remember stories of epic struggles and accomplishments far longer than the X's, O's, statistics, and win-loss records. Coaches should earn their ways into the hearts of their players by regularly telling stories which deepen appreciation for the game and team. Parents should regularly tell stories – even painful ones – as a means of helping their children remember the growth which has come as a result of participation in athletics.

- He performed miracles (signs).

All right! All right! Again, Jesus had an advantage here over student-athletes, coaches, parents, spectators, and officials. But all of us can recall times when we pushed ourselves well beyond our normal capacities to perform at epic levels in athletics. I am convinced that none of us exercises even a fraction of our abilities, because our lives are soft and "privileged." We could use some trials and persecution to sharpen our love for athletic games and the Lord who played a part in creating them in the minds of the inventors. And, through the power of the Holy Spirit, Jesus promised that we would do even greater things than even He accomplished, so we should claim that power on faith.

- He was a bold witness for God the Father.

Jesus was not a popular fellow in the First Century. He called the power-mongers of the time by names like vipers, white-washed tombs, and hypocrites – not exactly an endearing characteristic – but a necessary quality nevertheless, if people were going to "get the message." He was not concerned about His own safety. He simply obeyed the Father without condition. It's not as though He was a puppet on God's string, though. Jesus had free will – the same as any other human being – He simply chose to exercise His free will perfectly with the will of His heavenly Father. Adults pull back on their witness for Christ – for fear of being rejected or ostracized or worse in the American culture. We should not be surprised when committed Christian athletes, who are much younger than their parents and coaches, pull back on their witness as well. All Christians should pray the following prayer: "Father in heaven, please allow me never to desert Jesus when He calls me to speak about or for Him. Amen."

- He thirsted to honor and glorify God through all of His thoughts, words, and actions.

As I indicated earlier, Jesus said, "I tell you the truth: Anyone who has faith in me will do what I am doing. He will do even greater things than these." (John 14:12) Jesus also said, "I have brought you glory on earth by completing the work you gave me to do." Wouldn't it make sense that Jesus would enable student-athletes and coaches to do great things in the arena of athletics? Can you fathom doing even greater things than Jesus Christ?! Don't you want to?! To be a man or woman of honor in sports is to do great things for His glory. Again, we typically do not stretch ourselves outside our comfort zones. "Winning" and "losing" carried different connotations for Jesus. Matt Hill made some excellent observations about God's perspective about winning and losing in sports: "God does not show favor to you when you win. God's blessings are not conditional. He blesses people in defeat, too. Whether you win or lose, God is proud of your efforts. Coaches and student-athletes should not put their worth in the scoreboard results. Yes, we keep score, and we spend a lot of money on athletics, but we have a higher calling in life. The ultimate benchmark is not winning at Northwestern. The ultimate benchmark is bringing honor and glory to God. God is disappointed in me daily, but He is still proud of me."

- He did nothing to tarnish His testimony.

Jesus acted with absolute integrity. He was truth, so He could not act inconsistently with His character. He was holy. He was perfect. He gave evidence of all fruit of the Spirit. (See Galatians 5:32-33.) He finished strong. He was the living (and dying embodiment) of a line from one of His own parables: "Well done, you good and faithful servant! Well done! Enter into the joy of your Master! Ah, to hear those words, if I'm an athlete in competition, a coach representing Christ, a parent seeking to encourage and disciple my child, a Christian spectator wanting to lead others to a saving knowledge of Jesus, or a referee seeking to be an honorable arbiter in a contest. We should constantly pray that we will give no referee or opposing coach, player, or spectator reason to doubt our commitment to Jesus Christ.

- He pointed out the sinful behavior of others, speaking the truth in love.

The self-righteous power mongers of Jesus' time set up a woman "caught" in adultery, dragging her (but not the male adulterer) out before the assembly. Seeking to trap Jesus, the teachers of the law were stymied when Christ, omnisciently knowing their hearts and intent with this incident, asked any who were without sin to throw the first stone. Of course, they knew they had met their match, and the stones fell to the ground. Jesus asked the woman if any had condemned her. She answered no. Neither would He, Christ said. *However*, he also would not ignore her sin. He told her, "Go and sin no more." I can imagine her gratitude for her salvation at the point of capital punishment. As I have stated previously, we, too, should humbly hold people accountable for their sin and mistakes when involved in athletics. Regrettably, as I have detailed, people are overly harsh with those whom they believe have wronged them. Often, hard hearts are the root of people's unwillingness to forgive. We can speak the truth in love, healing relationships with humble hearts.

- He exhorted people to spiritual growth and faith.

Jesus cannot suffer people at the point of their lives. All of us have room to grown. The Word of God calls us all to be "conformed to the likeness of the Son (Romans 8:29)." He is a perfectly righteous and holy God Who desires growth and evidence of lush fruit in our lives. He repeatedly praised people who gave evidence of phenomenal faith. Athletes should grow through their participation in athletics. No effective coach would allow a player to stagnate if there were potential for greater athletic capacity for the "whole" player – body, mind, and soul.

- He behaved consistently at all times. There was no hypocrisy in Him.

The First Century culture was replete with examples of "godly" people who formulated layer upon layer of laws to follow but who could never keep all of those laws 100% of the time and who often behaved antithetically to the laws which God had given to His people. As has been stated before, Jesus was absolutely obedient to the Word of God, the laws of God, the will of God, and the ways of God. He did not act one way with a crowd and then differently with another. Today's world is filled with hypocrites. Pick up the news, and you'll read about any number of phonies. Politicians and celebrities are chameleons, changing views to suit the needs of unique audiences. The vast majority of people in our world would rather have the praises of men, pleasing them, rather than honoring and glorifying God, pleasing Him. Student-athletes, parents, and coaches should work hard to maintain a consistency of character, no matter the "audience." And, after all, the only audience we should seek to please is "The Audience of One."

- He demonstrated grace, forgiving others and bearing no grudges.

The power brokers of the Jewish culture had difficulty forgiving, because they did not enjoy personal relationship with God. Theirs was a religion of rules. Their hard hearts prevented them from loving and forgiving those who were difficult to love and forgive. Jesus forgave liberally. As has been stated previously, He did not ignore the sin which led to His forgiveness, but he was supernaturally able to forgive those who hated, reviled, and persecuted Him. Even from the cross of His own crucifixion, He was able to cry out, "Father, forgive them, for they know not what they do." What forgiveness! What compassion!! Forgiveness seems to be in short supply in athletics. We use each other to get ahead. We're not at all afraid to trample on others as we progress toward higher and higher levels of athletic achievement but lower and lower despicability of human ethics and behavior. Great athletes forgive their coaches and teammates. We learn from our mistakes and move on. We do not live in the past but, rather, celebrate the present as we anticipate a brighter future.

- His life was an example of perseverance.

Can there be a greater example of perseverance than Jesus Christ?! I think not! He could have easily stayed in heaven with His Heavenly Father, but He willingly gave up his position to be born into a simple life. Raised as a simple carpenter, Jesus grew up in the obscure and despised town of Nazareth. ("Can anything good come of Nazareth?" one of the disciples said before he believed in Jesus.) Jesus launched a public ministry which could not be compared to the ostentatious show of contemporary preachers, who wear Armani suits and use flashy PowerPoint shows when performing to thousands of congregants. Jesus was basically "homeless" as he prayed, walked, preached, spoke, taught, healed, and answered confrontations for three years. He was a human being who experienced thirst, hunger, disappointment, grief, and fatigue. The ending of his life included false arrest, a kangaroo court, multiple beatings, a scourging which turned smooth skin into "hamburger," the carrying of his own heavy object of execution, and crucifixion on that cross. Jesus was resolute to the end. He knew his purpose. He knew the mission. He persevered unto death on the cross for the remission of our sins. Athletics are fraught with disappointments, discouragements, hard work, missteps, losses, injuries, and sometimes even deaths of those we love. One of the greatest lessons learned in sports comes from the perseverance in overcoming these challenges. All participants in sports should offer encouragement to others who seek to persevere.

- He expressed joy in spite of his circumstances.

Jesus knew that His relationship with His Father was the most important element of His life, so he constantly sought to invest time, energy, and attention to that relationship. The lack of faith in others did not define Him. His possessions (few as they were) did not define Him. The resistance and opposition of others did not define Him. His mission in life (and death) defined Him. He knew His purpose, and He fulfilled that purpose perfectly. For the joy set before Him, He endured death on a cross. He even had joy when He was dying on the cross, because He knew that He had been obedient to God's perfect plan of salvation for those who believed in Him, and He was anticipating His return to the glories of heaven. "Happiness" is not the chief end of man. Nor is "prosperity" the chief end of man. The chief end of man is to know and worship God and to enjoy Him forever. Such a realization should bring great joy. With so much sin in the world, we know that we will never be absolutely "happy," but we can experience joy – in spite of our circumstances. Athletics should be characterized by greater quantities of smiles, laughter, genuine fellowshipping, and pure joy for the opportunities to celebrate each others' physical gifts. A recent "Wisdom for the Busy Coach" devotional had the relationship between gratitude and unhappiness right -- "Feeling down? Unhappiness can creep up from so many directions – a key player makes a poor choice that pulls her out of your line-up; you're stuck in a losing streak; tension has built up between you and a close friend. While we may try to stomp it out with our favorite cappuccino or trip to the movies, there is one surefire way to keep unhappiness at bay: *a grateful heart.* Next time you're feeling unhappy vibes, make a list of all the things you're grateful for, and, before you know it, those unhappy feelings begin to fade." (emphasis in original) An joy will replace unhappiness!

- He took an eternal perspective, not getting mired in the muck of his human life. He knew the glories of heaven lay ahead of His life on earth.

Jesus could see the picture on a jigsaw puzzle box. He knew the ultimate vision for life. And He realized that vision for His life. He modeled that which we should become. He looked into a future which would bring no more pain, fear, disease, discouragement, or sin. Because He was able to take the long view of life, He didn't get caught up in the picayune, day-to-day struggles. We, however, tend to live in the moment. We seek instant gratification. We are accustomed to "drive-through" service. Our views are so temporal. We often can only see one puzzle piece and don't know how that piece fits into the whole. We would rather not experience any adjustments to our schedules, and we attempt to resist any event which would make us unhappy. We take a short view of life in athletics. We're only satisfied by the most recent "win," experiencing despair if we don't have daily successes. Life is not easy. Life does not ever seem to go as we plan. Wins do not always come in bunches, because the statistical odds are against us. Taking a longer view of athletic events would allow us to put the losses and discouragements into perspective.

Jesus pulled people along at some point in a great progression –

- "Come and see."

This first level necessitated the least amount of commitment. Jesus was essentially saying, "Come check out the life I would ask you to live." If the disciple was ready, he moved to the next level of commitment.

- "Come and follow me."

At the "come and follow me" stage, the disciple was no longer an observer alone. He was now called into action. He had to go where Jesus went and attempt what Jesus did. In Jesus' time, this was known as "following in the dust of the Rabbi." The disciple sat at the teaching of the Rabbi. He learned and applied what the Rabbi taught him. The disciple did what the Rabbi did. The disciple was no longer a voyeur. He was a *follower*. If the follower was ready, he moved to the next level of commitment.

- "Come and be with me."

"Being" with the Rabbi and other disciples pulled a person into a closer relationship than "seeing" and "following." Being with one or more disciples caused a follower to question critical life values at their core. Questions were asked and answered. Stories and interpretations of those stories deepened the emotional depth of relationships. Men were doing life together

- "Come abide in me."

In John 15:5, Jesus spoke of Christians "abiding" or "remaining" in Him (depending upon the Bible translation). He used an excellent word picture. Branches which have a healthy connection to the main vine – and which are receiving all of the nutrients that come from water, fertilizer, and soil – will bear much fruit. Followers of Jesus are the branches. Jesus is the vine. Staying closely connected to Jesus through the power of His Holy Spirit allows us to bear much fruit for Him and for His glory. The stark contrast is apt – Apart from Jesus, we can do NOTHING. Broken branches or a damaged connection to the source of our spiritual nutrition will result in withered fruit or no fruit at all. So we must abide in Jesus. Of course, in this context, I have written exclusively about men growing spiritually together. Such was the culture of Jesus' time. But Jesus opened up this abundant life to ALL who would embrace Him as Lord. Women, children, taxpayers, and lower-class citizens like fishermen were suddenly able to follow a Rabbi – *the* Rabbi. And such is the case today. ALL can come and see, follow, be, and abide in Christ. Don't delay the journey. Walk in the dust of *the* Rabbi.

- Jesus conquered death.

A legend died 30-some years into the century which is marked by His life. But, as I indicated in the previous chapter, He did not remain lifeless! God raised Him from the dead! He is the only head of any organized "religion" who can make this claim! The Bible confirms this truth. Historians wrote biographically of him at that time. Archeology provides further evidence of His existence. Numerous people saw him die, and over 500 eyewitnesses saw Him alive again. Thomas, one of His disciples, felt the marks of his crucifixion, only then declaring, "My Lord and my God!" Because He died a death on the cross *in my place* – and because He conquered death – each of us who claim Him as Lord will live in his presence and worship Him for eternity! Jesus Christ really was – and is – and always will be – *the* perfect coach. I hope you will enthusiastically embrace Him as *your* coach. Athletes, coaches, and parents who depend upon this Life Coach will come to know an abundance which is quite different than the world's abundance. Difficulties do not go away when Jesus is the head coach, but our perspectives change, and we are better able to respond more joyfully to even the most negative of circumstances. Follow Him! Follow the greatest coach of history!

Allow me to conclude with the example of a man who understood Jesus Christ to be his personal Coach, a man who was a great ambassador for Christ. I am privileged to live in a state where Ed Thomas coached for many years. That name may mean nothing to you. Ed Thomas was a high school football coach. That's as "far" as he advanced in the profession. From a human standpoint, an observer would think that someone who ends his coaching career as a high school coach at 58 years of age has not really achieved greatness. But such an observer would be absolutely wrong about Ed Thomas.

Ed Thomas' coaching career was prematurely ended at the hand of a deranged shooter. One of his former players shot and killed Ed Thomas in his Aplington-Parkersburg weight room. Anyone would say that Ed Thomas died too soon. We could easily point to the indicators of his coaching success: 292 wins, National Coach of the Year, and an unusually high number of extremely successful National Football League players from this small Iowa town.

But those are not the true indicators of Ed Thomas' impact on others. Most importantly, he was a devoted husband to his wife and a dedicated father to his children. He was a leader beyond the football field in his school, church, and community. Just the summer before his death, he was the real AND symbolic leader of a town which re-built Parkersburg after a devastating tornado. His most important impact was on his own sons and the sons of Aplington-Parkersburg; he invested time, energy, and his life in the lives of those young men. He saw coaching as an avenue to help boys become men, and men they did become. Pallbearers at the funeral included Casey Wiegmann of the Denver Broncos, Jared DeVries of the Detroit Lions, Brad Meester of the Jacksonville Jaguars, and Aaron Kampman of the Green Bay Packers.

Following Coach Thomas' tragic death, heartfelt words of sadness and joy offered testimony of the coach's impact on the lives of so many. Green Bay Packers linebacker Aaron Kampman, who had played for Coach Thomas at Aplington-Parkersburg offered what I found to be the most powerful reaction to his former coach's death: "Coach Thomas was very special to me and many other young men from the Aplington-Parkersburg communities. His legacy for many will be associated with his tremendous success as a football coach. However, I believe his greatest legacy comes not in how many football games he won or lost but in the fact that he was a committed follower of Jesus Christ."

Iowa High School Athletic Association Information Director Bud Legg observed, "[His death] doesn't make any sense. Anybody that knows Ed knows what a terrific guy he (was). He's so dedicated to the kids. If you're going to pick an ideal person to coach your son, your daughter, your grandchild, it's Ed Thomas."

Tom Stone is a Hall of Fame coach at a similarly-small Iowa high school, Pekin-Packwood. He experienced great loss on the day of Ed Parker's death, saying, "It's a sad day for a great man, and it's a sad day for life in general. He touched so many lives. He brought out the best in so many people. He had a real knack in getting along with kids. The frightening thing is that it could happen to any of us. But of all of us, he'd be the last person you'd think it would happen to. It's been a very difficult morning for me."

Ken Winkler, a close friend of Ed's and a football coach at West Marshall High School of Iowa, said, "He is a great person who also happens to be a great football coach." The very successful head University of Northern Iowa football coach, Mark Farley, agreed, stating, "The hard part is this is a great man, not just a great coach, a great man. You can't find a coach in the state he hasn't had an impact on. He just represented everything that was good about coaching, good about representing kids."

Long-time U.S. Senator Charles Grassley of Iowa resides on a farm not far from Ed Thomas' community, and he remarked, "This is a tragic day. In our area of the state, it's hard not to know Coach Thomas. He was a pillar of the community. His success on the football field made him an icon in his profession, but the people who knew him will remember him most for his leadership off the field. His leadership to help pull up a community knocked off its feet by an F-5 tornado only a year ago will forever be etched in the minds of Parkersburg residents and Iowans across the state."

Al Kerns, a fellow coach at Aplington-Parkersburg offered a eulogy at Ed Thomas' funeral, saying, in part, "I don't think of the games won. I don't think of the countless awards he won. . . .All I know is that by being near him for over 30 years, he made the people around wish to become better." First Congregational Church Pastor Brad Zinnecker said of the large turn-out at Ed's funeral, "They recognized a man after God's own heart."

Ed Thomas' family accepted the Arthur Ashe Courage Award during the ESPY awards ceremony on July 14, 2010, as the parents of murderer Mark Becker applauded from their seats in Los Angeles' Nokia Theatre. Aaron Thomas, the coach's son, who now serves as Athletic Director at Aplington-Parkersburg High School, spoke in front of a national television audience after accepting a statuette from NFL quarterback Brett Favre. Aaron said, in part, "When you look at former winners and the company we've joined – from coach (Jim) Valvano, to the Tillman brothers, to Nelson Mandela – and to think that our dad and the example he set at doing what's right has led us into this category, we went through many tough times, but we had a great example from my father in how to handle adversity. . . .I never once imagine we'd bury my dad (after) being murdered. And I never once imagine we'd be at the ESPYs receiving an award from Brett Favre."

Coach Ed Thomas reflected the character of Jesus Christ. True to his calling, he had been attempting to mentor the troubled man who had murdered him. And the family of Ed Thomas gave witness to Ed's character and the character of Jesus Christ, forgiving Ed's killer and embracing that young man's parents and family as their ongoing friends in the same church where they had worshipped together for years.

From a human perspective, 58 years of life is a short life. But God had ordained that Ed Thomas' life would count for more in 58 years than many people can achieve during a much longer time period. Ed Thomas' influence on so many people is obviously more eternal than temporal. He now stands in the presence of His Savior. He finished life strong.

It's now time for you to finish strong as you move into the final phase of your reading experience. . . .

JOHN WOODEN ON THE SPIRITUAL REALM OF LIFE

"Some evangelical Christians think of me as being liberal, because they disagree with my decision to let my life speak for my faith. At the same time, liberals consider me to be way too conservative. I know you can't please everyone, so, on this issue, I haven't tried. I have only wanted to please God." (p. 40)

"I know church attendance alone does not make a person a Christian. It takes a personal relationship with our Creator, which comes about only through God's grace." (p. 77)

"In 1943, a friend gave me a small cross, and I've carried it in my pocket ever since. It's not a good luck charm or anything like that, but I held it in my hand during games, and I still grab it during times of tension. It reminds me who is in control and who I represent. It probably is a good thing for officials that I had that in my hand when a bad call was made. Although the phrase was not in vogue back then, in a way, the cross in my pocket spoke to me and asked, 'What would Jesus do?' in any particular situation." (p. 78)

"Physical conditioning is important. . . .But a failure to address mental, moral, and spiritual conditioning will limit even the best physical conditioning." (p. 125)

"I have never tried to change a person's faith. I saw that as God's job, not mine. I did encourage my players to stay open-minded, however, because those who were open-minded would give way to truth, and those who weren't wouldn't. I have always believed that what Christ said is truth, and that He is Truth." (p. 135)

"It is very difficult to be successful without a strong sense of spiritual well-being. I believe God wants us to be strong in our faith. Jesus said to seek Him first and then He would add all things. I have sought Him first and foremost, and I have tried to do my best. I am at peace." (p. 137)

"I don't think we are supposed to find our own truth. That's playing God. I believe in absolute truth and absolute sin, and the Bible is my standard for determining those absolutes. With that in mind, I believe that an inquisitive person is more apt to discover truth than someone with a closed mind." (pp. 70-71)

Chapter 17

Will This Model Work?

The positive sports culture I have described works best in a Christian school, college, or university, since everyone involved can fully express faith in the athletic arena. But this model, even if not overtly espousing biblical principles, will also work in ANY setting. Who among us does not want positive coaches? Who among us does not want our children to improve their skills and grow from their athletic experiences? Who among us would not want to enjoy a less critical, angry, destructive model of sports? Can teams still "win" with this model? Absolutely. The Bible challenges everyone to excellence. ("Be holy." And "Be perfect.") Pursuing a Christian model of athletics does not mean that competitors are milquetoasts or doormats. In this culture of athletics, everyone is exhorted to engage in fiercely counter-cultural competition a most worthy prize.

Paul in 1 Corinthians 9:24-27:

24 Do you not know that in a race all the runners compete, but only one receives the prize?

So run that you may obtain it. 25Every athlete exercises self-control in all things.

They do it to receive a perishable wreath, but we an imperishable. 26So I do not run aimlessly;

I do not box as one beating the air. 27But I discipline my body and keep it under control, ☐ lest after preaching to others I myself should be disqualified.

(1 Corinthians 9:24-27, English Standard Version)

Norm Evans, Offensive Tackle, Seattle Seahawks:

"I guarantee you Christ would be the toughest guy who ever played the game. . . .

If he were alive today, I would picture a 6-6, 260-pound defensive tackle

who would always make the big plays and would be hard to keep out of the backfield."

(In Joel Penner, p. 17)

Can we "win" this way?

The question really is "How can we *not* win this way?"

Some coaches believe this model of athletics to be too "warm and fuzzy," prone to be "soft" in its approach to competition. I beg to differ. We all see where "cold and prickly" has gotten us!

Some coaches are threatened by this more "honorable" system of sports, arguing that Christians believe themselves to be "better than others" when they make decisions which cost them points, games, and championships.

Here, I am indebted to Joel Penner's work on biblical competition. In his Master's thesis, he offered a comprehensive review of the literature on Christians' views of athletics. He rightly pointed out that Christians, as with so many activities of our lives, have experienced great difficulty integrating athletics into our Christian witness ("Athletic Competition: Loving God and Loving Your Neighbor," pp. 4-5). We too often compartmentalize our faith.

It is true that the original meanings of the words, compete and contest, are much different than contemporary connotation. "The words *cum* and *pedere* are the Latin derivatives of the word, compete. Together they literally mean 'to strive with rather than against.' Similarly, the words *con* and *testare* are the Latin derivatives of our word, contest. Together they literally mean 'to testify with another rather than against.' Somewhere in the centuries of the development of sport, the true meaning of athletic competition has been distorted." (Ibid., p. 37, emphasis in original) How refreshing if we returned the sense of athletics to those original meanings – to strive with rather than against and to testify with rather than against another!

Some Christians do not even believe Christians should be involved in athletics at all, taking a separatist approach to the activity. Speakers and writers have vehemently argued that competing in sports is not compatible with loving God and loving others. Numerous arguments have been made against Christians participating in sports:

- Sports "deny the Christian virtue of contentment" (Ibid., p. 7)

- Sports put Christian in situations which work against God's command to "love others" (Ibid., 7)

- Athletics contribute to the "fallenness" of mankind. (Ibid., p. 8)

- Competition in sports is "simply an ungodly attempt to gain security." (Ibid., p. 9)

- Physical pursuits distract from spiritual pursuits. (Ibid., p. 9)

- Athletics may hinder a child's development. "In a study performed by Robert Roos. . . organized sports participants tend[ed] to be less mature in their moral reasoning than other kids." (Ibid., p. 11)

Shirl Hoffman – a former athlete (fooball, basketball, track and field), official (soccer, basketball), college coach (basketball), and professor and administrator in university departments which prepare physical education teachers and coaches – offers cautions to Christians about sports:

"There are simply no easy, straight-faced, intellectually respectable answers for how evangelicals can model the Christian narrative – with its emphases on servanthood, generosity, and self-subordination – while immersed in a culture that thrives on cut-throat competition, partisanship, and Darwinian struggle. . . .If indeed sport is marching toward Gomorrah [the site of biblical destruction of life and property], it seems to have escaped the attention of large portions of the evangelical community, which continue to bask in the reflected glory of Christian athletes. . . .Rarely does the evangelical press ask touchy questions about tensions between the moral culture of Christianity and that of big-time sports. The silence is deafening. . . .evangelicals in the sports community have too often been followers rather than leaders, adopters of the dominant ethos rather than trendsetters who challenge it. . . .Frank Deford warned. . .'The bad things about athletics have rubbed off on religion. . . .Religion is like the tar baby – it's gotten stuck and the more it struggles the more tar it gets on it. There's the danger when anything moral plays with anything as public, as notorious, as celebrated as sport – you get stuck.' . .

.The call here isn't to eliminate competition, a treatment that would no doubt kill the patient along with the disease. . . .If sport played by Christians is to have a distinctive slant – especially sport sponsored by Christian institutions – it won't simply be sport done well, or played without egregious violations of the sporting code. It will be sport creatively structured and specifically crafted to express the joy of the faith."

As with any activity, excess can definitely skew athletic competition to the negative. For instance, Tim Challies of Oakville, Ontario asks whether professional sports are worthwhile for the Christian: "By our participation as fans, are we contributing to the sometimes shocking lack of morality, to the building of massive egos, to the idolatry of the athlete?" (http://www.amazon.come/Reason-Sports-Christian-Fanifesto/) Some Christian athletes are hypocrites, so they tarnish Christianity in their hypocrisy.

But the full range of activities in God's created order are venues for honoring Him. The great Dutch theologian and apologist Abraham Kuyper was absolutely correct when he pointed out that "there is not one square inch of all creation over which Christ does not declare, 'This is mine!" There should be no distinction between the sacred and secular of God's creation. As with any other part of creation, sin has tarnished the original design, and those committed to living out Christian principles through sports should "redeem" athletics for God's glory. Gary Warner confirmed this necessity when he stated, "Christians are called on to permeate the competitive sports process, and not run from it." (Ibid., p. 6)

Paul wrote about pressing on toward the goal to win the prize of eternal life (Philippians 3:12-14), language appropriate to the venue of athletic participation. ". . .Gary Warner believes that the seed of competition has been placed in people by God, and to deny this expression of self is to deny God's creation." He continued, "Paul is surely an advocate of competition – teeth-gritting, back-banding, leg-pumping, mind-setting, heart-willing competition." (Ibid., p. 14) Joel Penner asked, ". . .if Paul thought athletic competition and striving for victory to be ungodly, would he have so frequently utilized metaphors from the arena?" (Ibid, p. 19)

If anything, the Christian is a more vigorous competitor – competing as his "best self" against his previous best performance. Joel Penner wisely pointed out, "To hold back from investing fully and intensely into a game is to inhibit the freedom afforded by Christ which can be realized through the competitive experience." (Ibid., p. 36)

Sports provide a wonderful venue for instilling important values which will follow a child into adulthood. Rick Wulkow, Executive Director of the Iowa High School Athletic Association, had keen insights in this regard: "I look at it this way. So many of the values we want our kids to get through participation in activities are also the values we get when we read the Bible, go to church on Sunday, and listen to sermons. So many of the values correlate with how you treat people, how you're thankful for your abilities and opportunities. We need to understand why we have our values, our parents, and our opportunities. The Almighty is in this. We need to listen to our preachers and our teachers. I am now holding a publication called "Portals of Prayer." There's correlation of life to a Bible verse and prayer. There are lessons in 'life' which come through athletics. Leadership, pride, integrity, loyalty, teamwork – that's what spirituality is all about. If we have those values, we're going to be good people. The Truth is within us. It's how I have instilled values with my own children. As an official, I was one of these guys on a basketball court with 15,000-20,000 people standing at attention. I listened to the National Anthem, and I prayed for safety and everyone to have "success," not according to wins or losses. I did that every game. As a coach, even in defeat, I gave thanks for what we were able to accomplish. During each game, we displayed our talents, people were supporting what we were doing, and there was pride in our community. I feel there is something about that moment, reflecting upon that moment which makes us a better team, better family, better individuals."

If our definition of "winning" in athletics is helping others to gain strength of body, soul, and mind – and glorifying God – then we most certainly can all experience "winning" through athletics. And we should engage the culture, not separate from it. Athletics is a wonderful venue for community-building, a winning proposition for everyone involved. Chip Ingram espouses a template for authentic church community which can easily be overlain on athletics. The Fellowship of Christian Athletes is making application of this same r12 teaching. In this chapter, we will explore the development of positive athletic community by applying principles from a segment of Romans 12.

Bernie Saggau, former Executive Director of the Iowa High School Athletic Association told me, "Everyone wants to belong to a 'gang.' If they don't find a 'gang' at school, they'll find a different kind of "gang" away from school. Each one of us is hard-wired for relationship. Hermits and recluses are fighting their DNA. Life is not meant to be lived as Lone Rangers. We must "do life together." Athletics is certainly all about "doing life together." In sports, we experience the full range of the continuum between "the thrill of victory and the agony of defeat," as the old ABC Sports catch-phrase from my childhood goes.

Regrettably, ever-present electronic devices are buffering us from face-to-face community-building. Too many kids sit behind video games, computer screens, social networking sites, cell phones, hundreds of television channels, and more movies than can be viewed in a lifetime. Research projects are extolling the virtues of MySpace and Facebook as educational devices. We can reverse this tidal wave of technology which was intended to make our lives so much easier. Instead of achieving easier lives, we have become slaves to our idols. We worship the icons on the screens to which we have become too easily addicted. These electronic communities are only locking us down into our own minds, keeping us from depth of relationship which will feed our souls. We are mesmerized. And our relationships are superficial at best. But I say, "Stand apart! Be different!" Shut off the machines. Get out of your chair. Go open the door to a life of dialogue, listening, collaboration, partnerships. Get involved in sports. Kids can walk away from the over-organization of athletics to a simpler life at the playground, on the basketball court, in the swimming pool, on the bicycle, or simply hoofing-it to enjoy quantity time with friends.

We can be a part of "authentic community" through athletics. I am indebted to Pastor Chip Ingram for an idea whose time has come. According to Chip. . .

. . .Authentic community occurs when. . .

. . .the real you. . .

. . .meets real needs. . .

. . .for the right reason. . .

. . .in the right way.

THE REAL YOU
(Based on Romans 12:9)

Authenticity -- "Let love be sincere."

Show yourself for who you really are. No masks. No hypocrisy. Be willing to share the good, the bad, and the ugly of your life. Slow down and take the time to allow people to get to know the real you. Love God, and love others. While at athletic contests, truly love your own children, the coaches, the other parents, their children, and even opponents in these contests. Love your enemies and those who persecute you, Jesus said.

State Champion Tennis Coach Kirk Trow understands the need for coaches to nurture community in athletic programs: "People want connection. Parents want community in the most positive way. My parents are great.   When the kids connect, the outcomes are better. Coaches need to be responsive to their athletes. I initially had a reputation as spending all of my time with the top 2 or 3 kids. I changed that. They were right. I wasn't of any help for kids who were learning the game."

Purity – "Hate what is evil. Cling to what is good."

We must admit our own sin and shortcomings. We must come clean about our hang-ups and the anger of unfulfilled athletic dreams. We must not try to live our failed athletic experiences through kids. We must not push our kids too hard. We must not put winning ahead of our athletes' desire to enjoy the sports in which they are participating. We must not turn a blind eye to the indiscretions of others. We must hold every stakeholder of athletics accountable for their inappropriate behavior. That which is not addressed is essentially blessed. We too often engage in group-think, and it's time to step up like prophets to please the Audience of One.

AUTHENTIC COMMUNITY MEETS REAL NEEDS
(Romans 12:10)

Devotion – "Be devoted to one another in brotherly love."

Our children should not be our idols. The sun does not rise and set on our all-star athletes. Sure, we must love the kids, and cherish them as gifts from God. But we must hold our lives in proper balance. We must not allow athletics to be the god (lower-case g) we worship. Athletics is a cheap substitute for a family life which could be lived in more than one arena. Each of us must spend time with spouse and children and parents. We are to be devoted to activities other than athletics as a way of keeping our lives in proper balance.

Humility – "Giving preference to one another in honor."

As the great opening of *The Purpose-Driven Life* goes, "It's not about you." Life is about serving others. We need to look for ways to eliminate our self-serving to honor, affirm, edify, and encourage others about their talents and abilities. In an age of "psychological starvation," everyone involved in athletics is looking for positive reinforcement. We seek these "rewards" not for "behavior modification," but, rather, because we all have gifts which need to be extolled. Look to serve others in this way by humbling yourself and honoring others.

Authentic Community meets real needs. . .

. . .FOR THE RIGHT REASON
(Romans 12:11)

Motive – "Not lagging behind in diligence, fervent in spirit, serving the Lord."

We do not need to sacrifice intensity or the desire to win in sports. The Lord calls us to excellence in all chosen endeavors. He would expect nothing less than our best. We must constantly be looking for ways to honor and glorify Christ through athletics. For people to be successful in athletics, they most not lag behind in diligence, they must remain fervent in their motivation, and must, once again, serve, as though serving the Lord Himself.

Authentic Community meets real needs for the right reason. . .

. . .IN THE RIGHT WAY
(Romans 12:12-13)

Upward Focus --- "Rejoicing in hope, persevering in tribulation, devoted to prayer"

Our lives are not our own. God gave us life. Also, our talents are not our own. God coded our genes and chromosomes to allow us to run well, bump a volleyball, throw a block, stick a single-leg take-down, cut through water, sink a three-pointer, hit a ball, or kick a ball. We must be great "stewards" of our very lives and abilities, investing those talents in the community of competitors in athletics. Adversity will come. Physical injuries occur. Disappointment is certain. Not all "wins" are recorded on the scoreboard. Rather than protecting ourselves from the discouragement which comes from not achieving our goals in athletics, we must persevere through such heartaches. And great communities know how to uplift each other with prayer, psalms, songs of thanksgiving, and words of encouragement.

Outward Focus – "Contributing to the needs of the saints, practicing (pursuing) hospitality"

Again, we serve each other. We don't simply allow people to come to us. We seek them out with supernatural efforts to practice hospitality. We must get to know each other as student-athletes, parents, coaches, and officials. All of us should seek not to put the others at-odds but, rather, to build a network of people who are generously dedicated to the best which sports has to offer. The ferocity to win should still be present, but the greater ferocity should be reserved for a supernatural sportsmanship which allows us to walk away from a well-fought contest satisfied by the effort and grateful for the opportunity. It is not trite to say that others who are disabled of disadvantaged would give everything to play games and compete in athletics.

I have tried to make my case about The Great Sports Relationship Experience. I have argued for Authentic Community. Can we continue to act completely as "opponents" in life? It's hard to hate someone when I know her. Athletics unfortunately breeds a cool standoffishness which prevents unity and community in this unique culture called sports. We all have a choice. Once again, the line is drawn. Will we choose cavalier independence or community? Such is a choice for every man, woman, and child in our culture.

(Based on material from Chip Ingram's book, *Living on the Edge*, p. 191)

Chip Ingram has partnered with the Fellowship of Christian Athletes to offer r12 coaching, which is based on coaches and athletes (1) being surrendered, (2) separating from the culture, (3) constantly in a mode of self-assessment, (4) serving, and (5) responding supernaturally through the power of the Holy Spirit.

>
> *Surrendered* (Romans 12:1)
>
> In our relationship with God we offer him all that we are and all that we have.
>
> *Separate* (Romans 12:2)
>
> In our relationship with the world we live in the world while separating ourselves from its godless values.
>
> *Self-Assessment* (Romans 12:3-8)
>
> In our relationship with ourselves we develop an accurate view of ourselves and contribute to a local church's ministry.
>
> *Serving* (Romans 12:9-13)
>
> In our relationships with others we create genuine community that is built on authenticity and purity.
>
> *Supernaturally* powered (Romans 12:14-21)
>
> In our relationships with enemies we genuinely forgive and bless those who have hurt us.

Opportunities for online community and resources are available at http://www.r12coach.com.

As with any chosen activity, sports taken to extreme – to the point of being idols in our lives – can go against God's created order. Right attitude and right motivation contribute to sports being redempting in nature. Paul, for instance, emphasizes the spiritual over the physical pursuit and the physical prize in 1 Corinthians 9:25. We are to pursue a crown which will "last forever." Medals and trophies fade and deteriorate. Records are broken. Salvation results in an eternity lived with Jesus Christ!

This model of athletics, even if not overtly espousing biblical principles, will work in ANY setting. Who among us does not want positive coaches? Who among us does not want our children to improve their skills and grow from their athletic experiences? Who among us would not want to enjoy a less critical, angry, destructive model of sports? Can teams still "win" with this model? Absolutely.

"Whenever [Joe] Ehrmann speaks publicly about Building Men for Others – usually at a coaching clinic, a men's workshop or a forum for parents – someone inevitably asks about winning and losing: 'All this touchy-feely stuff sounds great, but kids still want to win, right?' 'Well, we've had pretty good success,' Ehrmann says. 'But winning is only a byproduct of everything else we do – and it's certainly not the way we evaluate ourselves.' Gilman finished three of the last six seasons undefeated and No. 1 in Baltimore. In 2002, the Greyhounds ranked No. 1 in Maryland and climbed to No. 14 in the national rankings. Much more important to Ehrmann is the way that his team ends each season when nobody else is watching. Before the last game, each senior stands before his teammates and coaches to read an essay titled 'How I Want to Be Remembered When I Die.'"

"Here is something linebacker David Caperna – reading from his own 'obituary'—said last year: 'David was a man who fought for justice and accepted the consequences of his actions. He was not a man who would allow poverty, abuse, racism or any sort of oppression to take place in his presence. David carried with him the knowledge and pride of being a man built for others.' The most important coach in America sat back and smiled. Win or lose on the field of play, Joe Ehrmann had already scored the kind of victory that would last a lifetime." (Marx, p. 3)

Chapter 18

Conclusion

Dr. Bob has "seen the light." He looks back on his career as a student-athlete and coach, knowing now that there is a better way. At the end of the book, he issues a challenge to everyone who has read the book to advocate for a new "light" in athletics.

Thank You, and Congratulations!

Our time has come to a close. Thank you for persevering through this analysis, and congratulations on completing a task which so many others are unwilling to even try.

Let's return to Coach Scott Kessler's template for coaching, and I will now assert more biblical truth into the model.

Christ is our rock. When the winds and rains of life come, He will always be the rock on which we stand. We are weak people in comparison to Jesus, but, in our weakness, His strength is made perfect in us. A great cloud of witnesses have gone before us. Their legacy cries out to us. We must remember their sacrifices. So many of them had faith but did not even realize all of their great rewards on earth. We must honor and glorify God in all that we do as participants in athletics.

Student-athletes, coaches, parents, spectators, and officials who claim Christ as Lord of their lives really do have an advantage in the arena of athletics. We are empowered by the Holy Spirit, and, as such, we should claim that power at heights beyond what we could ever typically ask or imagine.

Who are we? We are children of God, sons and daughters of the Most High King, children of the living God, and called to be His ambassadors on this earth, according to Coach Kessler (and me)! Is that the mental filter through which we strain all of our behaviors, or do we continue to act like so many other "Christians in the culture," who are "indistinguishable from the rest of the world?"

Why are we on this earth? We are here on this earth "to live for the praise of HIS glory, HIS goals, and HIS agenda, even when in conflict with ours," Coach Kessler so wisely points out (emphasis in original). God has stated in His Word that He will not share his glory with another, that we cannot serve him and self at the same time, and that, if we love the world and the things of this world, the love of God cannot be in us."

Coach Kessler also aptly asserts, "We are all going to die, and we are going to be dead sooner that we think, in most cases." Where are we going? Christians certainly do not believe death results finally in "ceasing to exist." Wholehearted followers of Christ are going to heaven to be with Him forever! Those who do not believe and place their trust in Jesus are going to hell, to live lives separated from God forever." Believing that there is a real heaven and a real hell guides our earthly decision-making.

Our legacy depends upon our perspective. All of the "stuff" of this world will burn up. We cannot take our possessions with us to heaven. Why we are drawn to participation in athletics is critical, "because eternity hangs in the balance."

- "Are our motives to win championships and [to] create a legacy of success?"
- "Are our motives to glorify God, whatever the cost to our reputation and career?"
- "Are our motives to glorify God, whatever the results or whatever our record?"
- "What matters?"
- "What lasts?"
- "Do we have adequate vision to impact the world for Jesus through sports?
- "What is your plan to realize this vision for Jesus? Is it a good plan? Are you executing the plan?"

John Steddom, the high school principal of my school, offered wisdom in commentary on the object of athletic competition –

"Does God care about athletics? Maybe in His economy, pursuing a state championship is worldly. What if he doesn't want to bless our efforts, because those efforts are intended to seek man's approval rather than His? If so, what does that mean about our participation in sports? Is it possible to pursue excellence, which I believe He calls us to, but not pursue a state championship? Is there another calling that we are not pursuing properly that would please Him more?"

John is asking good questions. Our responsibilities as Christians are to, in this order, (1) love God; (2) love others; (3) seek righteousness, be holy, be perfect; (4) serve the world; (5) conform to the likeness of Christ; and (6) expand the Kingdom of God by going, making disciples, baptizing, and teaching each other to obey everything which Jesus commanded. Along the way, there will be "championships." But we seek to wear a crown of righteousness, not a crown of worldliness, nor a crown of prosperity (as the preachers of the prosperity gospel would have us believe). We are fools for Christ and slaves to Christ, so that others might believe and come to a saving faith in Jesus. Ours must be an "abundance mentality," not a "scarcity mentality." Everyone wins who gives her all, no matter the score on the scoreboard.

Again, an earlier quote attributed to Coach Kessler applies – "If we win championships and don't teach individuals intentionally and strategically how to prosper in marriage and family and relationships and work, I would contend that we should seriously evaluate whether we should continue in this profession." Our legacy as a new part of the great cloud of witnesses is what we should seek. Our sole focus is to equip boys to become men and girls to become women. In an age of seemingly perpetual adolescence, the culture cries out for mature leaders and ambassadors for Christ!

Isn't success in athletics as much about exhibitions of character in a world which needs such examples? Our basketball team was ranked first in the state during the entire season – up to the opening game of the state tournament, which we lost. While disappointing, I am proud of the players, coaches, and spectators of that team for ranking #1 in sportsmanship among 10 teams in our athletic conference. Some might say that sportsmanship awards are for "losers." But I say that such conduct, particularly in the midst of so much excellence (26-0 heading into the state tournament), is even more special and the mark of "winners."

Put on love, joy, peace, patience, kindness, goodness, faithfulness, gentleness, and self-control. People all around us should see the fruit of the Holy Spirit of God. (See Galatians 5:22-23.) Put on compassion, humility, meekness, perseverance, forgiveness, and thankfulness. (See Colossians 3:12-15.) Put on authenticity, holiness, love, brotherly affection, honor, zeal, fervency, service, hope, hospitality, and harmony. (See Romans 12:9-21.) A football player can knock another player on his rear and then help him to his feet. That's character! That's sportsmanship! That's fruit! That's winning! That's success!

Finally, and perhaps most importantly, no spiritual analysis of abundance in life or athletics should neglect the topic of prayer. According to Coach Kessler, "Prayer is a necessary component of impact. This is spiritual battle.   . . . the enemy is NOT the opponent. . . .The enemy is the devil. . . .If you are not praying in quantity with and for your staff or other leaders [parents and players], there will be very little long-term impact, eternally-speaking." (emphasis in original)

Pray against the devil! Pray for yourself! Pray for the leaders in our culture! Pray for the student-athletes in our care! Pray for their parents, as they are entrusted to disciple their own children, teaching them to live lives of integrity! Pray for officials, that they might be objective and honorable in their work! Even and especially in secular settings, pray for systems of sport which so desperately need the light and truth of Jesus Christ! Amen! Amen!! And amen!!!

Finish strong! Don't start well, show staying power, and then fizzle-out at the end of your life. And you never know when the end of your life will come, so live each day to the fullest.

You say, "I can't do it." God says, "You can do all things." (Philippians 4:13)

You say, "I am not able." God says, "I am able." (2 Corinthians 9:8)

You say, "I'm too tired." God says, "I will give you rest." (Matthew 11:28-30)

You say, "I can't go on." God says, "My grace is sufficient." (2 Corinthians 12:9 and Psalm 91:15)

You say, "I can't manage." God says, "I will supply all of your needs." (Philippians 4:19)

You say, "I'm afraid." God says, "I have not given you a spirit of fear." (2 Timothy 1:7)

You say, "I'm always worried and frustrated." God says, "Cast all your cares on me." (1 Peter 5:7)

You say, "I don't have enough faith." God says, "I've given everyone a measure of faith." (Romans 12:3)

You say, "It's not worth it." God says, "It will be worth it." (Romans 8:28)

You say, "Nobody really loves me." God says, "I love you." (John 3:16 and John 3:34)

You say, "I can't forgive myself." God says, "I forgive you." (1 John 1:9 and Romans 8:1)

You say, "I can't figure things out." God says, "I will direct your steps." (Proverbs 3:5-6)

You say, "I'm not smart enough." God says, "I can give you wisdom." (1 Corinthians 1:30)

You say, "I feel all alone." God says, "I will never leave you or forsake you." (Hebrews 13:5)

You say, "It's impossible." God says, "All things are possible." (Luke 18:27)

(Author Unknown)

One of the greatest challenges for any author is to determine a title which accurately captures the essence of a book. I struggled mightily with that challenge. I originally titled this book, Light and Darkness.

You have experienced my attempts to contrast models of athletics which are "light" and "darkness."

Do light *and* darkness exist at the same time? In the arena of sports, I suppose you can most definitely respond in the affirmative. On any given day, we learn of noble and ignoble behaviors of participants in sports, so metaphorical light *and* darkness figuratively exist at the same time.

However, the physics of light and darkness really *do not* allow them both to exist at the same time. Light eliminates darkness, so the two phenomena are mutually exclusive.

Such is why I decided to entitle this book Light *or* Darkness. You make think this a minor distinction, the difference between "or" and "and." But it is anything but a minor nuance. Satan is the prince of darkness.

He came to steal, destroy, and kill. He is a deceiver. There is no truth found in him. He operates hidden in shadows. He is the author of confusion and division. He represents darkness.

Jesus declared Himself to be the "light of the world." His character is pure, righteous, holy; darkness is inconsistent with his being. His presence – His light – envelopes darkness.

As such, a new model of sports must envelope any of the darkness which currently exists.

You have a responsibility after reading this book.

Do you choose light, *or* do you choose darkness?

Avoid the darkness.

Light the world.

May God bless you in your commitment to lighting the world of sports!

Acknowledgements

God bless. . . .

You, who have invested your time and energy in the reading of this book. My greatest hope is that you will multiply the influence of this message through your own spheres of influence.

Pastor Michael Mudlaff, who gave me a writing refuge during my sabbatical leave at Westchester Presybterian Church in Urbandale, Iowa.

Andy Fjellman and Dave Nadler, who unlocked the text from its electronic prison!

Athletes who play with honor.

Mike Everitt, Tim McClelland, Eric Cooper, Ted Barrett, Scott Helverson, and Bill Spyksma – who gave me great insights about sports through the eyes of officials.

Giants *Bernie Saggau, Rick Wulkow, Mike Dick, Jim Hallihan, and Scott Raecker* – who gave so willingly of their time to me and who have been shining examples of leadership dedicated to honor in sports.

Parents of athletes past, present, and future – especially those at Des Moines Christian – who have read my manuscripts and encouraged me with their loving words and actions.

All of the *coaches* who are dedicated to using this positive model of athletics. *Cade Lambert* was particularly helpful as ideas germinated and grew into the final text. His uplifting post-game huddles are more meaningful to me than the games themselves! People like *John Wooden, Tony Dungy, Frosty Westering, Joe Ehrmann, Scotty Kessler, Andy Lambert, Chris Creighton*, and so many others have dedicated their lives to legendary legacies of discipling boys to become men and girls to become women.

John Jones and John Steddom, administrators who are unconditionally supportive of this culture of sports and all other activities at Des Moines Christian.

Jennifer Erickson and Matt Hill, who so carefully studied and edited my initial drafts.

My parents, *Trish and Willie Stouffer*, who have loved me unconditionally during all 52 years of my life.

My son-in-law, *Jacob Flinkman*, who played football under Andy Lambert's system of biblical coaching at Trinity International University in Chicago, who is a man's man, and who clearly adores and loves my daughter, Molly.

My daughter, *Hannah Stouffer*, who brings energy and excitement into our lives.

My daughter, *Molly Flinkman*, who is the real writer of the family, and who needs to tell her own story of redemption through words. (Check out Molly's intellect, spiritual depth, and excellence as an author at http://www.mollyflinkman.blogspot.com.)

My wife, *Cheryl Butler Stouffer*, who loves (and knows) sports and loves me. The grace of God is so evident in our marriage. Thanks, Cheryl, for allowing me to sit at a table for 40 hours while you and Hannah vacationed without me in the Florida Keys with Ted Cudnick, the NCAA basketball aficionado.

Most importantly, I acknowledge the great and glorious God – *the Lord and Savior, Jesus Christ* – for rescuing me when I was 36 years of age – and for daily growing me into His likeness. To Him be all praise and honor and glory! He alone is worthy of such praise!

Appendix

The Appendix includes multiple documents, including several written covenants which can be used in schools and sports leagues to solicit commitments from all stakeholders to behave more honorably in athletics.

Covenant of Athlete

- First and foremost, I will seek a vibrant, intimate, abiding relationship with Father God.
- I will pray for opportunities to make a difference in the lives of others.
- I will pour my life positively into others. I am willing to bear the messiness, inconvenience, and hardness of life for the sake of others.
- I am willing to humbly point out the sinful behavior others, speaking the truth in love.
- I will encourage the spiritual growth and faith of others in the context of this activity.
- I will attempt to behave consistently at all times.
- I will serve others.
- I will make sacrifices for others.
- I will forgive others, bearing no grudges.
- I will serve as an example of perseverance, and I will offer encouragement to others who share that example.
- I will express joy in this activity.
- I will take an eternal perspective with this activity, not getting mired in the muck of his human life.
- I will play with and for my teammates; I will make an absolute commitment to team play.
- I will play hard and physical WITHIN THE RULES.
- I will work hard to do my best in practice and in competition.
- I will be self-disciplined, avoiding the use of drugs and alcohol, for instance.
- I will make the sacrifices to reach high levels of success.
- I will speak positively to and about teammates and coaches at all times.
- I will have fun. I will keep my sense of humor. I will find joy in the simple and profound.
- Except in extraordinary circumstances, I will honor a full-season commitment to participation.

- I will keep life in perspective, not getting so tunnel-visioned in the present, and taking the long view. The joys of heaven await. We should not expect everything on earth to go well. We are aliens.
- I will live as a Christian 24/7/365! I am NOT a Sunday-morning-only Christian!
- I will be bold in my witness for Christ. I will not desert Jesus when He calls me to speak about Him.
- I will seek to honor and glorify Christ through all of my thoughts, words, and actions. I will be a man or woman of honor.
- I will not do anything which would tarnish my testimony. I will give no referee or opposing coach, player, or spectator reason to doubt my commitment to Christ.
- When I mess up, I will be broken, and sincerely admit my mistakes or sin.
- When a participant is injured or sorely disappointed, I will pray.
- I will play and let the coaches coach, the referees referee, and the spectators cheer FOR both teams.
- I will find joy in the hard-fought accomplishments of others, even if I am on the "losing" side of the scoreboard.
- I will be the member of a team which wins with grace. I will lose with dignity.
- I will genuinely shake the hands of opponents, opposing coaches, and referees.
- I will pray after the game with any Christians who desire prayer.

_____   _____

Signature   Date

Covenant of Parent

- First and foremost, I will seek a vibrant, intimate, abiding relationship with Father God.
- I will pray for opportunities to make a difference in the lives of others.
- I will pour my life positively into others. I am willing to bear the messiness, inconvenience, and hardness of life for the sake of others.
- I am willing to humbly point out the sinful behavior others, speaking the truth in love.
- I will encourage the spiritual growth and faith of others in the context of this activity.
- I will attempt to behave consistently at all times.
- I will serve others.
- I will make sacrifices for others.
- I will forgive others, bearing no grudges.
- I will serve as an example of perseverance, and I will offer encouragement to others who share that example.
- I will express joy in this activity.
- I will take an eternal perspective with this activity, not getting mired in the muck of his human life.
- I will be a positive supporter of all participants.
- I will work to keep my own behavior under control. I will stifle yelling and negative comments directed at players, coaches, parents of opponents, and officials
- I will be a good sport, and I will encourage sportsmanship of all others.
- I will hold others accountable when they are not acting in godly manners.
- I will speak directly with others to resolve any conflict.
- During my interaction with my child, I will place appropriate pressure on the him/her to perform at high levels
- I will remind my child to keep life in balance. Activities are not the end-all, be-all. I will help my child to keep life in perspective, not getting so tunnel-visioned in the present, taking the long view. The joys of heaven await. We should not expect everything on earth to go well. We are aliens.
- I will not shield my child from pain, disappointment, heartache, and negative consequences of their own behavior.
- I will NEVER physically confront any officials, parents, or coaches EVER, let alone in the heat of the moment. If correction is necessary for any party, I will take time to bring my emotions under control.

- I will give specific feedback about accomplishments to my child after practices and games.
- I will emphasize team over the individual.
- I will encourage everyone involved to have fun.
- I will live the sold-out Christian life 24/7/365! I am NOT a Sunday-morning-only Christian!
- I will be bold in my witness for Christ. I will not desert Jesus when He calls me to speak about Him.
- I will seek to honor and glorify Christ through all of my thoughts, words, and actions. I will be a man or woman of honor.
- I will not do anything which would tarnish my testimony. I will give no referee or opposing coach, player, or spectator reason to doubt my commitment to Christ.
- When I mess up, I will be broken, and sincerely admit my mistakes or sin.
- When a participant is injured or sorely disappointed, I will pray.
- I will let the players play, the coaches coach, the referees referee, and we spectators will cheer FOR both teams.
- I will find joy in the hard-fought accomplishments of others, even if I am on the "losing" side of the scoreboard.
- I will be the member of a crowd which wins with grace. I will lose with dignity.

_____   _____

Signature   Date

Covenant of Spectator

- First and foremost, I will seek a vibrant, intimate, abiding relationship with Father God.
- I will pray for opportunities to make a difference in the lives of others.
- I will pour my life positively into others. I am willing to bear the messiness, inconvenience, and hardness of life for the sake of others.
- I am willing to humbly point out the sinful behavior others, speaking the truth in love.
- I will encourage the spiritual growth and faith of others in the context of this activity.
- I will attempt to behave consistently at all times.
- I will serve others.
- I will make sacrifices for others.
- I will forgive others, bearing no grudges.
- I will serve as an example of perseverance, and I will offer encouragement to others who share that example.
- I will express joy in this activity.
- I will take an eternal perspective with this activity, not getting mired in the muck of his human life.
- I will be a positive supporter of all participants.
- I will work to keep my own behavior under control. I will stifle yelling and negative comments directed at players, coaches, parents of opponents, and officials
- I will be a good sport, and I will encourage sportsmanship of all others.
- I will hold others accountable when they are not acting in godly manners.
- I will speak directly with others to resolve any conflict.
- During my interaction with student participants, I will place appropriate pressure on the participant to perform at high levels
- I will remind participants to keep life in balance. Activities are not the end-all, be-all. I will help participants to keep life in perspective, not getting so tunnel-visioned in the present, taking the long view. The joys of heaven await. We should not expect everything on earth to go well. We are aliens.
- I will not shield participants from pain, disappointment, heartache, and negative consequences of their own behavior.
- I will NEVER physically confront any officials, parents, or coaches EVER, let alone in the heat of the moment. If

correction is necessary for any party, I will take time to bring my emotions under control.

- I will give specific feedback about accomplishments to participants after practices and games.
- I will emphasize team over the individual
- I will encourage everyone involved to have fun.
- I will live the sold-out Christian life 24/7/365! I am NOT a Sunday-morning-only Christian!
- I will be bold in my witness for Christ. I will not desert Jesus when He calls me to speak about Him.
- I will seek to honor and glorify Christ through all of my thoughts, words, and actions. I will be a man or woman of honor.
- I will not do anything which would tarnish my testimony. I will give no referee or opposing coach, player, or spectator reason to doubt my commitment to Christ.
- When I mess up, I will be broken, and sincerely admit my mistakes or sin.
- When a participant is injured or sorely disappointed, I will pray.
- I will let the players play, the coaches coach, the referees referee, and we spectators will cheer FOR both teams.
- I will find joy in the hard-fought accomplishments of others, even if I am on the "losing" side of the scoreboard.
- I will be the member of a crowd which wins with grace. I will lose with dignity.

_____   _____

Signature   Date

Covenant of Coach

- First and foremost, I will seek a vibrant, intimate, abiding relationship with Father God.
- I will pray for opportunities to make a difference in the lives of others.
- I will pour my life positively into others. I am willing to bear the messiness, inconvenience, and hardness of life for the sake of others.
- I am willing to humbly point out the sinful behavior of others, speaking the truth in love.
- I will encourage the spiritual growth and faith of others in the context of this activity.
- I will attempt to behave consistently at all times.
- I will serve others.
- I will make sacrifices for others.
- I will forgive others, bearing no grudges.
- I will serve as an example of perseverance, and I will offer encouragement to others who share that example.
- I will express joy in this activity.
- I will take an eternal perspective with this activity, not getting mired in the muck of his human life.
- I will be a positive supporter of all participants.
- I will teach for improvement of fundamental skills and understanding of the game, rather than primarily "motivating."
- I will insure that the participants are properly conditioned and that their wellness is at acceptable levels for participation at all times.
- I will be clear about expectations and antecedents to "playing time."
- I will be consistent in enforcing my expectations.
- I will love, encourage, and edify athletes; even correction will be done positively.
- Whenever possible, I will correct through "restorative justice" (over punitive measures).
- I will PRIVATELY address concerns with students, parents, and officials.
- I will speak positively about coaches and players at all times.
- I will forgive others.
- I will place the appropriate amount of pressure on athletes.
- I will work hard to keep life in balance for myself and the participants. I will keep life in perspective, not getting so tunnel-visioned in the present, taking the long view. The joys

of heaven await. We should not expect everything on earth to go well. We are aliens.

- I will assign value to players based on their status as "image-bearers" of God. ALL of the participants have equal value in the eye of the Lord!
- I will not "play favorites."
- I will encourage participants to work hard to win, but not at the cost of integrity or a positive experience.
- I will seek to develop all participants, not just the "stars."
- I will not yell negative comments to officials. My interactions with officials will be calm and objective in content.
- I will give specific feedback about accomplishments before, during, and after practices and games.
- I will behave with integrity at all times
- I will strive for excellence at all times, bringing honor and glory to God in all of my actions.
- I will encourage everyone to have fun. I will keep my sense of humor. I will find joy in the simple and profound.
- I will live as a Christian 24/7/365! I am NOT a Sunday-morning-only Christian!
- I will be bold in my witness for Christ. I will not desert Jesus when He calls me to speak about Him.
- I will seek to honor and glorify Christ through all of my thoughts, words, and actions. I will be a man or woman of honor.
- I will not do anything which would tarnish my testimony. I will give no referee or opposing coach, player, or spectator reason to doubt my commitment to Christ.
- When I mess up, I will be broken, and sincerely admit my mistakes or sin.
- When a participant is injured or sorely disappointed, I will pray.
- I will coach, I will let the players play, the referees referee, and the spectators will cheer FOR both teams.
- I will find joy in the hard-fought accomplishments of others, even if I am on the "losing" side of the scoreboard.
- I will be the member of a crowd which wins with grace. I will lose with dignity.

Signature   Date

Covenant of Official

- First and foremost, I will seek a vibrant, intimate, abiding relationship with Father God.
- I will pray for opportunities to make a difference in the lives of others.
- I will pour my life positively into others. I am willing to bear the messiness, inconvenience, and hardness of life for the sake of others.
- I am willing to humbly point out the sinful behavior others, speaking the truth in love.
- I will encourage the spiritual growth and faith of others in the context of this activity.
- I will attempt to behave consistently at all times.
- I will serve others.
- I will make sacrifices for others.
- I will forgive others, bearing no grudges.
- I will serve as an example of perseverance, and I will offer encouragement to others who share that example.
- I will express joy in this activity.
- I will take an eternal perspective with this activity, not getting mired in the muck of his human life.
- I will attempt to maintain sharp discernment about the action, rules, and progression of the competition.
- I will keep my emotions in-check during the heat of competition and at the point of controversial judgments.
- I will seek to listen actively during disputes, deescalating any argument when possible. At least so far as it depends on me, I will live at peace with everyone.
- During disputes, I will not use inflammatory words, and I will focus on the specific rule or reason for my judgment about enforcement of the rule.
- If I have made a correct judgment or interpretation of a rule, and a coach or player begins to unreasonably spew emotional arguments at me, I will not simply stand and take the abuse of this person. I will focus on the reasons and rules of my call, not the emotion of the moment.
- I will not draw attention to myself through overly flamboyant or aggressive movement, gestures, or comments.
- I will not "bait" participants, coaches, or spectators to anger by verbal or non-verbal means.
- I will seek to listen actively during disputes, deescalating any argument when possible. At least so far as it depends on me, I will live at peace with everyone.

- During disputes, I will not use inflammatory words, and I will focus on the specific rule or reason for my judgment about enforcement of the rule.
- I will strive for absolute fairness of judgment, no matter my negative or positive biases for coaches, participants, or teams.
- I will not attempt to form too close a relationship with any one coach or participant – in order to remove even the hint of favoritism.
- I will seek the assistance of fellow officials, when necessary.
- I will not be so proud or arrogant as to stand by an incorrect or missed call. My objective will always be to make the correct judgment, even after-the-fact, if such is permissible under the rules.
- At the end of a competition – whether I made correct judgments or missed calls – I will walk away knowing that I did my best, and I will not second-guess myself in future competitions.
- I will live the sold-out Christian life 24/7/365! I am NOT a Sunday-morning-only Christian!
- I will be bold in my witness for Christ. I will not desert Jesus when He calls me to speak about Him.
- I will seek to honor and glorify Christ through all of my thoughts, words, and actions. I will be a man or woman of honor.
- I will not do anything which would tarnish my testimony. I will give no other referee or opposing coach, player, or spectator reason to doubt my commitment to Christ.
- When I mess up, I will be broken, and sincerely admit my mistakes or sin.
- When a participant is injured or sorely disappointed, I will pray.
- I will let the players play, the coaches coach, the officials officiate, and spectators cheer for both teams.
- I will find joy in the hard-fought accomplishments of others.

_____   _____

Signature   Date

More about CHARACTER COUNTS! in Sports

"Winning Is Important, but Honor Is More Important. Quality sports programs should not trivialize or demonize either the desire to win or the importance of actually winning. It is disrespectful to athletes and coaches who devote huge portions of their lives to being the best they can in the pursuit of individual victories, records, championships and medals, to dismiss the importance of victory by saying, "It's only a game." The greatest value of sports is its ability to enhance the character and uplift the ethics of participants and spectators.

"Ethics Is Essential to True Winning. The best strategy to improve sports is not to de-emphasize winning but to more vigorously emphasize that adherence to ethical standards and sportsmanship in the honorable pursuit of victory is essential to winning in its true sense. It is one thing to be declared the winner, it is quite another to really win.

"There Is No True Victory Without Honor. Cheating and bad sportsmanship are simply not options because they rob victories of meaning and value and replace the inspirational high ideals of true sport with the degrading and petty values of a dog-eat-dog marketplace. Victories attained in dishonorable ways are hollow and degrade the concept of sport.

"Ethics and Sportsmanship Are Ground Rules. Programs that adopt Pursuing Victory With Honor are expected to take whatever steps are necessary to assure that coaches and athletes are committed to principles of ethics and sportsmanship as ground rules governing the pursuit of victory. Their responsibilities to demonstrate and develop good character must never be subordinated to the desire to win. It is never proper to act unethically to win

"Benefits of Sports Come From the Competition, Not the Outcome. Quality amateur sports programs are based on the belief that the vital lessons and great value of sports are learned from the honorable pursuit of victory, from the competition itself rather than the outcome. They do not permit coaches or others to send the message that the most important benefits

derived from athletic competition can only be achieved when an athlete or a team wins.

"Sports as a Setting for Learning. Sports provide an extraordinary setting for learning. Coaches who identify themselves as teachers ("teacher-coaches") place very heavy emphasis on assuring that the athletic experience supplements and enriches the academic education of student-athletes."

(From http://www.drake.edu/icd/ccii/ccii-in-sports/index.php)

A Very Different Game
Written by Bob Stouffer
Illustrated by Molly Flinkman

The azure blue of the sky was visited by fluffy cotton ball clouds.

Freshly-cut grass shined and smelled of summer.

The caked brown softball infield surface was marked by perfect geometry with lines of chalk.

A gentle breeze drifted invisibly and sporadically.

Several girls practiced hitting balls off batting tees, fielding and throwing in the lush green outfield.

Sweat beads formed on the forehead of the human coach who was instructing his softball players on this field.

But, outside the vision of this coach and these girls, a very different game was being played just beneath the thick blades of grass.

And, every so often, movement of very active insects reminded the humans that another group of living beings also visited and played in this park every day.

I walked over to Field 2 of the softball complex.

I got down on my hands and knees.

A creature jumped up from the grass toward me.

A grasshopper!

Had my movement startled her?

No, that wasn't it!

I looked closer.

I saw a couple dozen grasshoppers on their own softball field! (Who would believe me?!)

My attention drew to one team, their coaches, and their fans.

Ella stood by third base, drawing circles and shaking dirt through the ball glove of her hind leg.

Grace B. smiled a beautiful grin, as she loved everyone around her.

Grace C. was always cute as a bug's ear (whatever that means).

Bailey lovingly turned up her nose when – yet again – her coach called her by the wrong name, Grace.

Ireland hit off her left hind leg and smashed the ball above the grass line, hopping for dear life to first base.

Ashlyn showed her skill by helping to make all three outs in an inning by throwing with her front right leg to first.

Sam whacked the batting tee yet again, all four legs of her entire body gyrating in a circle, but she persisted, sending the ball tumbling yet again.

Coach Molly shared her positive words with everyone within earshot.

Jumping Coach Bob so enjoyed the ways that the girls listened, learned, improved, and had fun.

Mom grasshoppers, dad grasshoppers, grandpa grasshoppers, and grandma grasshoppers chewed and spit out their words of encouragement to all of the little grasshopper players!

They played. . .and they played. . .and they played. . .and they played. . . .

Our last game above the grass was over. The lights were turned out. The softball complex was ebony. I could no longer see the grasshopper game.

But they played on.

Long ago, I helped coach my daughter's softball team at that complex.

Who knows to this day whether those same grasshoppers aren't just beneath the waves of grass, playing their softball and jumping up into our world with joy!

The End

April 30, 2010

Hannah:

Congratulations on your efforts in the long jump and your three races last night at East High School! While I don't really know much about the long jump – and you don't, either at this point in that experiment – are you open to some "coaching" from your Dad? I hope you are open to my ideas. I should start by saying that I never ran track. The first track meet I attended was an eighth grade invitational at which I coached for Mason City's Monroe Junior High School. I learned about track by reading track and field magazines! Any success of our teams was due to the athletes, not my coaching!

That being said, I do hold my Iowa coaching license, and I did have a lot of success coaching football, wrestling, basketball, track, and baseball. I understood the principles of preparing an individual athlete and team for competition. Most of my expertise is in strength work, conditioning, and fundamental skill development (particularly in football and baseball). Since I won a state championship as a student-athlete, and I helped coach a state championship team as a coach, I have seen the highest levels of competition at the high school level, so I believe I am credible in "coaching" you a bit right now.

You are still young. Last night – and in previous meets – you have been running against bigger, faster, stronger, and more experienced runners. Eventually, you will gain even more physical strength and experience, so you will, I believe, be very competitive throughout your track career. I can already see that you are physically becoming stronger, simply from the natural maturation of a body which has gone from being a little girl to a young woman.

I do have some suggestions for your preparation. Practices are critical to your success in meets. Even though practices can be boring, your effort in practices will prepare you for competition. You've got to give great effort. I would describe myself as an average to above-average athlete physically. I have told you before that I had to work for everything I earned. My work ethic, intelligence for the game, and tenacity were the traits which carried me as an athlete. I worked VERY hard in practice. Hannah, if you work quite a bit harder (which is VERY possible) – and if you learn more about the nuances of track and field –

and if you get into greater competition shape – and if you continue with your own competitive drive, there could be no stopping you.

Your biggest challenge, though, in my humble opinion, is your concentration at meets. The ADHD probably contributes to your scattered thoughts on the afternoons and nights of concentration. And you also tend to distract yourself by being more interested in the social aspects of the track meets. Don't get me wrong. There's nothing wrong with enjoying the company of fellow athletes. However, to reach your optimal level of performance on the nights of meets, your focus must be on your events at-hand. Goofing around on the infield or in the stands – paying more attention to boys than to preparation – these things dull any sharpening intensity for competition. I probably went overboard in that regard when I was competing. I was super-fired up from the minute I got up on the morning of a game and especially just prior to and during the actual competition. No one could distract me. I had a singular commitment to doing my best. I had girlfriends in high school and college, but I concentrated on football, not my girlfriends, when game day came around.

You are young. You are learning. You are competing well. You are, perhaps, finishing in races about where you should as a freshman competing against upperclassmen. Your Mom and I are proud of what you have already accomplished. Still, I can't help but think that you could rise to a higher level (even this year) if you worked harder in practice, ate better, slept better, and prepared yourself mentally to have laser-focused concentration on the days of meets. You've got some great opportunities coming up. Give it your best. I can't wait to see how you do. God bless you, Hannah! You really have been blessed by God with remarkable athletic abilities.

I love you!

Bibliography

"Athletic Participation Survey, 2008-2009: Students Give Their Views," published by the IHSAA.

Black and English. *What They Don't Tell You About School Administration in Schools of Education.*

Blount, Rachel. "Roseville's Northwestern Puts Principles Ahead of Results," *Star Tribune*, 07 September 2010.

Bosman, Dave. "Set Example for Kids by Laying Off the Refs," *Des Moines Register*, (January 28, 2010).

Challies, Tim. "The Theology of Sports," September 23, 2009, http://www.amazon.com/Reason-Sports-Christian-Fanifesto.

Character Counts in Sports, http://www.drake.edu/icd/ccii/ccii-in-sports/index.php

"Coach Your Kids to Their 'Olympic' Best," The Dads @ Fathers.com, 26 February 2010

Coyle, Daniel. *The Talent Code: Greatness Isn't Born. It's Grown. Here's How.* New York:
Bantam Book, 2009.

Des Moines Register. (March 6, 2010) [article about Southeast Polk basketball player]

"Drake to Play First American Football Game in Africa," http://www.godrakebulldogs.com, 02 September 2010.

Dungy, Tony. *Quiet Strength.*

Ehrmann, Joe. *InsideOut Coaching Seminar Manual*, produced by Building Men and Women for Others, Inc., 2009.

Fornelli, Tom. "Bengie Molina Upset with ESPN," Internet, May 13, 2010.

Green, Dan. Finish Strong: Teen Athlete. . .Developing the Champion Within. Cited at www.simpletruths.com, 2008.

Gould, Daniel, Ph.D. Institute for the Study of Youth Sports website. Michigan State University.

Hoffman, Shirl James. "Sports Fanatics: How Christians Have Succumbed to the Sports Culture – And What Might Be Done About It," Internet, January 29, 2010.

i9 Sports, www.i9sports.com

Ingram, Chip. *Living on the Edge*.

Klemmer, Brian. *The Compassionate Samurai*.

Lambert, Cade. "A Coach's Perspective on Winning Big," www.dmcs.org, February 12, 2010.

Lorenzen, Al. "Where Do You Stand in Regard to Youth Sports?" A gathering of parents at Des Moines Christian School, August 25, 2009.

McCaslin, Caz. "Everybody Wins: Keys to Becoming a Successful Sports Parent," Living with Teenagers, 31 (June 2009), pp. 19-21.

McLean, Mickey. "High School Coach Gunned Down," *World* online magazine, (June 24, 2009).

Mariotti, Jay. "Cool Cat Stevens: Model for Future," FanHouse, April 4, 2010, http://jay-mariotti.fanhouse.com.

Marx, Jeffrey. "He Turns Boys Into Men," *Parade* magazine, August 29, 2004.

Marx, Jeffrey. *Season of Life.*

Moorman, Chick. *Stories for Dad's Heart.*

Papendick, John. "Meyer Retires," *American News*, (February 23, 2010), pp. 1A, 8A.

Penner, Joel. *Athletic Competition: Loving God and Loving Your Neighbor.* Deerfield, Illinois: Trinity International University, 2004.

Pitts, Leonard. "A Perfect Reaction to an Imperfect Call." *Des Moines Register*, (June 10, 2010), p. 13A.

Positive Coaching Alliance, www.positivecoach.org.

Quotes regarding Ed Thomas' death, http://jtlinder.wordpress.com/2009/06/24/ed-thomas-shooting-reaction/

"The Sara Tucholsky Story," Simple Truths website, www.simpletruths.com.

"Send the Right Message: When It Comes to Youth Sports, Strive to Keep It in Perspective," *Blue* magazine, Welmark, Inc., (Spring, 2010), pp. 18-21.

Smies, Kelly. "The Plague of Athletics," *The Diamond*, Dordt College, 30 September 2010, p. 6.

Travis, Clay. "After Memorable Sugar Bowl, Saying Goodbye to Tebow Is Sweet Sorrow," FanHouse.com, 02 January 2010.

Vealey, Robin S. "Communicating with Athletes: Timing Is Everything," http://coaching.usolympicteam.com/coaching/kpub.nsf/v/5mar05.

White, Rodney. "Overflow Crowd Mourns Slain Iowa Coach," *Des Moines Register* online, (June 29, 2009).

"Wisdom for the Busy Coach"

"Wisdom for the Busy Coach," [#2]

Wooden, John. *They Call Me Coach*.

The Author

Dr. Bob Stouffer is a fifth generation educator. He is the son of a kindergarten teacher and elementary school principal. He vividly recalls early memories of his voracious reading and writing. He focused his high school experience on his English coursework, although he was also an All-State singer, accomplished debater, and all-conference football player. Stouffer was an all-conference football player when he majored in English as an undergraduate student at Winona State University in Minnesota. Graduating Summa Cum Laude, he bypassed law school and began his career as an educator (currently in his 31st year). He coached football, holding the distinction of winning state championships both as a player and coach. He coached wrestling, basketball, track, and baseball. Eventually, he earned his M.A. from Truman State University and Ph.D. from The University of Iowa in Educational Administration, serving as an Associate Principal and Principal in public high schools of Iowa. He is known as "Dr. Bob" to the students, parents, staff, and community supporters he has served as a K-12 Superintendent of Schools at Des Moines Christian School since 2000. In addition, Dr. Stouffer has taught graduate level education and leadership coursework since 1994. He helped lead the founding of a new church in 2005 and the founding of a new Christian school in 2009. He is a frequent speaker and teacher in gatherings of men, married couples, educators, church congregations, and participants in various ministry organizations. He is a much-published author, and he has made numerous radio appearances, but this is his first book. He earned his Certificate of Ministry in 2009, and he is pursuing full Ordination through the Evangelical Free Church of America in 2012. Dr. Bob is the husband of 28 years to Cheryl and father to Molly, 24, Hannah, 16, and son-in-law Jake.

Made in the USA
Columbia, SC
24 June 2021

40932816R00143